Living Faith

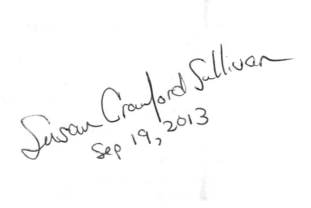

Susan Crawford Sullivan
Sep 19, 2013

Living Faith

Everyday Religion and Mothers in Poverty

SUSAN CRAWFORD SULLIVAN

The University of Chicago Press   Chicago and London

SUSAN CRAWFORD SULLIVAN is assistant professor of sociology and an Edward Bennett Williams Fellow at the College of the Holy Cross.

The University of Chicago Press, Chicago 60637
The University of Chicago Press, Ltd., London
© 2011 by The University of Chicago
All rights reserved. Published 2011.
Printed in the United States of America
20 19 18 17 16 15 14 13 12 11   1 2 3 4 5

ISBN-13: 978-0-226-78160-0 (cloth)
ISBN-10: 0-226-78160-7 (cloth)
ISBN-13: 978-0-226-78161-7 (paper)
ISBN-10: 0-226-78161-5 (paper)

Library of Congress Cataloging-in-Publication Data
Sullivan, Susan.
   Living faith: everyday religion and mothers in poverty / Susan
Crawford Sullivan.
       p. cm. — (Morality and society series)
   Includes bibliographical references and index.
   ISBN-13: 978-0-226-78160-0 (cloth: alk. paper)
   ISBN-10: 0-226-78160-7 (cloth: alk. paper)
   ISBN-13: 978-0-226-78161-7 (pbk.: alk. paper)
   ISBN-10: 0-226-78161-5 (pbk.: alk. paper)   1. Low-income mothers—
Religious life—Massachusetts—Boston. 2. Women and religion—Mas-
sachusetts—Boston. 3. Parenting—Massachusetts—Boston—Religious
aspects. 4. Religion and social problems—Massachusetts—Boston.
5. Church work with the poor—Massachusetts—Boston. 6. Church
work with women—Massachusetts—Boston. I. Title. II. Series:
Morality and society.
   HQ759.S835 2011
   306.6'774461083086942   dc22   2011014685

♾ This paper meets the requirements of ANSI/NISO Z39.48-1992
(Permanence of Paper).

To Gerry Sullivan
and William and Mary Crawford
with love and gratitude

Contents

Acknowledgments

It is difficult to know where to begin to start in thanking all the people who have contributed to this book. First and foremost, I am deeply indebted to the women who opened up their lives to speak with me in the interviews. It is my modest hope that this research will somehow in some small way contribute to making things better for them and others. I am also grateful to the ten social service programs that allowed me access to conduct interviews and especially thank Linda Going for helping to open the first doors in gaining access. I am also indebted to the pastors in this study, who gave generously of their busy schedules to speak with me.

Along the way, this project has received generous financial assistance from the Women's Studies in Religion Program (WSRP) at Harvard Divinity School, the Louisville Institute, Harvard Kennedy School's Multi-Disciplinary Program on Inequality and Social Policy and the Hauser Center for Non-Profit Organizations, and the College of the Holy Cross Research and Publications Committee. The 2009–2010 academic year spent as a WSRP research associate and visiting assistant professor at Harvard Divinity School was particularly instrumental in bringing this book to fruition. For all of this support, I am most grateful.

It has been a true pleasure to work with the editorial team of Doug Mitchell, Tim McGovern, and Erin DeWitt at the University of Chicago Press. Kathy Swain, as copy editor, has been wonderful to work with. Her careful eye is greatly appreciated. Alan Wolfe, as series editor, provided encouragement and support throughout the process of turning my manuscript into a published book. I also appreciate the contributions of other people at the University of Chicago Press, including Rob Hunt, Natalie Smith, and Joe Claude.

Years ago, Robert Wuthnow graciously welcomed me when I stumbled on his ongoing workshop on religion and culture while I was a master's student in public policy at Princeton. He introduced me to the study of the sociology of religion and has remained a source of advice and encouragement since. Theda Skocpol served as an invaluable source of support for this project from its earliest stages, helping me to formulate and clarify ideas and assisting with numerous practical issues. Chris Winship pushed me to think more deeply about churches and the urban poor; his influence on this book is tremendous. I am deeply thankful for their mentorship and guidance. Brent Coffin added important theological points of view in the early stages of the project. Ed Thompson and Susan Rodgers at Holy Cross, successive department chairs of the Department of Sociology and Anthropology at Holy Cross, have provided considerable support and guidance during the writing process. I am also grateful to them, and the Dean's Office, for facilitating and supporting the year's leave at Harvard Divinity School to finish the book. In general, I am fortunate to have wonderful colleagues at Holy Cross, both in my department and beyond. Other people who have provided encouragement include Marshall Ganz, J. Bryan Hehir, and Robert Putnam.

Numerous people have read and commented on all or part of this manuscript. The two reviewers from the University of Chicago Press, Jocelyn Crowley and Omar McRoberts, reviewed the manuscript very thoughtfully and thoroughly, offered many suggestions, and helped make it into a vastly better book. I am truly indebted to them. Robert Wuthnow, Susan Rodgers, and my Fall 2010 Harvard Divinity School seminar students (Women, Poverty, and Religion) also read a draft manuscript in its entirety, providing very valuable recommendations for better linking my findings with literature in sociology and anthropology of religion and religious studies. I am grateful to Joan Fouhy, Betsy Strines, and Mary Sullivan-Haller for reading the manuscript with a close eye for editing. Others who have read parts or all and contributed helpful comments as the book developed include Ann Braude, James Bryant, Ben Dunning, Jennifer Kiel, Margarita Mooney, Tanya Oldenhage, Solimar Otero, Lucinda Ramberg, Audrey Smolkin, Gerry Sullivan, and Ed Thompson.

Other people helped by generously sharing information. Robert Putnam provided me with information from his and Campbell's (2010) wonderfully thorough book, *American Grace*. Kenneth Pargament sent several lengthy e-mails explaining religious coping theory and its relationship to resilience. Brad Wilcox, Philip Schwadel, and Joseph Baker also were very helpful in e-mailing responses to my questions and offering information. Frank Kartheiser and Margaret Post were helpful in talking through issues of religion and community organizing.

Parts of the material forming this book were presented at annual meetings of the American Sociological Association, the Association for the Sociology of Religion, and the Religious Research Association. In addition, some of the material has been presented at Harvard Divinity School's WSRP Public Lecture Series and at the Boisi Center for Religion and American Public Life at Boston College. Thank you to the participants at these forums for helpful comments. A previous version of one section of chapter 3 was published in *Sociology of Religion* 67, no. 10 (March 2006): 99–108, and a previous version of some of chapter 4 was published in the *Review of Religious Research* 50, no. 2 (December 2008): 157–75. I appreciate the insightful comments from the reviewers for these journals and the permission from the journals to reprint the material in this book.

Several skilled research assistants helped in various stages of the project. Misty Koger-Ojure of Harvard Divinity School was an absolutely invaluable source of help and knowledge. Her thoughtful insights added considerably to this book. Harvard Divinity School WSRP research assistants Lauren Pawlak and Eva Payne helped in finding books and assisting in other tasks. Kristen Troy, a then undergraduate at Holy Cross, transcribed the pastor interviews with speed and accuracy. Sarah Lowe, a then Harvard undergraduate, skillfully scheduled interviews with the mothers and watched the mothers' children during interviews. Diana Barnes Philpott helped during the interview phase as well. Liz Ibazebo also contributed research assistance. Also, several wonderful women have helped watch my own children over the years, enabling this book to be written. In particular, I appreciate the love and care given to our children by Cayce Gray, Cheryl Gouin, and Annie Skrodzki. Back in the earliest stages of this project, the dining hall of Harvard's Eliot House provided a homey place to write. I appreciate the friendship of the many Eliot House workers I came to know. Their spirit infuses this book.

My family and wonderful friends are a tremendous blessing. My faith communities during the course of writing this book—St. Paul's Catholic Parish in Cambridge, Massachusetts, and St. Mary's in Shrewsbury, Massachusetts—have been a lifeline. The community experienced in these parishes allowed me to experience firsthand the social capital that supportive church congregations can engender. Monsignor Michael Rose and other pastors, Fathers George Salzmann and Manny Clavijo, friends such as Cedrine Bell, Annamaria Nickle, Kathy Notorianni, moms' group members, and other friends of both parishes have been a constant source of friendship and support. I also appreciate the listening ears of long-time friends such as Eric Chaskes, Claire Conceison, Cathy Osmera, and Odette Valder.

I reserve my deepest gratitude for my family. My father and mother, William and Mary Crawford, have stood by me throughout. Their constant prayers, encouragement, and assistance are profound, and profoundly appreciated. My sister, Sally Gillett, and her husband, Bernard, brother Tom Crawford and his wife, Yancey, and their families have been fantastic. I have received much encouragement from my wonderful in-laws, Dan and Lyn Sullivan, Dan and Jeanne Sullivan, Rich and Barbara Sullivan, and Mary Sullivan-Haller and Brandon Haller; my aunt Margaret Settipane; and many other members of my family. For this I am most grateful. My children, John Paul, Meg, Sarah, and Bridget, have brought unspeakable joy into my life and given me motivation. Last but by no means least, I profoundly thank my husband, Gerry Sullivan. Words cannot express my gratitude to him for his love and support, shown in countless hours spent discussing ideas, reading drafts, watching children, and many other contributions. Without him, this book would not have happened.

ONE

Introduction: Listening to Poor Mothers about Religion

Maria, a twenty-four-year-old single mother with three small children, is in many regards a highly religious Pentecostal. She says that her religion is "very, very, very important" to her. She prays many times a day and reads the Bible once or twice daily. She follows all of her religion's precepts regarding not wearing pants, makeup, or jewelry and not dancing or listening to nonreligious music. "Once you are in the religion for a long time, six months or a year, you will begin to forget about the makeup, the earrings, the bracelets, pants." Maria's previous coworkers asked many questions about her religion because of her noticeably different lifestyle.

Yet for all of the obvious salience of religion in Maria's life, she does not currently attend church. She used to be deeply involved in her Hispanic Pentecostal church community and attended services weekly. But after moving in with the father of her children, she was no longer welcome at church. "We are not married. We live together. I just like to call him my husband." Her religion "says that two people should not be living together if they are not married. That is one of the reasons why we are not in the church right now, because me and my husband are not married. So we have to get married in order to go back to church." Maria wants to go back to church but does not see marriage as a possibility in the immediate future. "Now is not a good time for us to get married. We have to keep going on with our lives and try to get our feet on the ground in order to do it." Maria has also recently moved to a long-term housing shelter for families, not conveniently located to her former church. She stays at home caring for the children, while her boyfriend helps support the family. Her church, she says, "is too far. I don't like to take my kids far away. It's just a mother thing. My church is all the way downtown."

When she was involved, Maria found her church community an invaluable source of practical assistance and emotional support. As a single mother on welfare, Maria had occasions when she needed assistance.

If you need help in any way, somebody comes to your house and tries to help in any way he or she can. You can ask for help from the people in church, especially the pastor. He may come to your house, or some other members of the church can try to help out in the best way they can. . . . When I didn't have a place to stay with my children, they helped me stay in the house of one of the sisters in the religion [fellow congregants]. . . . If I didn't have money to go buy milk for my kids, they would provide me with money sometimes. They will just go from house to house of the people in church and pick up things that would be probably helpful, that would go in your refrigerator, and they help you to get things until you get back on your feet.

Speaking about emotional distress, Maria explained, "If you are feeling stressed, you get down and you pray next to your bed. . . . Then if you don't feel the way that you want to feel when you get up, you call somebody from the church, and they will come to your house, and they will try to help you. They will try to give you a sense of focus. They help you a lot."

Maria occasionally visits her old church, but, as she noted, she is not welcome to attend regularly, as cohabitating violates church norms. The move to the family shelter removed her from the immediate vicinity of the church, and she does not have frequent contact with church members now. Lacking transportation and dealing with several very young children, Maria does not find it easy to get to church anymore. She summarizes, "The times that I want to go full-time to the church, it never works out . . . because it is too far, or because me and my husband are not married, or because of my kids." Thus, Maria currently practices her faith in an individual way, isolated from a religious community.

I interviewed Maria as part of my research on the role of religion in the lives of low-income urban mothers. She recounted her experiences as we sat in her small apartment in the family shelter, her toddler dribbling grape juice as he played with my eight-month-old son. Her story presents several paradoxes: here is a woman whose deep traditional religious faith is a defining part of her life, yet she does not attend church. Maria, like many other very poor urban mothers, has pressing needs that could in part be met by the spiritual, emotional, and practical support of a church congregation. Yet it turns out that, like Maria, even if women are highly personally religious, many do not regularly participate in organized religion. And although she is not currently part of a church congregation, religious faith pervades and shapes the ways in which Maria responds to challenges, parents her children, and makes meaning of her circumstances.

I did not set out to write a book about the role of religion in the lives of mothers in poverty. Originally I planned to explore the connection between faith and work for low-income mothers. As a new mother of an infant, I found myself surprised when talking with some highly educated mothers who used religious language and concepts to frame their decision to leave the labor force and care full-time for their children. These affluent and religious mothers viewed any use of child care and continuation of career as selfish at best, if not a downright rejection of God's will. But I knew welfare reform required poor mothers of very young children to work. What did low-income mothers think? I wondered. Certainly some of them were conservative Catholics or evangelical Protestants like these highly educated, affluent women who rejected the concept of mothers of young children working outside of the home. Did poor women simply frame these issues differently due to their economic circumstances? How did the requirements of welfare reform square with their religious convictions? I set out to explore these questions, conducting in-depth interviews with urban mothers who were on or had recently transitioned off welfare and, later, talking with pastors who ministered in poor urban areas.

I found that religion can influence poor mothers' conceptions of work, welfare, and motherhood. But what really struck me in the interviews was how personally religious many respondents seemed to be, yet they did not attend church. I saw how prayer and religious beliefs played a defining role in their daily lives, although organized religion often played little or no part. Unasked, mothers brought up how they had found it difficult to continue attending church after moving into a transitional housing shelter or how they had felt stigmatized at church for being single mothers or for some other aspect of their lifestyle. And although most did not participate in organized religion, they spoke repeatedly about how much they relied on prayer and faith in facing challenges such as securing housing and jobs, raising their children in dangerous neighborhoods, and trying to make sense of the difficulties they faced. Religious faith served as a lens through which many viewed and interpreted their worlds.

Everyday Religion

This book contributes to a growing body of research on "lived religion" or "everyday religion," that is, how people actually practice religion in their daily lives. David Hall notes, "We know next-to-nothing about religion as practiced and precious little about the everyday thinking and doing of lay men and women" (1997, vi). Scholars such as historians Robert Orsi and Marie Griffith, sociologists Meredith McGuire and Courtney Bender, and anthropologist Marla Frederick, among others, have produced ground-breaking work on lived religion. To study lived religion, states Orsi, "entails a fundamental rethinking of what religion is and of what it means to be 'religious.' . . . Religion comes into being in an ongoing, dynamic relationship with the realities of daily life" (1997, 7). Nancy Ammerman draws attention to everyday experiences of individual lives and the importance of understanding the social worlds where religious ideas and practices exist. Traditional ways of measuring religion, such as religious adherence and church affiliation, miss the many religious practices that occur outside of institutions, leaving much of actual everyday religion unanalyzed (Ammerman 2007).

Orsi calls us to rethink religion as a type of cultural work "concerned with what people *do* with religious idioms, how they use them, what they make of themselves and their worlds with them" (2002, xix). Religious practices thus have meaning only as they are related to how people actually live. "Religion is approached in its place within a more broadly conceived and described lifeworld, the domain of everyday existence, practical activity, and shared understandings, with all its crises, surprises, satisfactions, frustrations, joys, desires, hopes, fears, and limitations" (xiv). How poor urban mothers experience and live religion can be understood only from within the broader framework of their lifeworlds.

Religion and spirituality remain strong in the lives of modern Americans. A high percentage of Americans say that religion is very important (56 percent) or fairly important (25 percent) in their own lives, with women more likely than men to say religion is very important (66 percent to 51 percent). Fully 85 percent of African Americans say that religion is very important in their lives. Poorer and less-educated individuals are more likely to regard religious faith as very important (Newport 2006).

Forty-nine percent of Americans say they felt a strong sense of God's presence in the previous twenty-four hours (Gallup and Jones 2000). Six out of ten Americans say faith is involved in every aspect of their lives, and seven out of ten say they find purpose and meaning in life because of their religious faith (Gallup Organization and Center for Research on Religion and Civil Society 2003).

Given figures like these, why has so little sociological attention been paid to the role of religion in the lives of mothers in poverty? Although there have been many studies of mothers on welfare, there is a conspicuous lack of research on their participation in religion and its role in their lives. Such women's lives are difficult and challenging: juggling searches for housing and decent jobs, struggling to care for children, surviving on welfare or working at low-wage service jobs that often lack dignity and benefits, coping with family disruption, and perhaps facing physical or mental health problems or addictions. It seems likely that many poor mothers might involve faith in their daily activities and find purpose or meaning through religious faith. Frederick contends that social scientists emphasize race, class, and gender in understanding how people navigate their worlds, while neglecting spirituality. Yet, she continues, "among the faith-filled, faith in God navigates how individuals respond to almost all of life's circumstances" (2003, 3). To study the lives of such individuals without studying how spirituality operates in their lives misses a key part of what both motivates and constrains their actions. To study the lives of poor mothers without exploring the role of spirituality obscures how many understand and respond to their circumstances. Faith speaks to the life experiences of those for whom religious faith is important, providing meaning in life's experiences and helping to shape people's interpretations and actions (Frederick 2003). How is "everyday religion" practiced amid the hardships of motherhood in urban poverty?

Religion often comes to play a more prominent role in people's lives during times of duress (Pargament 1997). Thus, in part I focus on how disenfranchised women draw on religion in dealing with challenges and making meaning of circumstances. Given the lack of access to other types of resources that more affluent individuals take for granted, religion can become an important resource for poor women in negotiating the many demands of their lives. This book both joins and builds on earlier works, including Carol Stack's *All Our Kin* and Kathryn Edin and Laura Lein's *Making Ends Meet,* in explaining how low-income mothers survive and attempt to overcome circumstances.[1] While rejecting a utilitarian view that reduces religion to a mere coping mechanism, I contend that religion serves as a resource for a potentially large number of women.

In this book, I conceptualize religious resources as two types: institutional and cultural or personal. *Institutional religious resources* are resources associated with a church or faith-based organization, such as pastors, networks of fellow congregants, and material aid. Churches, first and foremost, exist so that people can worship together and experience the divine, acting as sacred spaces where worshippers can gain a sense of transcendence and connection with the divine. People join in communal worship, praying, singing, and receiving sacraments (Wuthnow 2004). In addition, social scientists find that aspects of congregations have provided important resources across a broad array of arenas, ranging from the civil rights movement to mental health. Churches provide opportunities for companionship and participation in social activities, and churches often serve as sources of friendship and social support to their members. Pastors can provide such assistance as help with personal problems, financial aid, and emergency shelter. Congregations may engage members in actions aimed at addressing social problems.[2]

In addition to church-based institutional resources such as pastoral aid or networks of congregants, religion also provides *cultural resources*—the beliefs, views, and symbols that people draw on to structure their experience of the world. Ann Swidler (2001) analyzes how culture shapes people's "strategies of action," a notion highly applicable to studying the role of religion in the lives of mothers in poverty. Religious beliefs provide a lens through which to interpret the world and a way to make meaning of life's experiences (Koenig and Larson 2001; Pargament 1997).

Because religion—in both its institutional and personal forms—has been shown to provide resources in many different types of situations, it seems highly likely that it would serve as a resource to very poor mothers with limited resources. My study indicates that impoverished urban mothers draw strongly on personal religious beliefs and practices and less frequently on institutional religion in confronting challenges such as navigating work and welfare, raising their children, and trying to make meaning out of difficult situations.

Religion, of course, cannot and should not be reduced to a resource, and it is not my intention to do so. My respondents who engaged in religious practices engaged in these practices because they believed in a divine being that they wished to worship and to whom they wished to grow closer. Their faith was important to them not because it was a resource but because it was a central part of who they were and how they viewed the world. Religion was not merely a resource for these women; it encompassed their lived experiences of culture and identity.[3] As part of living out faith in daily life, poor mothers engage religion as a resource, but this does not make up the totality of their lived religion.

Churches and the Urban Poor

An "everyday religion" perspective examining religion in daily life becomes especially important when studying disenfranchised women, as several studies note a gap between churches and the urban very poor. Contrary to popular wisdom that assumes churches serve as a haven for the poor, some survey research has found less-educated or poorer Americans to be less likely to participate in churches.[4] In a recent poll, 42 percent of Americans had attended religious services in the past seven days. Twenty-nine percent seldom attended, and 15 percent never attended (Gallup 2009). R. Drew Smith's (2003) survey of 1,206 residents of inner-city public housing complexes in four cities found that residents attended church at a considerably lower rate than the general population. Almost 60 percent of the housing project residents rarely or never attended church, despite the fact that in three of the cities the majority of residents were African Americans, who have higher attendance rates than the general population (survey data find almost 60 percent of African Americans attend nearly every week, and African Americans who never attend church are more likely to have lower levels of income and education).[5] Researchers drawing on a nationally representative survey of unmarried urban mothers estimate that two-thirds attend church relatively infrequently or never, although African Americans are most likely to attend regularly.[6] Another recent nationally representative survey found poor adolescents to be less likely to attend religious services and participate in other church-related activities and more likely to have no religious preference, compared to nonpoor teens (Schwadel 2008). Low-income white Catholics are considerably less likely to attend church than nonpoor white Catholics; strikingly, whereas the presence of children in the home usually promotes church attendance, this is not the case for poor white Catholics (Schwadel, McCarthy, and Nelsen 2009). In Penny Edgell's (2006) study of congregations in upstate New York, social class predicted church attendance controlling for other demographic factors, religious salience, and religious identity; those with high school or less education were less likely to attend services or participate in other church activities. Trends over time show declining church attendance among those without a college degree. Robert Putnam and David Campbell (2010) note that while church attendance rates among whites under age forty-five have been essentially flat since the 1970s, they have declined by about one-third for those without a college degree. For African Americans, church attendance has increasingly become middle class; attendance levels among college graduates have increased since the 1980s, and African American college graduates attend at higher rates than those with lower levels of education.

In looking for ethnographic evidence about church participation and poor urban residents, several scholars have observed low-income public housing complexes on Sunday mornings. They find few people coming and going, suggesting that residents are not attending church at high levels (Laudarji and Livezey 2000; Smith 2001). In Chicago, researchers found only one church out of twelve within walking distance of a low-income housing project that included project residents as participants and members (Price 2000). Omar McRoberts's (2003) *Streets of Glory* relates that very few of churches he studied in an economically depressed Boston neighborhood engaged neighborhood residents and their concerns; most members of the neighborhood's churches lived elsewhere, commuted to church services, and returned home. Attracted to the location by inexpensive rent, the majority of congregations in the neighborhood viewed "the street" as an evil to be avoided and from which their churches should be kept separate and safe. The isolated urban poor, claim Lincoln and Mamiya (1990), represent a serious challenge for the black church, and they argue that a reconnection must take place between the church and poor urban dwellers. Levels of church attendance are likely to be even lower among extremely poor women like those studied for this book, many experiencing housing instability and living in shelters; large-scale surveys generally cannot easily reach women in such circumstances.

Yet, as noted earlier, many of the women I studied had high levels of personal religious beliefs and practices, despite the fact that few attended religious services. Several earlier studies suggest that people of lower socioeconomic status engage in higher levels of personal religious devotion, such as private prayer.[7] More recently, low-income individuals were found more likely to pray frequently, controlling for other demographic and religious variables (Baker 2008). Another recent study concludes that despite lower levels of church attendance, poor adolescents are more likely than nonpoor adolescents to pray alone and read scriptures alone a few times a week or more, as well as to say that faith is important in their daily lives (Schwadel 2008). These findings raise questions about how everyday religion might play out in the lives of poor women detached from institutional religion.

Poverty, Religious Individualism, and Social Capital

Individualism and fluidity have been defining features of American religion over the course of the country's history; in the 1830s Alexis de Tocqueville was "very struck with the voluntary character of American religion and how easily people moved from one faith to another" (Roof 1999, 150). Scholarship analyzing American religion since the 1950s stresses its increased individualistic nature in recent decades. Robert Wuthnow's (1998) *After Heaven* analyzes how Americans have moved from a "spirituality of dwelling" rooted in religious congregations to a "spirituality of seeking." Richard Madsen (2009) calls religious individualism "the American religion" of the white middle class. Robert Bellah and collaborators' *Habits of the Heart* describes Sheila, a woman who called her faith "Sheilaism. Just my own little voice" (1985, 221). Bellah and his colleagues note how, disengaged from religious organizations, Sheila combined a belief in God with notions of the psychotherapeutic self to construct an individualistic religion emphasizing God's desire for people to love themselves and care for themselves and others. The authors raise concerns about a "kind of radical individualism that tends to elevate the self to a cosmic principle" (236). Furthermore, they claim that even many people in churches remain religious individualists, seeking personal support and emotional intimacy from churches and leaving their churches when such needs are not sufficiently met (232). However, studying baby boomer spiritual seekers, Wade Clark Roof (1999) points out that a culture of religious individual seeking and choice may strengthen, rather than weaken, religious commitment. Spiritual seeking may in fact be spiritually rejuvenating, and seekers should be taken seriously because they are engaging faith seriously. When people affirm religious faith and identity because they have chosen to do so, they often have greater understanding of their religious beliefs and a stronger sense of accountability (158). Madsen (2009) summarizes contemporary American religion as comprised of restless seekers moving about within an "archipelago of little islands of strongly held faith." He writes, "Restlessness is built deeply into the core of American religious culture. The restlessness is not so much a result of the weakness of faith. It is a result of the very strength of the fundamental premises of the American religious individualism. The more seriously that mainstream Americans follow their religious instincts, the more restless they become" (1296–97). Whether scholars view increased religious individualism with alarm or see it as an indication of spiritual strength, these studies share in common a focus on the middle class, generally the white middle class. White, middle-class, spiritually seeking baby boomers or "spiritual but not religious" young adults constitute the classic portrait of people who are interested in personal faith or spirituality but are not deeply committed to formal religious communities. Urban poverty, however, can also serve as an important, although understudied, pathway to religious individualism. Poverty leads to a religious individualism that stems from sometimes different reasons, is experienced in different ways, and leads to different consequences than that of the stereotypical restless American spiritual seeker.

In examining detachment from organized religion among the urban poor, this book also speaks to issues of social capital. In general, social and civic life in American communities have undergone great change in recent decades. Social capital—that is, social networks and the associated norms of trust and reciprocity (Putnam 2000)—has declined by a number of measures. Membership in civic and community organizations, participation in social activities, and informal socializing with friends have all declined since the 1950s. People are less likely to attend meetings on town or school affairs, entertain friends at home, get together with neighbors, or belong to clubs (Putnam 2000). Church participation also appears to have declined, although trends are debated. Putnam and Campbell (2010) find an overall pattern of modest decline in church attendance from the 1970s to the present. Also of significance, the percentage of young adults aged eighteen to twenty-nine who never attend church and say they have no religious preference has increased substantially since 1990.[8] Involvement in other church-related activities apart from service attendance has fallen since the 1950s.[9]

High levels of social capital have been linked to a host of individual and community benefits, leading some observers to view these social changes with concern.[10] Although scholars of social capital debate the degree of change in social capital, the causal mechanisms, how to interpret new forms of electronic community, and whether these changes are good or bad, most agree that a profound shift has taken place in American community life (Skocpol and Fiorina 1999).

According to Edin and Kefalas (2005), many Americans believe the poor make up for what they lack in economic resources by rich, satisfying relationships. Their research finds quite the opposite to be true. Among the young mothers they studied, many could not name one single person they considered a friend and were often emotionally distanced from and distrusting of family members as well. Other scholars note that where close connections in poor neighborhoods occur, they are not necessarily positive. When women must depend on neighbors and family for assistance, these relationships may create stress. Women may resent shouldering the burdens of severely troubled neighbors or relatives and crave more privacy and outside ties (Belle 1982; Weissbourd 2000). A study of mothers on welfare in public housing projects found women engaged in few friendships and trusted few people, instead complaining that their neighbors were nosy, jealous, loud, and bad mothers (Seccombe 1999). National surveys indicate lower levels of trust generally among the poor (Wuthnow 2004). In comparing extremely poor black neighborhoods and other black neighborhoods in Chicago (most of which were moderately poor), Wacquant and Wilson (1989) found residents of the extremely poor neighborhoods to be less likely to have a best friend, less likely to have a partner, and less likely to know most of their neighbors, belong to a voluntary organization, or attend church services. Sandra Smith (2007) claims that networks providing extensive social support have declined since earlier studies like Carol Stack's (1974) *All Our Kin*, citing more recent quantitative studies finding that the poor and African Americans give and receive less support than others. Family networks providing extensive support are uncommon among American families in general, but they are even more uncommon among the poor and African Americans. In particular, Smith highlights high levels of distrust and individualism among low-income African Americans. Overall, she summarizes, "most studies show a distinct social support disadvantage for the poor. . . . Relatively few appear to get the assistance that they need to get by" (2007, 31).

Social capital includes both "bonding" and "bridging"—close ties to those within one's community and cross-cutting connections with those outside one's community (Putnam 1993). William Julius Wilson's highly influential *The Truly Disadvantaged* (1987) argues that the exodus of middle-class and working-class families from inner-city neighborhoods and the subsequent decline of neighborhood institutions have resulted in social isolation for the extremely poor. In this view, concentrated neighborhood poverty results in isolation from the people and institutions of mainstream society and social pathology in the neighborhoods. Wilson's argument suggests that the urban poor not only lack high levels of close "bonding" social capital but also lack "bridging" social capital to connect them to those in mainstream society. Mario Small (2004, 2009), on the other hand, claims that poor neighborhoods and their residents vary in their levels of institutional resources and social isolation. People within poor neighborhoods have varying levels of relationship ties as well as linkages outside their neighborhoods, depending in part on how the institutions with which they interact are structured.[11]

In either case, religious institutions play an important role in poor communities. "Among the institutions of civil society, churches are often the last to leave deteriorating neighborhoods and dwindling communities and the first to return" (Foley, McCarthy, and Chaves 2001, 215). Religious congregations are fertile environments for the creation of social capital (Wuthnow 2002; Putnam 2000). Religious institutions can provide close personal ties as well as linkages beyond one's immediate neighborhood. People in churches have more access to social support and larger, more dense, and more satisfying social networks than those who are not in churches (Ellison and George 1994). Congregations in poor neighborhoods may maintain broader social linkages with other organizations, such as denominational bodies, interfaith organizations, and community groups (Foley, McCarthy, and Chaves 2001). Thus, when poor women of faith are disengaged from religious institutions, we must consider the implications for social capital.

Policy Context

Given the public policy emphasis on churches and religious organizations aiding the poor since welfare reform, the lack of scholarly attention to religion in the lives of low-income urban mothers is particularly perplexing. The aftermath of President Clinton's 1996 welfare reform law initially piqued my interest, eventually leading to this book. The 1996 Personal Responsibility and Work Opportunity Reconciliation Act (the federal welfare reform law) ushered in a sea change in American poverty policy. In addition to devolution, welfare time limits, and work requirements for mothers of young children, the new law also codified religion as a prominent feature in the battle against poverty. The law contained an important clause, the charitable choice provision, which encouraged and facilitated partnerships between states and faith-based organizations in the provision of social services. Formerly, large religious charities operated under strict provisions separating their social services from their faith activities. Under the 1996 welfare reform law, mechanisms were set in place to help government agencies contract with explicitly religious organizations, including congregations. These groups can use religious principles in programs or hire only coreligionists, though proselytizing, requiring participation in worship, or turning away beneficiaries on the basis of religion is prohibited. In January 2001, President George W. Bush established the White House Office of Faith-Based and Community Initiatives to further government partnerships with and "level the playing field" for faith-based organizations. Twelve federal agencies—including the Departments of Labor, Commerce, Justice, and Health and Human Services—now have a Center for Faith-Based and Community Initiatives. Thirty-six states and more than a hundred cities have liaisons or offices for faith-based and community initiatives. Faith-based initiatives have been supported and criticized by both liberals and conservatives. Elements of Bush's faith-based initiative did not meet with legislative success, and he used executive orders and changes within federal agencies to advance its agenda. Most controversial have been the executive orders exempting religious organizations from nondiscrimination clauses (Wright 2009).[12]

President Obama has kept a faith-based office, creating a new version of it in February 2009 and naming it the White House Office of Faith-Based and Neighborhood Partnerships. The new office has refocused and expanded its influence and reach, and rather than the previous office's focus on religious organizations competing for government grants, the mission now highlights policy matters and partnerships. President Obama asked the revamped office to focus on four priorities: engaging community groups in economic recovery and the fight against domestic poverty; promoting responsible fatherhood; reducing abortion and preventing unintended pregnancy; and increasing interreligious dialogue and cooperation. President Obama established a new Presidential Advisory Council on Faith-Based and Neighborhood Partnerships, composed of twenty-five members (with a range of political beliefs) who serve one-year terms. The council represents religious leaders from a wide variety of religious backgrounds—including Catholic, mainline Protestant, Evangelical, Jewish, Hindu, and Muslim—as well as other influential nonprofit leaders. The advisory council is led by the faith-based office director, Pentecostal minister Joshua DuBois. Both the faith-based office and the new advisory council work as part of the Domestic Policy Council.[13]

A 2009 Pew survey found that 69 percent of Americans supported houses of worship and other religious organizations applying for government funding in order to provide faith-based social services, with people aged eighteen to twenty-nine even more likely to support it. Only 25 percent of Americans oppose government funding for faith-based services. More Americans say that faith-based organizations are better able to feed the homeless, provide services to the needy, provide counseling to prisoners, and mentor young people than government or other nonprofit organizations. Democrats are now more likely than Republicans to favor religious congregations seeking government funding to provide social services (Pew Forum on Religion and Public Life and Pew Research Center for the People and the Press 2009).[14]

Advocates of faith-based social services, who include high-profile members of both political parties, consider religious organizations such as congregations and faith-infused nonprofits to be ideally situated to provide social services. After welfare reform, new fundamental assumptions now operate to govern public discourse. Poor, low-skilled mothers of very young children will be self-sufficient wage earners supporting their families, with welfare a temporary measure organized and implemented at the state and local levels. Religious providers will be on board to work with government and help enable poor mothers to achieve economic independence.

Whereas most of the discourse on faith-based social service provision has centered on the attributes of religious service providers or the constitutionality of government partnerships, I see an underlying message in the discussion. Sixty-two percent of Americans in public opinion polls cite the power of religion to "change people's lives" as a reason to support government funding of faith-based organizations (Bartkowski and Regis 2003, 9). Considering that the morality of women on welfare has long been suspect in the United States, I contend that some advocates of faith-based programs imply that religion itself may somehow help poor mothers of young children improve their work ethic, take responsibility for their lives, and become contributing self-sufficient citizens. Outside of whatever benefits religious social service providers and church volunteers might provide to help women leave welfare, religion itself is seen as a good for poor mothers.

This study is situated within this post-welfare reform cultural context emphasizing faith-based assistance to the poor. Lost in the public policy debates are the voices of poor women themselves, because researchers have not sat down to listen to what they say about religion. Knowledge of how these women participate in religion and incorporate it into their lives receives little notice in welfare reform circles, even as faith-based welfare-to-work job training programs have increased. Government officials pursue faith-based initiatives with little understanding of how poor women actually practice religion.

Experiencing Reality, Acting in the World

This book addresses a substantial and important gap in knowledge. Existing sociological research on poor mothers essentially neglects their lived religion. This is despite the fact that these women face many stressors and that previous research has found religion can serve as a resource for people facing difficulties, as well as the fact that recent public policy has emphasized religion's role in aiding the poor. First and foremost, then, this book aims to present the overlooked voices of low-income urban mothers about religion and its role in their lives. Listening carefully to what these women say about religion, providing a forum for their voices to be heard, and understanding their "everyday religion" drove my interest in writing this book.

Second, in considering everyday religion and low-income mothers, this book aims to further develop theory about religion and poverty. Classic social theories of the religion of the poor emphasized denial, escape, and focus on the afterlife. Karl Marx ([1843] 1978) presented the religion of the poor as an otherworldly escape that blinded the oppressed to their present miseries and prevented them from acting on their interests, thus serving the interests of the wealthy.

Religious suffering is at the same time an expression of real suffering and a protest against real suffering. Religion is the sigh of the oppressed creature, the sentiment of a heartless world, and the soul of soulless conditions. It is the opium of the people. The abolition of religion as the illusory happiness of men is a demand for their real happiness. The call to abandon their illusions about their condition is a call to abandon a condition which requires illusions. The criticism of religion is, therefore, the embryonic criticism of this vale of tears of which religion is the halo. (54)

The comfort afforded by religion, Marx's "illusory happiness," keeps the oppressed pacified and blind to the injustice of their circumstances, keeping them from rebelling and disrupting the social order.[15] Max Weber ([1915] 1991) contrasted the privileged classes' "theodicy of good fortune," legitimizing their good fortune, with the lower classes' "theodicy of suffering"—a theodicy of withdrawal and escape that focuses on otherworldly concerns (271). Freud's ([1927] 1961) *The Future of an Illusion* described religion as infantile wish projection and an illusion, rooted in the wish for the guidance and protection of a powerful father and for immortality. He called religion "the universal obsessional neurosis of humanity; like the obsessional neurosis of children" (55). Freud saw religion as a consolation for the suffering caused by nature and humanity. H. Richard Neibuhr (1929) described the religion of the poor in terms of "churches of the disinherited," with intense emotional personal religious experiences and an emphasis on the afterlife over this world (26). The deprivation thesis of twentieth-century American social theorists (e.g., Glock 1964; Davis 1949) viewed religion as consoling or compensating the poor for their lack of worldly success, comforting them in their suffering. These older ways of theorizing religion and poverty emphasize religious faith as *compensating* the poor for their lack of material accomplishment or success. Religion in this view consoles people and provides them with justification for their poverty. Because religion keeps people passively relying on a divine being and awaiting a better afterlife, it prevents them from acting in their own self-interest to improve their situations.

However, religion can serve as an "amphetamine" of the masses, as well as a possible opiate.[16] Turning away from a focus on religion as compensation for deprivation or denial of reality, more recent scholars have found that religion can provide a powerful lens for framing injustice, a network of resources for mobilization, and a worldview promoting hope and action. Aldon Morris's (1986) study of the origins of the civil rights movement showed the role churches played in social action for justice. Major actions such as student sit-ins and the Montgomery bus boycott were organized through churches, which provided leaders, organized masses of people, well-developed communications, finances, and space to hold meetings. Documentary film footage of the era shows Martin Luther King Jr. and other ministers exhorting boycotters using language of religious justice, while "the masses" prayed and sang in churches to sustain their energy to continue the boycott (Public Broadcasting System 1987). In 1974, Ernesto Cortes founded COPS (Communities Organized for Public Service) in San Antonio, a coalition of congregations composed primarily of Catholic parishes and financially supported by the Catholic hierarchy. COPS cultivated lay leaders, often women, in low-income Mexican American parishes. Mobilizing its widespread religious base, COPS engaged in nonviolent though often disruptive tactics that forced the white elites in power to address drainage issues in poor neighborhoods, allocate money to services and infrastructure in neglected neighborhoods, and attend to other pressing issues affecting the community (Warren 2001; Rogers 1990). In studying faith-based community organizing in California, Richard Wood (1994, 2002) shows how elements of religious culture such as theological worldviews and congregational liturgies can foster political activism and social change.

Although social scientists no longer contend that religion serves only as "compensation" for the poor, most sociological studies of religion and poverty have focused more on organizational aspects, such as faith-based community organizing, social movements, or social service provision. Few social scientists have deeply explored how the poor draw on faith in interpreting circumstances and how religion influences action in the social context of daily life. Some excellent exceptions include Margarita Mooney's (2009) study of Haitian immigrants and Marla Frederick's

(2003) ethnographic research among poor African American women church members in the rural South. These studies examine the role of everyday religion in personal transformation as well as in larger political action. Mooney shows how religious faith rooted in church communities provides Haitian immigrants with hope and resilience in their immediate circumstances, while also motivating some to reflect and act on larger social problems affecting them. Supported by church leaders and working through small prayer groups in the congregation, hundreds of church members in a Haitian congregation in Miami had been mobilized to participate in grassroots political action addressing social concerns.[17] Frederick explains how religion can not only engender personal strengths such as gratitude and empathy but also foster "righteous discontent" that leads some people to political engagement. Encouraged and supported through the networks of their church and other community organizations, some of her respondents engaged in faith-inspired political activism in education, public health, and other concerns in the public sphere.

Frederick rejects, however, the dichotomy between religion as "accommodation" or "resistance" by examining women's creative agency in areas of their personal lives. This perspective is valuable for assessing the role of faith in the lives of the mothers I studied, whose faith fueled no broader social action. They drew on religious faith in primarily personal ways, in trying to parent more effectively or gain strength to deal with housing searches or job stresses. In addition to dealing with overwhelming stresses in their lives, my respondents were disconnected from organizations that might challenge individualistic understandings of their situations or help engage them in broader efforts. The examples of faith-based social action in low-income communities mentioned above show people working not alone but through their churches, prayer groups, and other organizations. My respondents were mostly isolated from such organizations and often utterly overwhelmed contending with their myriad day-to-day demands. The fact that their religious faith fueled not activism but attempts at personal perseverance and growth amid adverse circumstances does not mean, however, that their religion serves a compensatory "opiate of the masses" function. This book looks at religion as low-income mothers themselves experience it in their day-to-day lives. The fact that their religious understandings and actions do not necessarily accord with what social activists would wish raises the question: Who is walking in community with these women whereby other interpretations or actions might be experienced?[18] Largely isolated from church, civic, and community groups, and often isolated even from family and friends, my respondents drew on religious faith as a source of personal strength and perseverance.

This book thus takes a more micro examination of the role of religion among low-income women. From the disciplinary perspective of psychology, Kenneth Pargament has articulated a framework for how religion can foster resilience in individuals. Pargament (1997) argues that while religion can serve a defensive role (passive, a type of denial, compensation, focused toward comfort and anxiety reduction), religion can also motivate people to engage problems positively and proactively. Feeling a sense of spirituality, feeling connected to and supported by a divine being, feeling like one is working with God in addressing problems, getting support from one's congregation, engaging in "benevolent religious reframing"—these expressions of religiosity can help people take positive action and find meaning in crises (290). This framework also takes into account ways in which people can engage religion harmfully. Some types of spiritual struggles, such as feeling rejected by one's congregation or feeling punished by or abandoned by God, can cause harm and exacerbate problems. Empirical research finds people to engage religion in helpful ways more often than in harmful ways, however (Pargament and Cummings 2010).

In order to further develop sociological theory about religion and poverty, research analyzing a variety of populations is needed, including people not involved in churches. How does religion frame people's worldviews within social contexts of poverty? What roles does religion play in people's daily lives? The population considered in this book is low-income urban mothers of young children, for the most part single and not involved in churches. Adding a study of this particular population to the few existing recent studies that speak to issues of religion within the lives of the poor extends sociological theory and knowledge.

Listening to Women

This book is primarily based on forty-five in-depth, semi-structured interviews with mothers living in urban poverty in and around Boston, as well as fifteen in-depth interviews with urban pastors in a nearby city who have considerable experience ministering within poor urban neighborhoods. The women in the various social service programs where I recruited for the study were overwhelmingly from a Christian religious background (for some, very nominal), and a few women had no religious background.[19] Recruiting emphasized that women did not have to consider themselves religious to participate in the study, and the study ended up including women with a range of belief and practice, including none.

To situate the study in the context of welfare reform, I focused on mothers of young children (with at least one child age six or under) who were on or had recently left welfare.[20] I chose in-depth interviewing for the methodology because survey research would likely fail to fully capture a complex and nuanced understanding of how and why these mothers integrate religion in their daily lives. Furthermore, this population of women is not always well represented in surveys; lacking stable housing, they are likely to be underrepresented in large-scale surveys. In the interviews, women spoke candidly about the role of religion in their lives, covering such painful and difficult areas as domestic violence, drug abuse, the loss of children to child protective services, and incarceration. In-depth interviewing about religion allowed me a unique window into their lives, and I feel privileged that women were willing to divulge and process often-intimate information with a stranger.[21] For their part, many of the mothers said they were grateful to have participated in the study and to have had the opportunity to share their stories, reflecting on their lives and the role religion plays. Although this book discusses religion affecting poor women's lives in many and often profound ways, my respondents were ordinary women, not religious zealots wearing their religion on their sleeve. Had a researcher or ethnographer been studying these women's experiences of something such as welfare, for example, or another related topic, without specifically probing in-depth about religion, the ways in which religion factored into their life experiences may well have gone largely unnoticed, especially as most did not attend religious services. In-depth interviewing focused on the role of religion in women's day-to-day life experiences provided a lens to start uncovering everyday religion.

I recruited women from long-term family shelters that provided other social services (five programs offering support such as education, job training, child care, and housing search assistance); non-live-in welfare-to-work job training and job search assistance programs (two programs); and three other social service agencies.[22] I surmised that recruiting through social service agencies rather than through churches would provide respondents ranging from those who were motivated by religious faith and attended religious services frequently, to those who had some involvement with faith and religion, to those for whom religious faith played little, if any, role in their lives. Generally, almost every eligible person at a given agency on a given day volunteered to do the interview if there was time. Women from a variety of backgrounds participated in the study, including those who said they were not religious and for whom faith seemed to play little or no role in their lives. I emphasized that I was there as a researcher, not as a representative of any religious point of view. For analysis, the interviews were fully transcribed and coded, and to maintain confidentiality, pseudonyms are used throughout the book (appendix A contains brief descriptions of the thirty-seven women quoted in this book). The findings from individual women are buttressed by interviews with urban pastors who collectively have worked with thousands of low-income mothers over the many years of their ministries. See appendix B for a description of the methodology and the interview questions.

The Mothers

Thirty-eight of the forty-five women were receiving public assistance at the time of the study (for most, welfare, although a few received Supplemental Security Income).[23] All but two of those not receiving public assistance at the time of the study had transitioned off welfare in the recent past. Only two women were long-term welfare recipients; most had gone onto welfare with the birth of a child and were aware of welfare reform time limits. Many were involved in job training programs, job searches, or both. Participants represented various racial, ethnic, and educational backgrounds. Eighteen women described their race/ethnicity as white, ten as black, twelve as Hispanic, four as mixed race, and one as Native American.

Forty-two of the forty-five women were single. Four of these women were separated or divorced, and the rest were never married. This book says relatively little about men. This is in part due to my original research focus on women's experiences of religion, welfare, and work; I did not specifically probe women about their relationships with men. On the other hand, women did not often bring men up in the interviews, despite the fact they initiated discussion on numerous other topics. In addition to the three respondents who were married, several women cohabitated with partners, but most did not. Some made passing references to boyfriends. A few respondents ventured that they had fled abusive situations of domestic violence. Because women on welfare experience domestic violence at much higher rates than the general population, it is likely that a considerable number of my respondents had.[24] The father of the baby of at least one mother was in jail. A few women mentioned boyfriends or boyfriends' mothers as people who encouraged their faith. One mother specifically pointed to her baby's father as the person responsible for her turn away from faith and church, vowing to never let a man do that again.

Survey data indicate that although 80 percent of poor unmarried women are romantically involved with their baby's father at the time of the child's birth, half of these relationships will end before the baby turns one; two-thirds will have ended by the time the child is three (Edin and Kefalas 2005, 74). Men often do not participate in the raising of children once the relationship with the mother has ended and often pay no child support (Nelson 2004; Edin and Kefalas 2005). The relationships between poor women and the fathers of their children fail for a number of reasons, among them drug addiction, alcohol abuse, infidelity, domestic violence, criminal behavior, and incarceration. Mothers hope that having a child will lead the fathers to a more stable and responsible life of maturity and commitment, but this hope often fails to materialize (Edin and Kefalas 2005). Low-skilled urban men have few employment opportunities in good-paying, legal occupations (Wilson 1987, 1996). Although this is one factor contributing to the decline in marriage (as women do not view these men as good marriage prospects), it also means that men's involvement in family life does not eradicate hardship. In my research, even in the cases where the fathers were involved and supportive, their contribution was not enough to keep the families out of severe financial hardship. The three married women in the study were all living with their spouses and children in long-term shelters for homeless families. Although their spouses were employed, these men did not earn enough to avoid the family's becoming homeless. Thus, whether fathers played an active part in family life or were nowhere to be found, women still experienced profound need that led many to seek religious support. Overall, the role religion plays in low-income single mothers' relationships with men—their baby's fathers as well as other boyfriends and partners—is a topic needing further attention and future research.[25]

Fourteen women had not completed high school, twenty had a high school degree or GED, and eleven had some college. No one had completed college. Almost half lacked permanent housing and were living in long-term family shelters offering various social service supports. The others lived in apartments with relatives, in a government-subsidized apartment complex for low-income women, or in other living arrangements; a number of these women also experienced housing instability in the form of problems with relatives or leases. Their ages ranged from late teens to early forties, with a median age of twenty-six.

Religious backgrounds also varied. Seven women described themselves as Catholic; nine described themselves in an evangelical tradition such as

Pentecostal, nondenominational Bible church, Seventh-Day Adventist, or Baptist; and one came from a mainline Protestant church. Twenty-nine of the women told me they had no religion or were not currently practicing any, but the majority of these women would fall into the category of "unchurched believers" (Hout and Fischer 2002). Eighty percent of the women who said that they had no religion or were not currently practicing said that religion was of medium or higher importance in their lives; more than 75 percent of these prayed privately; and 85 percent had been raised at least nominally in a religious tradition.[26]

Overall, twenty-one women said faith or religion was very important to them, eighteen said it was of medium importance, and six said neither personal religious faith nor organized religion was important to them. Twenty-eight women prayed very frequently—once a day or more; nine mothers prayed several times a month; and eight rarely or never prayed. Despite the relatively high level of personal faith practices and beliefs, few of the women I interviewed attended religious services regularly. Only seven of the forty-five women attended services once a month or more often; nineteen attended infrequently on holidays, and nineteen never attended at all.

I will note here that with regard to qualitative research and generalizing findings, I interviewed a particular sample of women, of Christian (or no) religious backgrounds, in the urban Northeast, mostly not involved in churches, and in need of social services and welfare. Recruiting through social service agencies led me to varied levels of religious beliefs and practices, but it also brings up issues to be considered. First, these women needed social services, shelter-based housing (for about half the sample), and welfare. Given the bureaucratic hassles, paperwork, strict requirements, and sanctions of welfare after welfare reform, women are not eager to enter the system. Some who do become discouraged with the bureaucracy and demands and leave welfare (Hayes 2003). Similarly, few women are eager to live with their children in a homeless shelter. Thus, most of the women interviewed were women without other options. Their levels of social support are perhaps lower than those not needing such services. My study speaks to a particular population, and there are other mothers in poverty who have not shared the experiences of my respondents.

That said, forty-five interviews, selected the way the women were selected, allow the development of meaningful, powerful qualitative characterizations of a variety of spiritual and religious perspectives and struggles. While one might assume that mothers from such diverse racial, ethnic, and religious backgrounds would not have much in common in terms of how they experience religion in their daily lives, the commonalities turn out to be striking. Although not generalizable in a statistical sense, these characterizations are conceptually robust and theoretically useful. Particular patterns among the women emerge because these patterns exist. Other people living in poverty in other areas face similar social environments and share similar belief structures.[27] Pastors interviewed for the book, with many years of experience in low-income urban neighborhoods, affirm the insights and experiences of the women interviewed.

In terms of language, I write about the study participants in the text but sometimes generalize the language to speak of mothers in poverty more broadly. This does not literally mean *all* mothers in poverty and should not be taken that way. Given statistics and qualitative findings on church attendance and the poor, high levels of religious belief and prayer in the United States, the insights of the pastors interviewed for the study, and number of urban mothers who are very poor or on welfare, the findings do, though, speak to a potentially large group of women.[28] The voices of the mothers studied raise important insights that people interested in religion and urban poverty must consider.

The Primacy of Motherhood

First and foremost, the women interviewed identify as *mothers*. Motherhood is at the very core of their self-concept and their understanding of their place in the world. Their lived religion cannot be analyzed apart from motherhood; motherhood shapes the narratives and religious meanings with which they imbue their lives. Previous scholarship contends that poor mothers highly value motherhood, often making it the primary focus of their lives. In her study of mothers on welfare, Sharon Hayes (2003, 84) notes, "Children and caregiving are a part of almost every sentence that comes out of the mouth of welfare mothers: nearly always a part of the stories they tell, the explanations they provide, the dreams they render, and the services they seek." The adolescent mothers that Edin and Kefalas (2005) studied credited their children for all that is positive in their lives. For these young mothers, children provided motivation and purpose in life; a deep, important, and lasting relationship; someone to love them; and a role through which they can prove their worth. The transformational experience of motherhood in some cases helped bring order to chaotic lives, as some gave up partying, drugs, or "running wild" on the streets in order to accept the responsibility of raising children. According to Edin and Kefalas, motherhood provides a sense of identity for poor women in different ways than it does for more affluent women. While more affluent mothers find identity in motherhood and experience joys in rearing their children, middle-class mothers also have greater access to a wider range of social roles to provide validation and satisfaction—"few middle class women approach mothering with such a great sense of need, and few see their children as very nearly the sole source of their fulfillment" (2005, 183).

I stumbled across the primacy of motherhood among my respondents very early in the research process quite by accident. Many of the interviews took place in the mothers' homes, including apartments within long-term family shelters. Because women had to have young children in order to be eligible for the study, I brought a research assistant to interviews in mothers' homes to entertain the children. One day early on, my own babysitter was ill, and I had to bring my then-eight-month-old son along to be watched with the respondent's children. The presence of my son changed the tone of the interview as compared to earlier ones, making it more open and effective. I began bringing my son along regularly to be entertained along with the respondents' children. Women seemed to relate to me much more as a fellow mother juggling the stresses of work and raising children than as a university researcher. They offered numerous child-rearing tips on topics ranging from feeding to teething to getting a baby to sleep through the night. As I was a new mother compared to most of the study participants, they had plenty of advice to offer. A shy, soft-spoken seventeen-year-old Latina mother readily initiated a conversation about infant eating habits and provided tips. One twenty-one-year-old white mother in a long-term family shelter eagerly ran to the back bedroom to get children's videos that her three-year-old daughter had outgrown and gave them to me. Although I initially hesitated internally on accepting them (surely there were other women in the shelter with need of them, and I could afford to buy them), I accepted them. This perhaps allowed us to interact more as mothers who had something to share with each other rather than just as academic researcher and homeless shelter–dwelling respondent. I had not expected the rapport that the presence of my son would elicit with the study participants, who seemed much more at ease talking with another mother of young children. Shared motherhood, of course, does not erase class or racial differences, nor do I pretend that I know how it feels to walk in these mothers' shoes. However, the mutual experience of motherhood did seem to open up an avenue for my respondents to speak with me in an open way, as people who shared some aspect of their disparate lives.

Looking Ahead

Subsequent chapters delve into the "everyday religion" of low-income urban mothers. Chapter 2 provides three key building blocks in understanding poor mothers' everyday religion: theories of religion, resilience, and harm; religious practices; and the role of churches. Chapters 3 through 5 analyze everyday religion in three major areas of daily life: work, parenting, and making meaning of circumstances. Chapter 3 looks at welfare and work, examining how religious beliefs and practices can frame women's views of work and welfare, as well as their experiences in the low-wage workplace. Chapter 4, on parenting, looks at how mothers draw on both personal faith and institutional religion in raising their children. Chapter 5 turns to more internal processes, examining how mothers draw on the cultural resources of religion in trying to understand and make meaning of difficult situations such as homelessness, unplanned pregnancies, joblessness, and poverty. Chapters 6 and 7 focus on the factors contributing to relatively low levels of formal religious participation despite high personal religiosity among the mothers interviewed. Mothers brought up logistical challenges hindering attendance, in addition to (for some) feeling stigmatized and unwelcome at churches due to factors such as single motherhood or poverty. Chapter 6 analyzes these reasons for nonparticipation from the viewpoint of the women and chapter 7 from the viewpoint of urban pastors. The conclusion steps back to take a broader look at everyday religion in the lives of mothers in poverty, considering implications for churches, public policy, and social service and community workers.

In the text, following the language of the women interviewed, I mostly use the words "religion," and "religious." Scholars debate the definitions of and distinction between "religious" and "spiritual."[29] In current popular definition, "religious" and "religion" usually pertain to formal organized religion, and "spirituality" connotes personal experiences of meaning and the transcendent. Religion, furthermore, has somewhat negative connotations (narrow, routine, going through the motions, dogmatic, intolerant), whereas spirituality has positive connotations (deep, real, personal, reflective, tolerant, inclusive) (Frederick 2003; Zinnbauer et al. 1997). The women I studied used the terms "religion" and "religious" as well as the term "faith" throughout in referring to both their personal spirituality and organized religion. (Only one respondent, a recovered addict who used the language of twelve-step-type recovery groups, described herself as "spiritual but not religious"). This book uses the term "religion" to discuss both personal faith and organized religion and sometimes uses the terms "spiritual" and "spirituality" interchangeably with "religious" and "religiosity." Because the women interviewed were from Christian or, in a few cases, no religious backgrounds, the findings speak to the Christian religion. The term "religion" in the text thus pertains to Christian religion—as that is what the data allow—although it is likely that some of the findings would apply to low-income mothers of other faiths.

Women most often talked about God when they spoke of religion; this book will follow their language when unpacking their narratives. As later chapters will detail, the most common image of God was that of father, a loving supportive father who cared about their everyday lives. Some respondents held an image of God who was a father still loving but also at times disappointed in them. In living out their daily parenting challenges, the women developed their image of God as more of a coparent helping them to parent more effectively and acting as a father to their children. Less than a quarter of the women interviewed spoke specifically of Jesus. For those who did, their images of Jesus varied. No one seemed explicitly to imagine Jesus as fulfilling the role of their absent spouse, despite the fact that the image of parenting "together with God" was fairly common. Jesus was most often referenced as example, savior, and fellow sufferer. Mothers from both Catholic and Protestant backgrounds mentioned stories of Jesus in the Bible as examples for how one should live; this was the most common way Jesus was mentioned in interviews. Devout women with evangelical experience emphasized Jesus as Lord and Savior, Jesus coming into their hearts, confidence in an afterlife with Jesus, and the importance of thanking Jesus. The vast majority of my respondents did not emphasize Jesus' suffering and death, although those who did used this image of Jesus in profound and meaningful ways.

Studies of women and religion increasingly call attention to the importance of the lived experience of ordinary women's lives, yet a "lived religion" exploration into the lives of low-income urban mothers is sorely lacking in existing scholarship. I hope this book will be useful not only to scholars of religion, gender, and urban poverty and policy but also to clergy, policy makers, social workers, and community workers. This intimate account, drawn from listening carefully to those among the poorest of the poor in the United States, aims to provoke both reflection and action.

TWO

Building Blocks: Theory, Religious Practices, and Churches

Jane, a forty-year-old white woman with four children ages three to fifteen, is a devout, born-again evangelical Christian. She stopped attending church services when her family encountered housing difficulties and the Assembly of God church where she and her husband were very active members would not help out. Having stopped participating in organized religion due both to disappointment with the church and to transportation issues (the family moved to a long-term family shelter, which was some distance away), Jane now relies on prayer and her strong personal faith as she confronts her numerous challenges. She believes that God is ultimately in control of her circumstances, despite the necessary actions she takes to improve her situation.

I was going to church, but I stopped. I was going to an Assembly of God church. . . . I stopped going when I became homeless. . . . When I had my old pastor, we could [get help]. . . . If you were in need of something, he was right there to help you out with it or counsel you if you needed counseling. . . . But then with my second pastor, we couldn't. . . . It was just the way he did things, you know, which we didn't agree with. We believed that you should help people out. . . . I think the churches should help out more, definitely. It's like they are hypocritical. . . . I think that's why we left the church, too, because you see that.

It's up to God. God has a plan, and I don't know what . . . but I just trust in God. . . .
The housing search workers here are really great, and I just pray that we just get an apartment as soon as we can. We are just doing the work that we need to do and just believing
and trusting in God. . . . God is in control of my circumstances. I am the one filling out
the applications and doing everything, but he is the one who is going to say where I
am going to live, where I am going to be. God is in control, not me. I am doing the
work, but really it's God.

Although homeless mothers on public assistance such as Jane may
not be involved in organized religion, many live out a strong everyday
religion in confronting challenges.[1] Given the fact that so few women
interviewed attended religious services, I was genuinely surprised at the
extent to which they involved religious faith when tackling adversity.
Three-fourths of those who never or very infrequently attend church
services did so, as did all who attend once a month or more. Again and
again in talking with women, I was struck by how often they talked about
the ways religion helps them navigate their many hard circumstances. In
finding apartments, enduring current living conditions, or getting children back out of protective state custody, religion is brought to bear in
the complex situations of women's everyday lives.

This chapter serves as a chapter of "building blocks" fundamental
to analyzing how lived religion operates in the social context of single
motherhood and urban poverty. Before turning in subsequent chapters
to specific sites of lived religion, I here lay out some analytical and conceptual tools. These tools provide an understanding of theories of religion, resilience, and harm; spiritual practices; and the role of churches.

Theories of Religion, Resilience, and Harm

As noted in the book's introduction, the religion of mothers in poverty
should not be viewed merely as a mechanism to deal with problems.
Faith is important to women because they believe in God, not because
they view it as a problem-solving tool. Psychologist Kenneth Pargament
indicts social scientists as being particularly vulnerable to this misconcep-
tion, for seeing religion as "one among many tools in the human arma-
mentarium for solving problems" (1997, 132). Rhetoric about faith-based
social services often falls into this trap by emphasizing the instrumental
utility of religion in changing people's lives (Unruh and Sider 2005; Bane
2000). To consider it thus does women a great disservice. Religion and
spirituality can provide meaning, rituals, community, and guidance for

living, throughout the full range of life's experiences (Frederick 2003; Pargament 1997). Theories of religion, resilience, and harm, however, prove important in understanding poor women's lived religion. People are more likely to draw on religion during particularly stressful episodes, when they are pushed against the limits of their own power. As part of how people understand the world, religion can structure how people interpret and respond to difficulties (Pargament 1997).

Scholars have defined resilience in many ways, but most definitions incorporate the notion of being able to move forward in the face of adversity. Resilience is "the ability of an individual to adjust to adversity, maintain equilibrium, retain some sense of control over their environment, and continue to move on in a positive manner" (Jackson, Firtko, and Edenborough 2007, 3). Another definition of resilience describes it as "a dynamic process encompassing positive adaptation within the context of significant adversity" (Luthar, Cicchetti, and Becker 2000, 543). Research on resilience has primarily been concerned with children and youth, examining how some children and adolescents experience favorable outcomes despite such adversity as child abuse, parental neglect, and poverty. Research on resilience has expanded, however, outside of child development to study resilience in adults facing illness, bereavement, trauma, natural disasters, and other adversities, as well as resilience in families experiencing stressors.[2] Being resilient in the face of hardship, tragedy, or trauma is characterized by "a stable trajectory of healthy functioning over time, as well as the capacity for generative experiences and positive emotions" (Bonanno 2004, 21). Resilience is considered both a trait (a combination of physical factors and personality traits that allow people to be resilient) and a process (Jackson et al. 2007). Environmental and cultural factors affect resilience. Sustainability is an important dimension of resilience pertinent to mothers in poverty, who endure chronically stressful situations.[3]

Engaging religion positively and proactively in dealing with adversity has been found to help promote resilience.[4] Two key factors influence whether someone will engage religion in contending with problems: the degree to which religion is available to a person (i.e., how religious they are, how much their orientation to the world is shaped by religious faith) and the degree to which they think religion will help provide a sound solution to the crisis or adversity they face (Pargament 1997).[5] Because religion becomes a more prominent resource for people with limited access to other types of resources, women, the elderly, people with less education and income, and African Americans are more likely to engage religion in problem solving. The "positive" ways in which people draw on religion in facing adversity include appraising an unwelcome situation through a benevolent religious frame, feeling guided by and supported by God, feeling connected to and supported by one's religious congregation, and feeling a sense of religious meaning (Pargament 1997).

Several extensive reviews of empirical studies note the wide variety of contexts and populations in which research has found religiousness to be associated with greater self-efficacy and active problem solving: people with different forms of cancer, HIV-positive African American women, people after a terrorist attack in their city, caregivers of people with dementia, people with mental illness, and others. Studies find religion to serve as a source of strength for people who have experienced trauma. Religion can foster resilience through several pathways. It can help provide people with a sense of meaning in adverse life events or situations. It can buffer negative emotions such as depression. Religion can promote "relational resilience," as religious people often have more social networks and social support. Furthermore, religion can serve as a force for personal transformation during crisis or adversity (Pargament and Cummings 2010; Pargament 1997; Pargament and Park 1995). Limited studies of low-income adult populations have found religion and spirituality to foster resilience, including among older African American women who are homeless, African American women exiting prostitution, low-income Latinos, Hurricane Katrina survivors, and others.[6] Low-income single mothers facing welfare time limits, stressful low-wage jobs, child-care problems, violent neighborhoods, lack of affordable housing, and family problems can feel pushed to their limits every day, with many events seeming out of their control. With limited means and few alternative resources, theory predicts that these women would be more likely to draw on religion in solving problems and trying to develop and maintain resilience in light of ongoing hardship.

Although empirical studies find that religion is more often engaged in helpful ways, religion can also be engaged in harmful ways. People experiencing struggles such as doubt, feeling rejected by church members, or feeling angry with, abandoned by, or punished by God experience more negative outcomes and contend less successfully in the face of stressful life situations.[7] Engaging in these types of spiritual struggles has been found to be deleterious across a variety of populations and situations. Cancer patients doing so report overall lower quality of life, and caregivers of terminally ill patients doing so have greater risk of depression and anxiety. People recovering from a serious illness or injury who engage in "negative" manifestations of religiosity are more likely to develop anxiety (Pargament and Cummings 2010). If on top of an adverse life event, individuals feel punished by God, abandoned by God, or alienated from their congregations, or if they experience other forms of "negative" spirituality, then their outcomes can worsen.

Whether religion is engaged beneficially or harmfully, this way of theorizing about religion significantly differs from the "compensation" theories put forth by earlier generations of social theorists. Religion can still be used in a defensive, passive, and "denying of reality" manner, but it can also be engaged in a proactive, strength-giving manner. In drawing "positively" on elements of religion in confronting challenges, people are active, not passive. They are not merely consoled, comforted, or pacified, but they actively work "collaboratively with God" to take action. Instead of denying reality, people accept that a real negative situation exists but reframe the situation through the lens of religion to gain strength to act, find meaning in hardship or trauma, and perhaps experience personal growth and transformation (Pargament 1997). Religion interpreted in a harmful manner also cannot be easily categorized as "compensation." This framework provides a considerably more complex way of looking at religion than seeing it as either compensation or a problem-solving tool.[8] The social scientist must seek to understand how religion operates within the context of individuals' social worlds.

Religious Practices

Religious or spiritual practices, the activities that people deliberately undertake to deepen their connection to and relationship with the divine, form the heart of living faith. Examples of these practices include prayer, worship, devotion, and observance of sacred time (Wuthnow 1998; Roof 1999). Prayer and devotional reading are the central spiritual practices for most people, practices that are in many cases "life-transforming" (Wuthnow 1998, 169). Religious practices relate to theories of religion and resilience because it is partly through religious practices that people develop or maintain resilience in light of difficult situations.

Prayer

Survey data indicate that nine out of ten Americans pray at least sometimes. Seventy-five percent say they pray at least daily, a somewhat higher number than the two-thirds who say they prayed in the past twenty-four hours; these figures indicate high levels of prayer among American adults (Gallup and Jones 2000). Among those who pray, 95 percent believe their prayers are heard and answered (Gallup and Lindsay 1999). Theologians, clergy, social scientists, and others have laid out an array of ways to conceptualize prayer. Poloma and Gallup (1991) categorize prayer as ritual, conversational, petitionary, and meditative. Older people, particularly older Catholics, are more likely than younger people to engage in ritual prayer, which includes such practices as praying memorized prayers, reading prayers from devotional books, and saying the rosary. The most common type of prayer is conversational prayer, where people talk to God in their own words, asking for guidance, blessing, and forgiveness, as well as offering thanksgiving. Petitionary prayer for material things is more likely employed by those who are poorer and have less education. The combination of material need with strong personal faith is especially likely to produce this type of petitionary prayer: evangelicals and other people who say religion is very important to them are more likely to engage in petitionary prayer for material things. About half of Americans who pray engage in meditative prayer, a more contemplative form of prayer that includes trying to listen to God and spending time adoring and worshipping God (Poloma and Gallup 1991). A recent nationally representative survey asked people what they prayed for during the last time they prayed: your family (89 percent); someone you know (75 percent); relationship with God (66 percent); general world concerns (62 percent); confessing sins (61 percent); personal health (57 percent); praise or adoration (49 percent); someone you don't know (47 percent); and financial security (33 percent) (Baker 2008). These data also indicate that lower-income groups, as well as African Americans, are more likely to engage in prayer for financial security, material needs, and health issues than their nonpoor counterparts. African Americans and women pray with greater frequency than other Americans; some studies show the poor pray with greater frequency as well.[9] It is thus not surprising that prayer plays an important role in the lives of low-income urban mothers.

Prayer narratives reveal how people conceive of the divine, view their relationships with God, and understand the role God plays in their lives. Prayer narratives are deeply embedded as a part of a person's cultural and religious background, as well as their social locations (Black 1999). Prayer, says Orsi (1996), is always situated in specific locations of social power. In prayer, people come into intimate contact with the limitations and contradictions intrinsic to their environments. Through prayer, the self seeks to understand and be understood (Orsi 1996, 186–87). What are the prayer narratives of poor mothers? With these women located within a social environment of severe poverty, housing and job instability, and concern for their children, two key themes emerge: petition and gratitude. These narratives take a conversational style, usually reflecting an image of God as a loving father and women's trust in God's love for them.

Prayers of petition marked the most common type of prayer for my respondents, often prayers for concrete material assistance in desperate situations such as homelessness. Maria (introduced in the opening vignette of chapter 1) recounted, "When I had nowhere to go, and I would ask God, 'Please, if you are not doing it for me, do it for my kids. I don't want my kids—I don't want to be sleeping in a car.' I never got to that point because he was always there to help me." Often quoting their prayers directly, mothers expressed how they asked God for housing and jobs and for help in finding child care and in passing their GED exams.

In addition to petitionary prayers for material assistance, poor mothers beseech God for help with emotional or mental health problems. Women on welfare are more likely than the general population to struggle with depression, anxiety, and other mental health conditions.[10] Circumstances in poor women's lives make them vulnerable to mental health problems; homelessness, domestic violence, job-related problems, problems with children, and health concerns can all provoke episodes of depression and anxiety. Some women also suffer from major mental health disorders, such as bipolar illness or severe clinical depression. The vast majority of women I interviewed prayed for emotional or mental health.[11] Elaborated Ann Marie, a twenty-four-year-old white Catholic who rarely attends Mass: "I ask God for help every single day . . . to keep my depression from kicking in. . . . I am a manic depressive. Every morning I just ask for a good day. . . . Last night I was depressed. I was just laying on the couch. This morning when I got up, I just asked God for a better day." Women with serious mental health problems do not necessarily rely solely on prayer as opposed to receiving medical treatment. However, they manifest a strong belief in the efficacy of prayer to help them contend with these illnesses. These mothers find prayer helps them feel less stressed, depressed, and anxious, in line with some social science research that finds religious beliefs and practices to be associated with less depression and higher levels of life satisfaction.[12]

These prayers of petition reveal the women's trust in God and their worldview that envisions God as actively engaged in the world. As Poloma and Gallup (1991) note, "It takes a great deal of faith to make requests for tangible objects" (33).[13] Prayer expresses poor women's trust that God cares about their circumstances no matter how powerless or insignificant they feel in the world and no matter how hopeless situations seem. Robert Orsi (1996) writes of the hopeless moments that led the Catholic women he studied to pray to St. Jude, the patron saint of hopeless causes. "In hopelessness, the devout encountered the limits of their social world to provide them with comfort, assistance, and solace, and acknowledged the shortcomings of the well-established categories of meaning in helping them understand their experience" (64). Low-income urban mothers frequently come up against situations in which they experience the limits of their social worlds to provide help and peace. They turn to God for help in seemingly hopeless situations, whether they are losing their housing or their jobs or their children to child protective services.

Mothers' prayers of petition reach out beyond their own immediate needs. Women pray for other people in their lives, asking God to help them, bless them, and keep them safe. Like many parents, the main "others" mothers in poverty pray for are their children (discussed in detail in chapter 4 on parenting). Children usually mark the central concern in their lives, and motherhood is for many the most salient part of their identities. Mothers pray fervently for their children to be safe, to stay on the right path, and to keep away from street life. Children are furthermore the only others that the interviewed mothers mention praying with informally, engaging in prayer with another person.

Low-income mothers pray for those who help them, such as shelter staff workers and other social service personnel. Juliana is a twenty-year-old Latina mother of one- and two-year-old daughters; she is on welfare and living in a family shelter. She explained, "I ask him to bless those in [the shelter] that have given me a roof over my head." In some cases, shelter workers and other social service providers are the objects of prayer for religious conversion or growth. Jane, one of the few mothers I interviewed who was zealously evangelical about sharing her faith with others, prayed for shelter workers to gain or grow in their faith in Jesus. Although shelter workers may not realize that some of their residents are praying for them, the fact that they are reflects the complicated relationships that can exist between social service personnel and those they serve. Praying for shelter workers and other social work personnel provides a unique twist on the balance of power. Mothers are not the dependent ones but rather the ones intervening to help bring down the power of the divine on behalf of social service workers who hold power over their homeless or welfare clients.[14] Petitioning God on behalf of others also provides poor women with something tangible they can do for people around them. Margarita Mooney (2009) notes the powerful role praying for others played in the lives of the Haitian immigrants she studied. Even those who could not materially help others could pray for them, transforming them from receivers to givers (77).

These prayer narratives of petition spring forth from a cultural context of severe hardship and insecurity. With situations at times feeling out of their personal control, mothers' pleading to God for help becomes for them an empowering act. Through prayer, women of faith "tap into" a divine power that they believe is greater than that of the forces against them. While events may seem overwhelming or even hopeless, mothers feel they can address God, beseech God, and perhaps influence God through the act of prayer (Pargament 1997, 294). Acting via petitionary prayer as a conduit to bring divine power, protection, and favor on the people in their lives gives women a greater sense of agency.

Prayer narratives of gratitude help bring coherence to poor women's lives, and many of these women express prayers of profound gratitude to God despite difficult circumstances. Whether situations were improving or still dire, my informants appeared to follow the biblical dictum "in all circumstances give thanks" (1 Thess. 5:18 [New American Bible][15]). Rhonda, a twenty-nine-year-old African American Baptist who attends church services with her five-year-old son about once a month, constantly invoked gratitude to God throughout her interview: for her job, her boss, and a myriad of other things in her life. Previously on welfare for several years, Rhonda now had a social service job and a much better situation, although she is still a single mother living in a poor, unsafe neighborhood and struggling to pay her bills. She said that she is always "thanking God that I'd made a place for myself and my son to have a roof over my head despite all I've gone through." She emphasized the need "to be grateful for what you have; work hard for what you want; thank God for waking up in the morning and having working limbs." Rhonda's prayers mark her genuine gratitude to God for helping her traverse the difficult path she has encountered in moving from welfare to work and from housing problems to shelter, and she also thanks God for her health, her son, and another day of life. Women who have persisted in the face of hardship to have situations improve give thanks and glory to God. Shantelle is a thirty-eight-year-old African American mother of seven (three children ages five, seven, and nine, and four much older children). When I interviewed her, she had been homeless and in shelters for ten years and was now living in a long-term family shelter with excellent supportive services (including help in her search for permanent housing). She explained, "My life has been wrecked for the last ten years. There has been nothing been going my way. Practically everything has been bad. It seems like things are turning around for the better, so I think about God every single day. Something good happens to me, I thank God."

Women such as Shantelle and Rhonda express gratitude for their improved circumstances, though the improvement is relative and life is still quite challenging. But even women who do not cite any recent improvements and who are in the midst of very difficult situations still find many things in their lives for which to thank God. They emphasize the importance of not complaining, despite the things they might have to complain about. Juliana, experiencing many difficulties living in her shelter, related, "Every night I pray, and every morning I wake up and thank the Lord for giving me another day of air. To live life. I thank him." Children are a primary source of women's gratitude, as evidenced in a quote from Maria: "When I see my kids getting up and giving me a smile every morning, that's amazing. You know that God is in your home." Women believe that nothing is too small to give thanks for. Sheila, a twenty-one-year-old African American mother of a two-year-old, was neither raised with nor practices any organized religion. She explained how one has to give thanks to God for all the little things in life: "A lot of people think that it should be a [bad] situation for them to pray. You should pray regardless. Thank you that I'm living another day. It's not when you're caught up in the corner about to get shot and you start praying. . . . I pray all the time just to say thank you for anything. I just bought some groceries, thank you. Things are going to happen. There are always people worse off than you."

Most of all, poor mothers living in precarious situations emphasize the need to give gratitude to God for the gift of life, for living another day. Marla Frederick (2003) found that the churchgoing African American women she studied in a poor rural part of North Carolina expressed profound gratitude to God in spite of facing difficult circumstances. Her respondents, like mine, constantly expressed sheer gratitude for life itself. According to Frederick, gratitude becomes a way to express faith and endurance in the midst of difficult situations, reflecting the women's belief that God has always provided for their needs and will do so again. Gratitude recurs as a theme among the few studies that, like Frederick's, have delved into the inner spiritual lives of the poor. Helen Black's (1999) study describing elderly African American women in poverty looking back over their lives found women to feel themselves blessed and grateful despite their long years of hardships.

Grateful for groceries, for a smile from their child, for working limbs, for a roof over their head, for another day of life, poor faith-filled mothers make gratitude a central part of their everyday spirituality. Gratitude serves many functions. First, it reflects women's deep belief in and appreciation of a loving God's provision for them, as well as their sense of God's care despite their challenges. Gratitude in this sense is indeed an expression of faith and endurance, as women remind themselves through gratitude of the many ways in which God cares for them and meets their needs. Second, a spirituality of gratitude affirms that women's lives have value despite what society at large believes about poor single mothers on welfare. Gratitude serves in this capacity to claim the worth that comprises their lives, even if it is something as small as a smile from their child.[16] In gratefulness to God, women reflect on the good things about lives that many in the larger society would see as marginalized as best, if not downright dysfunctional.

Gratitude, however, can be tempered with fear, and as such, women also employ it in hope of keeping further negative events from occurring. While mothers are genuinely grateful for things they do have, they are keenly aware that things could be (and likely have been) worse. Thus, women emphasize that they have to be thankful and not complain, lest God in his displeasure for their ingratitude would allow things to get worse. Said Rhonda, "God giveth and God taketh away. I may think my house looks terrible and the foundations need work, but he can make it so that the foundations would totally collapse and I wouldn't have it at all." Sheila echoed a similar sentiment: "If you always complain about every little thing, God can and will take that away from you. If you are showing him that you are not appreciating anything that's being done. . . . Let me not complain about this. There are other people worse. . . . When you think things can't get any worse, believe me, it can." Sheila's observation that many people have worse situations than hers is no mere consoling platitude but reflects women's fear underlying their precarious situations, which could always take a downward turn. For these mothers, the God who gives is also the God who can take away, and women must appreciate what has been given. Despite continuing hardship, they believe gratitude for what is good in their lives serves to keep God from sending or allowing bigger catastrophes.

While prayers of petition and gratitude mark the most common prayer narratives, poor mothers also engage in other types of prayer. Some interviewees mentioned spending time worshipping and praising God in their private prayers. Several mothers spoke of how they prayed for forgiveness of sin, and it is likely that a number of others do so as well, as surveys indicate that low-income people are more likely to pray for forgiveness of sin (Baker 2008). Women make promises to God in prayer, such as one mother who, encouraged by her priest to do so, promised

God in a prayer that she would complete her GED program after dropping out of several others. What does it mean to make a promise to God in prayer? This form of prayer involves the divine in women's goal setting, transforming ordinary goal setting into a sacred pact with God. Women are not only deciding themselves that they aim to attain a certain goal but are making a sacred promise that they will do so. The stakes are set higher, as women do not wish to disappoint God by breaking their promise, and thus they may be more likely to persist.

Poor mothers' prayer narratives reflect a God who is both compassionate and judgmental. Analysts of American religion emphasize that a transformation has occurred in how most Americans view God. As Robert Wuthnow describes, the contemporary American God "is a God of love, comfort, order, and security. Gone is the God of judgment, wrath, mystery, and punishment" (1994b, 7). Alan Wolfe writes that the language of damnation and sin has been replaced by empathy, understanding, and nonjudgmentalness; the Lord to whom Americans turn "rarely gets angry and frequently strengthens self-esteem" (2003, 3). Sociologist Marsha Witten (1993) argues that a therapeutic culture has turned Protestant images of God from "judge" to "daddy." My respondents hold images of God that do not fall neatly into either of these categories. God is both loving and judgmental. Their primary image of God is that of a caring, tender, loving father who is deeply involved in the details of their everyday lives. They believe God hears their prayers and understands the hardships they face and will help them and be with them. To them, God is close, intimate, a divine friend. A subtext to their prayer narratives, however, is a God who judges, who is a stern father. The same loving God is also at times a strict and disappointed father, a God who can allow or send bad things their way. This is seen in some women's assessments of themselves as sinners, in those women who feel they have fallen short of God's standards in certain areas of their lives, and in those who remind themselves that ingratitude risks God's displeasure and punishment. However, the image of God as a caring father intimately involved in women's lives is clear in both cases. Even a disappointed God is seen as a loving father who has women's best interests at heart, much like a human father disappointed in his child's behavior.

As a religious practice, prayer is easily accessible, no matter how marginalized the women's circumstances. In addition to its accessibility, the confidentiality of prayer makes it attractive for mothers seeking guidance. Some mothers perceive prayer as more helpful than talking to others, because they do not necessarily want to share their problems with their friends or family. Gabriella, a seventeen-year-old Latina mother who stopped attending her Pentecostal church at age eleven, explained: "Like, when you pray, it's like you're talking with God, and if you don't want to tell your problems to nobody, you're just praying. And God knows, and he's not going to tell nobody, either. . . . Everything I'm thinking in my mind, I take it out. I feel like I'm talking to somebody, so I take everything out, then I feel better." Gabriella, who left school after seventh grade and is now on welfare and studying for her GED, prefers to share her problems with God, as opposed to her mother (with whom she lives) or her friends. She feels reassured in her knowledge that God is not going to gossip or tell anyone. In prayer, women believe they are talking with someone who understands their problems and wants to help them and will keep their thoughts and struggles confidential.

Are Prayers Answered?

Does God answer? Many women would say the answer is a resounding yes, though not always how and when they want. The mothers studied see God as answering prayer in two main ways: most often by them working "in partnership with God" and sometimes through "miraculous intervention." Brenda (age twenty-one, white, raised nominally Catholic, does not attend Mass) illustrates the "miraculous intervention" model. She told a dramatic story relating her belief that God had directly intervened to get her child back from state protective custody. "What court-appointed lawyer do you know who will get an eighteen-year-old mother back into the same shelter that they just kicked you out of and get your child back in two weeks? That is an act of God. It was like he [the lawyer] was a little angel." In her interpretation, the court-appointed lawyer served as an angel, carrying out a miraculous act of God. Several mothers spoke of God's miraculous intervention in healing their sick children. Isabella, a twenty-seven-year-old Latina Catholic and mother of two, believed God brought her daughter out of a coma: "My daughter, she's sick, and then one day she have asthma attacks, and she was in a coma for one week, she don't open the eyes. So I made a promise here, I go [to church] every Sunday." At the time of the interview, Isabella was still continuing her practice of attending Mass every Sunday in gratitude for her daughter's healing. Although women view events—healed children, jobs, children home from state custody—as a result of direct divine intervention, they usually also have taken actions to help make things happen. They interpret the results of prayer as miraculous and gratefully offer thanks to God, but women are actors with agency.

Most often, mothers believe that God answers prayer by engaging them in an explicit partnership, whereby they and God work together, enlisting the help of social service agencies and others along the way. This finding fits well with earlier research observations that people often see themselves as working "collaboratively with God" to address problems (Pargament 1997). Maria believes that after her desperate prayer about her housing situation and not wanting her children sleeping in a car, God showed her the next steps to take. "When I had nowhere to go, and there was nobody who could take me into their house for any other reason, the only thing I had in mind was, go ask for help from the government. And that's what I did, and they got me a place, and here I am." Maria interprets her placement in an apartment in a long-term family shelter as an answered prayer coming from God, an answered prayer that required her to take the initiative to go to the government and for the agency to work with her in finding a placement. She credits the "partnership with God," the fact that it was after *praying* that she thought to turn to the government, for bringing about the good outcome. Other respondents shed further light on what it means to work "in partnership with God." Tamika, a highly religious twenty-six-year-old African American mother neither raised with nor involved in organized religion, is participating in a job training program. She stated: "I believe in that saying, 'Make one step; he [God] makes the second.' Yes, you make your first step, and God will make the next step. You might think you have a hard time making that first step, and you may not be motivated to make it, but if you made that step . . . the second step will be that big blessing you have about what you can accomplish." Women believe that God asks them to take that first step but partners with them to bring about accomplishments and answered prayer.

The idea of working "collaboratively with God" is not limited to the poor and is one key way that people in general engage religious faith in contending with challenges.[17] Yet given the lack of access to resources and the daunting challenges to be faced, "partnering with God" can serve as a particularly powerful framework for disenfranchised people. Helen Black (1999) describes the "covenantal partnership" between God and her poor and elderly African American respondents, whereby the women see themselves as co-actors with God. Margarita Mooney (2009) notes the notion of working with God among poor Haitian immigrants. As a partner, low-income single mothers believe that God helps them find solutions to their seemingly intractable problems, solutions that often involve social service agencies or government officials. Although the women take such actions as filling out housing and job application forms and engaging in education or job training efforts, they believe it is their partnership with—along with assistance from—God that brings results. God wants active partners willing to try hard to take necessary steps toward finding positive solutions to problems. In turn, they believe God hears their prayers and blesses the efforts they make.

God, however, does not always seem to answer prayer, sometimes leading to anger with God and a loss of faith. Sally is a black/white twenty-nine-year-old Catholic social service worker, and, three years before I interviewed her, she had stopped her regular Mass attendance on taking a job that required her to work on weekends. She discussed how she temporarily lost her faith when she transitioned off welfare several years earlier: "They [welfare officials] cut you off completely with nothing. You could say to them, 'I can't find a job.' They don't care. . . . I was going to church. I would say [to God] help me, help me, help me. But nobody was helping me, and my prayers weren't working. You know I always had my little cross and prayed every night, so it's like I lost faith in everything." At this crucial juncture in her life, Sally was praying desperately, with children to support, no job, and no welfare, yet prayer yielded nothing. Furthermore, she was holding up her end of the partnership, looking for a job while simultaneously petitioning welfare officials for mercy. No matter how much women take initiative and act on their situations, solutions may not be forthcoming. Shantelle recounted a recent period when unanswered prayer led to loss of faith: "Nothing was going my way. I don't have an apartment, and I have been homeless for ten years. Every place I live is temporary. So I ain't had that much faith in God. Why should I have that much faith in God? I had some, and then things kept getting worse, so no, I didn't have none at all." Mothers pray, yet still find themselves unable to find housing, cut off from welfare with nowhere to turn, or unable to find a decent job.[18]

In interviews, women talking about "anger with God" or loss of faith portrayed it as either an intermittent reaction or something they had experienced in the past that they no longer felt.[19] Vicky (age thirty-four, divorced mother of one, Native American, recovering alcoholic, nonattending but deeply prayerful Catholic) noted her intermittent anger with God: "I notice if I stop praying or sometimes I get angry because of my situation, I get mad at God. I don't feel good when that happens." Similarly, Elisa, a twenty-three-year-old Latina mother of three small children, stopped her frequent attendance at Pentecostal services three years earlier when she ran into transportation problems. She described how stressful episodes provoke temporary loss of faith: "Sometimes when I am stressed out, I don't have no faith at all. I'm like, 'God, why are you doing this to me? Why is this happening to me?' I think he's not there for me. But then after, when I'm really calm, I know that he's there for me." A more common reaction than anger or temporary loss of faith to seemingly unanswered prayer was the women's belief that God *is* answering their prayers, even though they do not see the results at the moment. Although they request specific things of God, they believe God's ways are higher than theirs. Shantelle, grateful to be in her current shelter with supportive services but still waiting for permanent housing, asserted, "I guess he do things in his own time and in his own way." In this framework, God cannot be confined to providing only one solution and cannot be expected to answer prayer only in the way desired by women (Black 1999). Thus, what appears to be a bad outcome can also be considered answered prayer, as God answering in "his own way." This interpretation is not limited to the poor. Writing about middle-class evangelical women in a parachurch organization, Marie Griffith (1997) described women "yielding to God's will, even when it conflicts" with their own desires. For example, when a loved one dies despite prayers for healing, women "interpret such events not as 'failures' but as lessons rich in meaning, summoning opportunities for renewed faith" (87). As I analyze in detail in chapter 5 on meaning making, this type of religious framing allows low-income mothers to re-interpret suffering in ways that bring them spiritual coherence.

Peace and Transformation

Surveys show that a third of Americans who pray experience a deep sense of peace and well-being regularly as a result of prayer and that another almost 40 percent do so occasionally (Poloma and Gallup 1991). Poor mothers turning to prayer often gain a sense of comfort and peace. Elisa explained how prayer gives her comfort in the housing shelter. "Some-times I feel really, really sad. Sometimes all of a sudden, I'll just start cry-ing. I feel sad because this place [the shelter] is driving me crazy. I think that God is not with me, but then I ask him, 'Why am I feeling like this?' So I pray to him, and I feel better, and I know that I'm still going to get out of here, and everything is going to be better for me and for my kids. Then I just realize that he's there, and he's going to help me feel better. So that helps me calm down." Prayer allows women to derive comfort from their belief that God is with them, that they are not alone, and that things will get better. The belief that they are never alone is particularly important for struggling single mothers and was highlighted by many of the women I interviewed. Although their difficulties feel overwhelming, most believe that God is a loving father who cares about their suffering, loves them deeply, and walks with them and helps them. They derive peace from the belief that God will be with them and never leave them alone.

Prayer yields more than comfort and peace. In analyzing the prayer narratives of middle-class evangelical women, Marie Griffith found that a woman's sense that God listens to her and understands her sufferings gives birth to a new sense of self. "New possibilities for identity emerge within old constraints" as women are "healed, transformed and set free" (1997, 77–78). Prayer can lead to transformation. Poor mothers find in prayer new identities as strong people who persevere, who face their problems not alone but working in partnership with a God they view as loving and involved. Most of my respondents, and likely many poor urban mothers overall, frequently pray for strength. In believing that God answers these prayers, women actually feel stronger, more capable, and more able to act in the world. Women transformed by prayer may view themselves not as stigmatized and scorned welfare mothers but as children of God, a God they believe strengthens them and works with them to help bring about their goals. Women reach out and pray for others, whether those others are their children or their social workers. Women express gratitude to God for life, for their children, for the good things they believe God has given them. These prayers of gratitude and prayers of petition for others transform them from those who need to those who have something to offer others (Frederick 2003, 214; Mooney 2009).

Prayer, Faith, and Action

Critics may contend that poor women employing religious faith to help deal with problems could lose initiative to take necessary actions. In keeping with previously mentioned studies that find religion helps people proactively engage problems, my respondents decry a passive approach. Stated Jennifer, a twenty-year-old white Catholic who attends Mass only on holidays, "I would pray, but I wouldn't wait for something to come to me, like God is going to have this come to me. I would go out and do it myself." Women believe prayer yields God's help, but God helps by empowering women to act, opening doors, and working through social service personnel and others. Under these conditions, religion serves as an element of women's cultural framework that promotes action.

Even women focusing on the afterlife, commonly stereotyped as resigned to the state of affairs in the world, instead often use their faith in the hereafter to motivate action. Jane explained:

But, thank God, there is a heaven, and this isn't it. Thank God this isn't it. Thank God there is more to this, you know, and that's our hope. That's our hope, as Christians, that we know that this isn't the eternal place we are going to be. There is a heaven, and God will help us get through this part, troubles and illnesses, whatever, whatever it is, hard times. You know where you are going, you know that you are going to go to heaven with Jesus, and I think you have that confidence and that just helps you to be stronger and more Christlike than if you didn't have him. . . . It gives you strength to get through the time that you are going through.

Rather than creating passive, disengaged acceptance of their current life situations, the promise of eternal life with God in heaven often gives women confidence and strength to tackle their daily challenges and work to improve their lives on earth. Although they believe that earth is difficult and that heaven with Jesus will be better, the knowledge of heaven gives believers such as Jane not only endurance but also confidence and strength. It is not an either-or dichotomy, heaven or earth, but heaven *and* earth. In a context of extreme deprivation, thoughts of heaven can provide a spirit of resilience and perseverance in the here and now.[20]

Sacred Reading: "The Lord Is My Shepherd, I Shall Not Want"

As with most other religious believers, mothers in poverty adopt prayer as their primary religious practice. However, sacred reading also plays an important role in the lives of some people. Ninety-two percent of American households own a Bible, and 59 percent of Americans report reading the Bible at least occasionally. Thirty-seven percent of Americans read the Bible at least weekly (Gallup and Simmons 2000). Women are more likely than men to read it, and young people are less likely than older people to read it (Barna Group 2001).[21] Believers engage in spiritual reading to seek divine guidance and to grow in their knowledge of the divine.

Among my respondents, as in the general population, women in evangelical churches or from evangelical backgrounds are particularly likely to integrate Bible reading as part of their religious practices. The practice of reading scripture provides an important avenue for poor women who value its guidance to gain what they perceive to be "God's perspective" on their situations. Rhonda turns to the Bible when she is depressed because she does not trust her friends to give her good advice. The Bible, she says, provides truth, whereas friends wishing to avoid hurting her feelings may not.

I like to do it [read the Bible] especially when I get depressed as opposed to if I was going to call on my girlfriends, and they give you an answer. . . . They want to comfort you because they're your friend. You know, some people don't know how to give effective advice. . . . It [the Bible] brings you back to reality. . . . I thank God and say this must be the godly way to do it, as opposed to the way of the world. . . . When I know I'm dead wrong, and it's something I said or I've done, I could call a girlfriend to confide in her, "Oh, you know what I did?" She would agree with me . . . when I know deep down inside that's not right. . . . The Bible has more truth or guidance, as opposed to a girlfriend, who may not be objective as my friend, because she doesn't want to hurt my feelings.

Women such as Rhonda perceive the Bible as providing them with guidance on the right way to do things, the "godly way" as opposed to the "way of the world." Sacred scripture, they believe, engenders knowledge of the right way to live in a world surrounded by distractions and temptations. In addition to guidance, spiritual reading provides strength and comfort. Several mothers directly quoted scripture during interviews, such as "The Lord is my shepherd," from the Twenty-third Psalm. This psalm and others, written in the first person and expressing intimate cries of pain and notions of God's love, help, and protection, emphasize to women in writing that God is with them no matter how difficult their struggles. In the spiritual practice of sacred reading, mothers may seek out specific passages particularly salient to their own struggles. Carrie, a thirty-five-year-old white nonattending Catholic, is the mother of two children, a six-month-old at home with her and an eleven-year-old removed previously by child protective services. She likes to read passages from the Bible about forgiveness of sins. "I tend to read. This way I feel I am healing myself, and it is relaxing to me." Seeking out and reading biblical passages about forgiveness helps Carrie to feel healed and forgiven. Also intriguing is that she sees the reading as her "healing herself," as opposed to God healing her. She is perhaps aware of the proactive work she is doing in seeking out biblical writings about forgiveness. The act of sacred reading can serve as an act of self-efficacy. Carrie described in the interview a prayer she keeps with her to read when she is feeling stress. "God, I see your footprints in the sand as you walk beside me and hold my hand, then as I go further I don't see your footprints. Jesus said, 'My child, that is because I am carrying you the rest of the way.' "[22] Reading this prayer helps Carrie to feel reassured that instead of abandoning her, Jesus is in fact carrying her during difficult moments.

Low-income women may rely on more vague knowledge of the Bible to provide strength. LaToya, a thirty-five-year-old African American who was not attending services at the time of the interview, drew on knowledge of the Bible to endure the difficulties she encountered in her shelter program. "When I have situations like being here [the shelter], and I just want to give it up, give up, you know, and just walk out, and, you know, then I pray to God, and then I feel like God is talking to me, 'Stick it out.' You can hear this psalm, 'Everything is going to be okay.' And I find myself not wanting to leave." What psalm does she mean? "Everything is going to be okay." Why psalms? LaToya clearly knows that some psalms speak words of comfort. Before going to prison for selling drugs, LaToya, a mother of seven children ages six weeks to thirteen years, had previously been an active congregant in her black Baptist church. Perhaps she has knowledge of psalms from her time in that congregation, perhaps she has read them on her own, perhaps they were something from her childhood religious socialization, or perhaps she has heard a televangelist speak of them. Released from prison yet feeling "a sinner before God" and avoiding church, LaToya retains a deep knowledge of the intent, if not the actual content, of the scripture she cites. The assurance and comfort she draws from that knowledge, combined with her belief that God is telling her to stick it out in the shelter, help her to persevere.

Despite the high percentage of Americans who own a Bible, polls indicate widespread ignorance about its contents. Only half of American adults can name any of the four gospels of the New Testament; 10 percent of Americans believe that Joan of Arc was Noah's wife (Prothero 2007). Yet a number of biblical ideas and sayings have entered into more general use. The mothers studied drew on broader cultural knowledge of the Bible, evident in their veiled and not-so-veiled references to it. In trying to explain hardship, Jane used a verbatim reference to a verse from the gospel of Matthew in the New Testament, saying, "And things happen to everybody. You know, God says the rain falls on the just as well as the unjust" (Matt. 5:45). Although evangelicals such as Jane are more likely to know and quote specific verses, Catholic as well as Protestant women exhibited knowledge of Bible sayings, especially those that have become more general cultural maxims. Ann Marie said God would not put her with her boyfriend who has seizures if she were not able to handle it and help him—possibly a veiled reference to a verse from the First Epistle of Paul to the Corinthians in the New Testament ("God is faithful and will not let you be tried beyond your strength" [1 Cor. 10:13]) but also a general cultural maxim that "God will not give you more than you can handle." Other examples of maxims derived from the Bible that mothers cited include "You're not supposed to judge" and "God says you have to work to eat." As a primary resource for devoted time set aside for reading or as a more general source of religious knowledge, the Bible plays a role in how some low-income mothers interpret and respond to their situations.

Spiritual practices, argues Robert Wuthnow (1998), call people to take an active part in their own spiritual development by seeking God in regular prayer, reading and deliberating on the meaning of sacred scriptures, seeking counsel of others, and trying to grow closer to God. "The point of spiritual practice is not to elevate an isolated set of activities over the rest of life but to electrify the spiritual impulse that animates all of life" (198). Drawing on my research, I suspect that the spiritual practices of many low-income mothers are deep and rich, whether or not these women are involved in organized religion. In conducting the interviews, I was particularly struck by the religious practices of Sarah, a thirty-one-year-old African American single mother, who despite not having attended church services since she was a teenager, talked of God constantly throughout the interview, prayed throughout the day, read the Bible daily, and devoted all day every Saturday for prayer in the spirit of "keeping holy the Sabbath." A woman such as this would be categorized as a "nonchurch attendee" in a typical social survey. This characterization would overlook the myriad and profound ways in which she engages in religious practices in living and making sense of her everyday life (McGuire 2008).

Even if they themselves do not engage in spiritual practices, most of the mothers interviewed believed these practices are important. Faith and religious practices are seen as a foundation, something to keep women anchored and be the best people they can be, despite hardship. Martina, a forty-three-year-old Latina raised Catholic, used to pray, read scripture, and attend Mass at earlier times during her adult life, but was no longer doing any of these at the time of the interview. She said, "Faith, I believe, is there to remind you and to help you about your virtues and your morals. . . . It keeps you stable. . . . It reminds you of how to be with other people and reminds you to be a good person despite the sacrifices and the heartache that you go through." Almost all of the few mothers who, like Martina, said that religion or faith was not important to them went on to talk about its importance: how it helped them previously in their lives, how they saw it making a positive difference in the lives of friends, or how engaging in religious practices could have kept them away from mistakes they had made. Although these views of religious faith may seem instrumental or utilitarian, the desire to want to be a strong, stable person in the face of hardship is commendable, and many wealthier people engage in religious practices for similar reasons (Pargament 1997).[23]

Beliefs, Practices, and Harm

As is clear from the previous section, poor mothers engage in religious practices in ways that can foster a sense of self-efficacy and agency. But poor women can also interpret elements of religion detrimentally, both in a larger macro sense and in a micro sense. Survey data suggest that women in poverty may be more likely than their nonpoor counterparts to feel abandoned or punished by God, although the majority of poor women do not feel this way.[24]

A "negative religious worldview" is exemplified by Brenda, who told me, "I know once I leave this hell, I will be going to somewhere a lot better. I don't believe in hell. I think this is hell. This is terrible. I don't understand the world, and I don't really want to. I'm just living in it until I go to a better place." As a single mother of a three-year-old and product of the foster care system, Brenda has seen more than her share of hardship. Her quote here illustrates compensation or social deprivation theory; in the words of sociologist Kingsley Davis (1949), "The greater his [man's] disappointment in this life, the greater his faith in the next. Thus the existence of goals beyond this world serves to compensate people for frustrations they inevitably experience in striving to reach socially acquired and socially valuable ends" (532). Brenda's comments suggest a negative religious worldview that might lead to passivity and depression. However, Brenda's larger religious discourse reveals much more than a negative worldview and otherworldly compensation for social deprivation. Her remarks coexist with other religious ideas promoting resilience, in beliefs that God helps her with stress and job performance. Nor is she sitting around and passively rejecting the world—Brenda is pursuing education and training, with the goal of being a social worker for children in foster care. The positive ways in which she employs religion coexist with, and, I would argue, outweigh, the negative.

Mothers in poverty, like other Americans, sometimes employ "demonic reprisals," which can be a negative and passive way of drawing on religion (Folkman and Moskowitz 2004). Seventy percent of Americans believe in the devil (Newport 2007), and the role of the devil is an important part of certain conservative Christian religious traditions. Satan, in this framework, desires to wrest Christians away from God and works both within individuals' psyches (through temptations and deceptions) and through external events to draw people into sin (Nelson 2005). For my respondents, the devil's temptations lay mostly in the realm of the psyche, where some believe Satan goads them to despairing thoughts about their situations and their future. Explained Elisa, "When you leave God, the devil attacks you more. . . . The devil is there to attack you. Like whenever you feel lonely, sad; the devil, he sticks things in your head to tell you that you did something wrong, that's why you feel like that." Mothers such as Elisa believe that Satan brings hopelessness, self-loathing, and despair by working through moments of loneliness and depression.

When women either consciously or through distraction withdraw from God, they find the ever-prowling devil ready to pounce.

Demonic reprisals, although considered a harmful religious interpretation by some social scientists, can also evoke resilience and strength. Griffith's compelling portrait depicts middle-class women evoking strength from engaging in "spiritual warfare" with Satan. Satan tempts women into fear, discouragement, and other sin, but as they stand fast and fight against Satan, God empowers them to defeat him. "In choosing to obey God's will rather than give into Satan's temptations, women are rewarded with the God-given authority to banish Satan and to render him virtually power-less" (1997, 193). Griffith portrays these women as also using their power to fight against the devil's influence in their family lives and in the broader society. They do not just pray for God to help but actively resist Satan "as soldiers waging war" (185). Similarly, poor women thinking about Satan or the devil find the act of "resisting the devil" empowering. Naming their feelings of hopelessness and helplessness as "of the devil" allows the mothers to categorize such feelings as things that are "not of God." Believing themselves vulnerable to the devil's attacks due to moving away from God, they try to reconnect with God via prayer and actively employ positive religious beliefs to "fight Satan." Blaming the devil for internal feelings of despair and hopelessness transforms such feelings into an external enemy against whom women can fight.

Where low-income mothers' religious interpretations seem most likely to become harmful, in a micro sense, are the negative ways in which some draw on religion in viewing themselves and their situations. About a quarter of my sample expressed religious guilt, often about their failure to participate in organized religion. This guilt ranged from what seemed to be minor expressions all the way to profound expressions of guilt deeply affecting a sense of self. Some women believed themselves to have failed God either in past mistakes or in their current life situations, as evident in their discourse: "God would think I'm a bum," "I'm a sinner," "God was disappointed in me," "God sees me doing nothing." Mothers sometimes feel abandoned by God. A number feel rejected by church communities. Women who engage in high levels of these types of spiritual struggles will likely find their problems exacerbated. These types of religious interpretations are associated with negative outcomes, such as greater levels of depression, poorer physical health outcomes, and poorer dealing with difficult life events and circumstances (Pargament 1997).[25] Some women's religious views exacerbated their sense of failure in not living up to societal norms with regard to such things as welfare use or child rearing, as subsequent chapters will address. These mothers feel they have failed not only in the eyes of society but also in the eyes of God, thus carrying an even heavier load of shame and guilt (Griffith 1997).

Negative religious interpretations can be fluid or more fixed. For example, an individual may experience feeling abandoned by God, something a number of low-income mothers experience at various points in their struggles with housing difficulties or welfare. Yet for most, this does not seem to be a permanent state, and such acts as prayer or seeking spiritual support, combined perhaps with circumstances improving, allow this feeling to pass. In other cases, women struggling with deep negative religious interpretations due to guilt or other things seem to experience these types of religious attributions over longer courses of time. Negative ways of engaging religion also coexist with beneficial ones, leading women to draw strength from religion in one area of their lives (for example, parenting or work stress) and to interpret it more harmfully in other parts.

Thus, the everyday religion of some mothers in poverty includes interpretations that can be harmful. Poor mothers overall, however, seem to follow patterns observed in earlier studies on various populations. People draw on religion in proactive and life-enhancing ways, and people may engage in harmful types of spiritual struggles that exacerbate already difficult circumstances, with positive ways of engaging religion occurring more often than harmful ways.

Sources of Religious Culture

Sociologist Ann Swidler (1986) argues that culture serves as a "tool kit" from which people construct strategies of action. Culture, in this interpretation, consists of "symbolic vehicles of meaning" (273), such as beliefs, worldviews, and rituals, as well as more informal practices of daily life, such as stories and language. To see culture as a "tool kit" is to see it as a repertoire of symbols, beliefs, and worldviews that people draw on in organizing action. The culture available to individuals both shapes and constrains their strategies of action. Religious culture—personal faith practices, religious beliefs, and religious knowledge—can be part of a repertoire from which people draw on in organizing action, whether or not they attend religious services. Actions can be both motivated by and constrained by the religious lens through which one views the world.

Where do poor women obtain the religious culture that serves as part of their "repertoire of capacities" (Swidler 2001, 81)? In general, people's sources of religious knowledge are diverse. Childhood socialization is an important source of religious understanding. The family is the most important agent for the religious socialization of children.[26] Through words and example at home, and through church involvement and religious education, many parents try to give their children a religious worldview. Most Americans (including most of the women interviewed) have been raised at least nominally in a religious tradition. My interviewees gained religious understanding in childhood from the faith of their parents, grandparents, and other close older relatives. For some, domestic religious images in their childhood homes—such as holy cards, pictures of Jesus, or statues of the Virgin Mary—reinforced particular religious worldviews. Through childhood family socialization, women absorb religious narratives that are carried into adulthood and that shape their images of God. Poor women's experiences in churches, both as children and later as adults for those who participate as adults, provide a further source of religious cultural knowledge. The Bible is a source of religious knowledge, especially for Pentecostal and evangelical women. Other religious media, such as pamphlets, religious books, and televangelist programs, also transmit religious culture.[27] Some women learn religious values from friends and other people such as coworkers who "witness" or otherwise try to provide spiritual knowledge.

Thus, in drawing on religious culture, mothers in poverty draw on whatever knowledge they have gained about religion from their upbringing, environment, exposure to religious media, and previous or current church involvement. In my research, specific denominational teaching seemed less important than a loose basic knowledge of Christianity, broadly construed. Although I found women from Catholic backgrounds more likely to reference sacraments and women from evangelical backgrounds more likely to quote the Bible, poor American mothers across a variety of backgrounds drew on surprisingly similar elements of religious culture in negotiating their everyday lives.

Overwhelming majorities of Americans claim that people "should arrive at their religious beliefs independent of any church or synagogue" and that one can be a good Christian or Jew without attending religious services (Reeves 1996, 61). A recent nationwide study found that 71 percent of Americans pick and choose their religious beliefs, with higher numbers of people under age twenty-five doing so. Rather than fully accept beliefs taught by organized religion, people choose their religious beliefs and tailor them to suit their individual needs (Barna Group 2009). Low-income women's religious repertoire is steeped in such widespread cultural religious autonomy. Mothers locate the most relevant source of religious legitimacy within their own personal experiences and observations. When their personal observations or experiences contradict church or clergy teaching, many women are quick to cite the church or clergy as wrong. Prayer and personal reflection provide authoritative indications of God's will. Women experience God separately from, and sometimes in opposition to, churches and official doctrine.[28]

Poor women, like other Americans, act as moral and theological agents, interpreting what they believe to be right through the lens of their own standards of ethics and justice. In this manner, some serve up quite pointed critiques of churches. As noted earlier, Jane left her Assembly of God church when the new pastor would not help her family when they ran into difficulties that led to homelessness. As opposed to the previous pastor, who believed in "helping people," the new pastor's approach did not meet Jane's standard of Christian justice. Calling churches "hypocritical," Jane referenced the book of Acts in the New Testament, describing how the early Christians shared with one another so that nobody went without. Here Jane offers a sharp critique of the materialism of wealthier Christians:

Like these people that can be living in these big houses, and even, say, their kids are grown up, or whatever, they don't need these big houses. What do they need these houses for? They can either live in smaller houses, or even apartments. Or two cars, or you have two cars; why do you need two cars, or three cars, or you need a boat? . . . I think a lot of the material stuff is just too much. It's good to have extra things. It's nice to have things like that. I am not saying that, but if there's people that are going without those basic needs, I think that something should happen. I think that people should step up to the plate and say, wait a minute, and they should give. They should help out.

Wealthy Christians, in this framing, should not be living in huge homes, owning three cars and boats, when their poorer counterparts lack any home or car at all. The Bible, Jane indicates, calls for wealthier Christians to share with the poor so that no one has to go without their essential needs being met. Anticipating protest from a fictitious wealthy Christian, she goes on to critique American individualism from the perspective of her understanding of Christian faith: "You might say, 'Hey, I did this. I had to work hard to get to where I am. I did it. Why can't you do it?' . . . Like I said, that scripture verse, it is in Acts 2, that it says they all got together, and they saved their possessions, and they sold everything, and they gave it so that everyone had an equal share." Here Jane imagines a wealthier Christian telling her that he or she has worked hard to gain those large houses or boats or cars and that she too needs to work hard to succeed. Jane exhibits her understanding of the meaning of the American Dream, whereby success and failure are attributed to individual effort

(Hochschild 1995). This, of course, would indicate that she and her family are poor and homeless because they have not tried hard enough. Yet Jane, a mother living in a shelter, shifts power here in contradictory and meaningful ways, defying expectations. As a moral agent, her righteous understanding of who God is and what it means to be a Christian is violated by pastors who will not help families in need. It is violated by wealthy Christians invoking their hard work to justify their individualistic enjoyment of excess material goods while fellow members of their community lack basic needs. This is not a woman who is too busy for church or who feels unwelcome in church. She left the church because it did not meet her standards of Christian love and justice. She perceives moral righteousness to be on her side, not on the side of the church or wealthier Christians.

Although a number of mothers served up critiques of some aspect of organized religion (sometimes to contrast one favorably against another), my respondents did not reflect on broader structural issues in American society, with the exception of Jane speaking against society's materialism, consumerism, and unwillingness to help the poor. Instead, poor mothers' cultural religious repertoire most often reflects the adoption of an American ideal of self-sufficiency. In interviews, some women quoted a supposed Bible verse, actually found nowhere in the Bible: "God helps those who help themselves." (Surveys show that 80 percent of Americans believe that this is a saying from the Bible [Griffith 2009].) Many mothers in poverty think they have to make it all happen, "alone with God." An analysis of their religious discourse reveals almost no mention of any structural issues that shape their lives and contribute to their many difficulties.

Faith, Prayer, and Hope

Within individual lives, religion often proves a powerful component of a disenfranchised woman's cultural repertoire. Mothers perceive faith to be affirming and inspiring, providing hope amid dire situations. The words "faith" and "hope" play a prominent role in poor mothers' religious narratives. In trying to analyze these concepts, particularly in trying to understand "hope," I sought out dictionary, social science, and theological definitions.[29] But it is listening to the voices of the women themselves that allows understanding of what these constructs mean for them. "Faith" for these mothers means a belief and trust in a God who they perceive loves them deeply and is involved in the everyday circumstances of their lives. Consistent with studies connecting faith with higher levels of hope, poor single mothers contend that their belief in God gives them hope that things will improve.[30] Faith is transformed into hope via women's spiritual practice of prayer. Faith—their belief in a loving God—leads mothers to pray, and their prayer yields hope. What, then, is hope? Women did not speak of "optimism" ("a broad and diffuse sense of confidence about goals"[31]); they spoke of hope.

The religious discourse of urban mothers in poverty is filled with the language of hope. Vicky stated, "It's a struggle being a single mom, low income, with a lot of worries. Sometimes I need to know that we've got a roof over our head, we've got some food in the fridge, and that's enough for today. . . . I ask God for a lot of help during the day with different situations. . . . [Faith] gives me hope that things are going to change." Liz, a twenty-one-year-old white mother who was raised Catholic and now attends Mass only on holidays, said, "When I'm depressed, I do pray for a better outcome of the situation. . . . It gives me a feeling of hope . . . hope that everything is going to turn out well in the end, that everything is going to be okay." For Magda, a twenty-two-year-old mixed-race black/white Episcopalian who stopped attending weekly service upon moving to a shelter with her sixteen-month-old son, prayer gives "hope that the next day is going to be okay." Psychologist C. R. Snyder and colleagues (2002) define hope as "a cognitive set involving an individual's beliefs in his or her capability to produce workable routes to goals and beliefs in his or her own ability to initiate and sustain movement toward those goals" (666). This definition does not capture the essence of the women's narratives of hope. "Hope" is grounded in women's perception of God as a loving father and is intimately intertwined with religious faith. For a few particularly personally devout mothers, hope is more explicitly tied to Christian themes, such as the hope of heaven or the resurrection of Jesus after crucifixion. "Hope," for most of the women, is a *confident* expectation that things will work out through the help of a God who they believe loves them and cares about them. As Jane explained, "My hope is in Jesus. It's not the same kind of hope like a human hope that you hope it happens, like maybe it will, maybe it won't. It's a hope that you know it will. It's a different hope. It's a knowing hope. It's awesome." Faith, mediated by prayer, brings hope to mothers in poverty, both for their daily needs and in the resolution of their longer-term situations. Far from providing mere comfort (although it does provide comfort), this hope grounded in faith helps women take actions toward making a better life for themselves and their children. Whether or not they participate in churches, faith provides many women with hope that they will someday have better housing, better jobs, better relationships, and a good environment in which to raise their children.

An emphasis on the relationship among faith, prayer, and hope in the lives of the mothers studied by no means negates a larger prophetic role of religion in challenging unjust social structures, the call for religious communities to stand in solidarity with the poor in combating injustice, or the role of faith-based community organizing. This does not mean, however, that understanding women's sense of hope and agency within their own social contexts is unimportant. Marla Frederick writes, " 'Hope' does not necessarily bring substantial change in people's material reality. It does not force political or economic change, just as gratitude does not necessarily result in large-scale change for the common good. What hope and gratitude do produce, however, is endurance and therefore the possibility of change in the midst of adversity" (2003, 73).

The Role of Churches

The third building block begins to lay out the various roles that churches can play in the lives of poor urban mothers. Despite the fact than only seven of the mothers in the study attended church once a month or more, churches played roles in various ways. Several themes are highlighted here: the notions of sacred space and spiritual experience, churches as providers of social and material resources, and faith-based social service provision.

Churches exist first and foremost as places for people to worship and experience the divine. Despite a cultural shift from a "spirituality of dwelling" to a "spirituality of seeking," Americans believe that the sacred exists more readily in particular contexts, such as in buildings set aside and consecrated for worship (Wuthnow 1998). Nancy Ammerman's non-ideological, not highly religious "Golden Rule Christians" found a sense of the divine in church: "The church's 'sacred space,' along with the 'sacred time' set aside for worship, seems to combine for many into an opportunity to set priorities in order, to 'feed the soul' . . . and to know that they have been in a presence greater than themselves" (1997, 207–8). Some low-income mothers thus perceive church as a sacred space, a place set apart from the chaos of daily life, where they can go to encounter God. These women sometimes have profound spiritual experiences in churches, both alone and with others, experiences that help them feel renewed and whole.

Although Brenda does not attend religious services, she will go sit alone in a nearby open church when she is experiencing anxiety:

I'll be like stressing to the point where I am going absolutely insane. Then I'll go to church, and, you know, I will pray. I really don't even know how to pray. I don't know if there is any certain way to pray, but when I go, I just go and I just talk to him as if I am talking to myself. I talk to him, and I say so much. When I leave, I feel like everything has just been cleansed. I feel so much better. I know I believe in God, and I know he hears me, so just me being in the house of the Lord and letting it all out, and no one else is around me popping this in my ear or popping that in my ear. It is just me and what I'm saying, and I am talking. When I leave, I feel like I got answered in a way.

"Just me being in the house of the Lord," as Brenda says, provides some women with a sense of transcendence and connection with the divine. Although Brenda also prays in her apartment at the long-term shelter in which she lives, she feels a deep sense of connection with God sitting alone in an empty church, pouring out her burdens and worries. She and women like her see church as a sacred ground, a place of silence and devotion, and a place where they feel they can encounter the divine.

"Being cleansed" is a common theme that emerges from women's descriptions of transcendent experiences in churches, whether these experiences happen alone, as in the case of Brenda, or with other church members. Juliana did not grow up going to church and currently does not attend church except as a guest; approximately once a year she goes to a Pentecostal church with her boyfriend's family. She spoke of feeling "cleansed" after her profound religious experience visiting the church with her boyfriend's mother.

I could not stop my crying. I cried like a baby for hours. It kept going and flowing and flowing. They asked me if I wanted to go to the front and have the pastor pray for me. I had never done that before. The whole church is like, "Come on, it is okay. You are more than welcome here; you are like family." So I went up front, and it was just this feeling that I just could not believe. I went to the front, and he started praying for me. . . . The pastor was telling me, because I guess God was talking through him, that he knew what I was going through. That he knew I was going through a great deal of a lot of struggle. That everything would turn out fine. It was a beautiful experience that I will never forget. It was so good that if I was to go outside and see a person I did not like or that I did not get along with or just anything, I would go and make peace with them. I felt so cleansed after all that crying that I did, and I felt so at peace that—you know it was just so beautiful. It was a beautiful experience. I just could not believe it. All I could see was the light.

Women having these types of experiences believe they are made clean, or purified, in the sacred space of the church. Feeling alone with God and releasing burdens and anxieties, or intensely experiencing the divine among a congregation, women describe peace, wholeness, and a sense of connection with God in these transcendent moments. (Somewhat ironically, Juliana feels like she cannot belong to this church and attend regularly because of its Pentecostal restrictions—she thinks, likely correctly, that she would need to give up smoking, grow her hair long, wear no makeup or jewelry, wear only dresses, and so on.)

Although women more often connect "cleansing" in a church setting with healing of emotional burdens as opposed to sin, the importance of church as a sacred space can be seen in the way in which mothers may struggle with notions of sin, repentance, and forgiveness. The view of church as a sacred space intersects with some poor women's visions of themselves as sinners in different ways. This is illustrated in interviews I had with Shantelle and LaToya, both of whom told me they stopped attending church due to a sense of sin and separation from God. Shantelle believes she needs God's forgiveness in order to get back to church. She needs to be purified before entering into the sacred space. Although she asks God every day at home for forgiveness, she does not yet feel forgiven. Until she feels forgiven for her sins, she does not feel worthy to enter the sacred space. LaToya, on the other hand, believes she will find God's forgiveness in the sacred space. While she has not yet done so, she says she needs to go to church in order to ask and gain God's forgiveness for her transgressions. Church, then, for them is not just another building but a holy place set apart that both requires God's forgiveness to enter and enables the granting of forgiveness. This sacred space both purifies sinners and requires purification.

While churches provide a setting where women may experience a sense of the divine in deep religious experiences, liturgies and sermons—sometimes more prosaically—can speak words of comfort and peace to mothers in poverty. Ann Marie does not often attend the Catholic church where she was raised due to difficulty controlling her young son during Mass and a sense of separation from a church lifestyle. Despite these barriers, Ann Marie does not feel unwelcome to participate in the liturgy. She has known the priest, who baptized her as a baby, all her life, and she was given baby items for her child from the parish. So Ann Marie occasionally attends Mass when she is sad or depressed. She states, "Going back on welfare is depressing. I do use my religion . . . going to church, just listening to a Mass. Then I know I'm not the only one that has this horrible downtime in life. . . . No one's got this most perfect life in the world, even if they're married or something." Participation in religious rituals connects individuals, allowing them to transcend normal boundaries and experience unity (McGuire 2002). In keeping with this Durkheimian notion, participating in communal worship and listening to sermons and scripture readings can allow poor women to feel connected with a broader community. The realization that all humans face some struggles helps them to feel less alone in facing theirs. Both form and content of religious worship can impact low-income women facing hardship. Some mothers find that rites of familiar liturgical prayers or songs of praise lift their spirits. They find scripture passages and sermons to speak of God's presence in the world and love for them.

Social and Material Support

Churches can comprise an important form of social and material support for the poor, and about a quarter of my respondents sometimes received such support from their current or former congregations.[32] The most common types of aid they sought and received from their congregations included assistance and counseling from pastors and help from other church congregants through emotional support, transportation, and meals. Pastors provide particularly important support. Taylor, Chatters, and Levin (2004) write of the important role clergy play in the black church, responding to the needs of members by securing supports and services such as food, emergency shelter, and financial assistance, as well as providing guidance in dealing with life problems.

Pastoral aid is well illustrated in my research by the case of Maggie, a thirty-two-year-old white single mother of three-year-old and ten-year-old daughters, who was not working at the time of the interview.[33] A very devout practicing Catholic, Maggie attends Mass two or three times a week and, with her older daughter, participates in a weekly Bible study designed for parents and children. She feels very welcomed and included in the parish community as a single mother. She lives near the church and does not mention any logistical issues limiting her ability to participate. Maggie receives strong encouragement from her parish priest about her goal to get a job working with special-needs children. "Father Murphy said to me, 'You get your GED and go into your program that you really want to do. And then you could get a job with that training.' . . . So many times I went to GED programs, and I'd always end up stopping. . . . Father Murphy made me promise in a prayer that I will stick to this." Maggie also talks to her priest about how to handle many other aspects of her life. "I talk to the priest, and he's helping me. . . . I talk to him about insurance, feelings, friends."

Maggie relies on personal religious practices as well; for example, she prays frequently about completing her GED. "I just pray to God that—let me get through this; let me pass all my tests, and so I can receive my GED, and go on to what I want to do." In Father Murphy, however, Maggie clearly has a resource that her counterparts who rely solely on personal religious practices do not. Father Murphy persuaded her to start yet another GED program and actively encourages her to persevere so that she can get the GED and pursue her dream of working with special-needs children. In addition, she goes to him for advice for other things in her life, ranging from friendships to insurance. Other mothers had received support and assistance from their pastors when their children were taken into child protective custody, when they ran into housing difficulties, or when they needed temporary help with food or bills. Jennifer described her former priest: "The priest that used to be in my church was really good to me. He was really good. He did help you find jobs and stuff."

Clergy serve as an important source of assistance for people dealing with emotional health problems. The poor, who may lack access to mental health professionals or distrust them, especially turn to clergy for help in this area; African Americans often consult pastors as their only mental health resource (Taylor, Chatters, and Levin 2004).[34] Maggie, who receives so much aid from Father Murphy in dealing with her practical life challenges, also finds him very helpful in contending with her severe clinical depression. "If I have a day that the medicine don't want to work for me, that night I will go see Father Murphy and talk to him about why am I depressed. And after I tell him and everything, he talks to me then, and he blesses me." She feels free to call him whenever she is having a crisis situation with her depression. "He says, 'Is everything okay?' I will say no. I really need to talk to you. May I come down and make an appointment? He says, 'Come down now.' He's never turned me away." Again, Maggie has church-based means to aid with her mental health problems that exceed the religious resources of women relying on personal religiosity. Presumably, Father Murphy is also able to connect her with medical help when problems arise beyond the scope of his ability. For other women, a sense of connection with a pastor can diminish a sense of isolation and aid in well-being, even in the absence of seeking direct assistance with emotional problems.

Besides pastors, poor women facing difficulties find support from other church members.[35] It is hard to think of another institution in which women could participate (outside of a supportive family or perhaps a network of close friends and neighbors) that would do the things described by my respondents: bring meals, do chores, help with transportation, and shelter them during a housing crisis. Aletta—a black/Latina twenty-two-year-old with three children ages five, three, and one—is one of the few married women in the study. She spoke of the extensive material support available at her Seventh-Day Adventist church, where her family had attended services twice weekly until moving away to a long-term transitional housing shelter and stopping all church participation. "They give you a voucher for Star Market to buy food. They give you transportation; they do carpooling. They do a lot of stuff at my church. They do fund-raisers for certain people. . . . I will be calling them for stuff when I get my apartment." Church members further serve as important sources of assistance in emotional well-being for poor mothers.[36] Church friends may provide spiritual encouragement for women experiencing anxiety or depression, encouraging them to persevere, to have trust in God, and to be at peace.

The sense of community engendered by a supportive pastor and congregation provides low-income women with substantial social capital. Explained Maggie, "I was having a really bad time struggling with depression and stuff, and I felt like sometimes that there was no way I'm going to make it. . . . It's a goal, and sometimes I feel like I'm just not going to do it. . . . It's just the church helps me to feel like I can do it." Although Maggie's remarks do not sound much different from those of the mothers who state that personal prayer or God helps them feel they can accomplish a difficult task, Maggie's sense that the *church* helps her feel she can do it reveals the myriad of church-based supports available to her. Churches provide members with material, emotional, social, and spiritual support. The fact that poor single mothers often lack other substantial sources of such support or social capital can make churches an especially critical resource for them.

Mooney (2009) describes churches as moral communities where the poor can enter into caring and sharing relationships with others. In these moral communities, people are called to serve one another, and the poor reach out to serve as well as be served. In this way, Mooney asserts, the poor can more readily accept material assistance from churches, because they are embedded in relationships that affirm their dignity as children of God. In church communities, low-income women enter into relationships with others as fellow children of God. A few of my respondents described their churches or former churches or friends' churches as families. Mothers in poverty receive from their churches, but they give to other members as well, whether in praying for them or offering concrete assistance. Maggie, for example, receives tremendous social, material, and spiritual support from her religious community, but she participates as a fully belonging member, not as only a needy "other" awaiting a charitable handout.

Sometimes church participation can also serve as a source of distress. As analyzed in detail in chapters 6 and 7, both mothers and pastors indicate that single mothers in poverty may encounter judgmental people at church who make them feel stigmatized and unwelcome. Pastors may say things in sermons that women find damaging. In addition, people in churches may form cliques, church duties can be demanding and stressful, and members may feel criticized. Churches can be sites of gossip, rumors, jealousy, shunning, and ostracism (Taylor, Chatters, and Levin 2004; Ellison et al. 2009). Negative interactions in congregations can harm mental health, provoking stress and depression. Excessive demands by a church for time, money, and energy take a long-term toll on mental well-being (Ellison et al. 2009).[37] These types of negative experiences in congregations, if they occur, limit the ability of churches to play a positive role in the lives of women who experience them.

Even without negative interactions, low-income women feel disappointed when churches do not provide desired support. Mothers may request assistance but find their churches unresponsive. In larger congregations, people can attend services without getting to know the pastor or other congregants, making church-based support more difficult. For example, although Isabella attends Catholic Mass every week as part of a promise she made to God after her child recovered from an asthma-related coma, she knows no one at her parish. Her one attempt at receiving job-related help from a fellow parishioner failed. "One time I go to the church, somebody told me about their job. I called the lady, I told her I lived in the shelter, and I want to work for her. She told me, 'You call me,' but she never give me the job."[38] However, smaller congregations where members are well known may be unable or unwilling to provide the kind of assistance that low-income women need and want. Rhonda related how she and another friend—a longtime, very active church member in their black Baptist church—did not feel comfortable asking their church for help:

But when I first started attending the church, my lights got turned off, and so did my neighbor's, the one who asked me to come to church. And she didn't ask the pastor [for assistance], and she had been a long-term member. Now, I didn't feel comfortable, because I just started going, so I got the money from other resources, but I found it quite shocking that she didn't ask the pastor for any help. . . . It's not like our family members have $300, $400, or $500 just laying around for someone to borrow. . . . You give to the church, and she's there all the time, and believe me they're always passing the plate around to collect money, so why wouldn't you ask? I guess that kind of set the tone for me, where I wouldn't feel comfortable asking the pastor for help for anything like a bill because she wouldn't, and she's been a longtime member.

Although this church will provide rides in bad weather, they do not provide more extensive support that women desire.

Women want and need more than rides to church from their congregations. They direct criticism at churches perceived to fall short in assisting people in need. Poor women, especially those who are involved and connected with their church communities, feel disappointed when desired assistance is not forthcoming. Lacking family members with resources, they believe their church families should be there to support them. Varying church norms and resources, however, shape what requests will be supported and what will not; norms can also prevent women from even asking. Churches may be unwilling to help meet their needs, or women's needs may go too far beyond what the church can provide. Women who have contributed financially to their churches, an act that often entails sacrifice for poor women, feel especially let down and angry when the church will then not assist them during a time of need.

Church-Based Social Services

The National Congregations Study indicates that 58 percent of U.S. congregations, which make up 78 percent of all church attendees, provide or support some type of social service—most commonly food pantries, food drives, and clothing banks. Most service provision required limited or no contact with the people being served. Controlling for other factors, larger congregations and congregations with larger budgets do more social services, as do congregations in low-income neighborhoods. Mainline Protestant denominations do more social service than conservative Protestant churches and Catholics. Along the same lines, theologically liberal congregations offer more social services than those that describe themselves as theologically conservative (Chaves and Tsitsos 2001). Previous studies yield mixed conclusions on the role of race. Cnaan and Boddie (2001) found that black churches provide more services than other congregations, including services for at-risk youth, health care, child care, and education. Chaves and Tsitsos (2001) argue that predominantly African American congregations do not, on average, do more social services than predominantly white congregations, although African American congregations are more likely to provide certain services, such as mentoring and job training. African American churches are more willing to collaborate with government in offering social services (Chaves 1999; Cnaan and Boddie 2001). All in all, congregations provide substantial aid to their communities.[39]

Most of the research about church provision of social services to the poor has centered on how churches provide social services, church willingness to collaborate with government, and the constitutionality of such partnerships. There has been little research from the point of view of recipients. A survey of 2,077 lower-income respondents in Pennsylvania found that people seeking assistance from congregations were more likely to be regular churchgoers. Seeking church assistance was most closely associated with seeking spiritual aid. Faith-based social service organizations differed substantially from churches in that people sought out financial assistance, child-care assistance, food and shelter, and emotional assistance. (Faith-based social service organizations were also more likely to attract regular churchgoers, but the relationship was not strong, showing that these types of organizations attract clients beyond regular churchgoers.) Churches received higher mean effectiveness measures from recipients and had marginally higher trust measures compared to public welfare agencies (Wuthnow, Hackett, and Hsu 2004).

My interviews indicate a range of reactions to congregation-based social service provision. Some women do not feel comfortable receiving social services from churches. For example, Marilyn—a thirty-two-year-old white single mother who, although Catholic, does not pray privately or attend Mass—said: "I know churches help people, but I wouldn't feel comfortable doing that. Maybe it's pride. I'd feel bad about myself. I'd rather go to a state agency than to a church." Some women believe there is an implicit expectation for church participation in exchange for receiving social services, making them unwilling to turn to churches if they are not members. (As Claire, a twenty-eight-year-old white mother and former Catholic who now attends a Baptist church once or twice a month, put it, "I think it would just be rude. Asking them for something and then not going to their church.") Furthermore, some women, including four of my respondents, do not realize that churches even provide social services. For women in these categories, the availability of church-based social services means little, as they either feel wrong using them or do not know of their existence. Most of the mothers interviewed, however, were aware that churches provide services and did not believe they had to be part of a congregation in order to receive them. Explained Brenda:

I am not a church member, and I feel fine when I go to the pantry. I don't act all ignorant like I'm just coming here for the food. I am not like that. There are people out there like that. When I go, I pay my respects. I say hi; I carry myself well. I thank them for everything that they could do for me. "I know I'm not a part of your church. You still help me out. God bless you. Thank you very much." [*SCS: They are not asking people to be part of their church?*] They don't. That's an act of God.

Yet few of my respondents went to church-based food pantries or used other social services provided by congregations, bearing out the finding by Wuthnow, Hackett, and Hsu that church-based social services are most often sought by regular churchgoers. Although church-based social services are another available resource to assist low-income single mothers who are struggling, these resources seem more readily sought by women already attached to churches.

Help received from faith-based social services is appreciated, whether provided through religiously affiliated nonprofits or churches.[40] However, for those distant from organized religion, use of faith-based social services does not generally connect the users to broader congregational communities. Rebecca, a thirty-four-year-old white Catholic, was very grateful for the assistance she received from faith-based nonprofit organizations: "The Salvation Army paid my rent one month. Catholic Charities paid my rent one month. So if it wasn't for those church organizations, I would have been screwed." Yet Rebecca feels uncomfortable in her own parish because of being on welfare. Vicky regularly gets food vouchers from a Catholic parish and likes the church members she has gotten to know from their volunteering. When she attempted to attend Mass, however, she perceived the priest's homily to vilify both single mothers and drug addicts. As a single mother and former alcohol and drug addict, she felt unwanted and did not return to church services again. Some scholars of urban religion contend that when churches engage the poor, they are likely to engage them more as social service clients than as members of the congregation (Smith 2001; Price 2000; Laudarji and Livezey 2000). A study of churches near a Chicago housing project found that although the churches provided social services, the number of project residents being "woven into networks that bridged the social isolation of the poor" was "exceedingly small" (Laudarji and Livezey 2000, 104).[41]

As sacred spaces and moral communities, churches are places where low-income mothers can experience the divine through times of quiet prayer, group worship, and engagement in give-and-take as members of a shared community. Churches can further provide resources to poor women via pastors, other congregants, and social services. However, perhaps in part due to acceptance of American ideals of individualism, combined with rejection by or critique of churches for some, poor mothers who are personally religious but not active in congregations do not generally seem to consider what church participation in a supportive congregation might offer. The mothers interviewed speak of the strength and hope they derive from prayer, but few mention pastoral, congregational, or spiritual support they might lack. This is true even of women who have formerly been very involved in churches and experienced considerable support from those church communities. By and large, personally religious mothers who are not connected with churches seem content with their reliance on personal religious practices and cultural religious knowledge in confronting the challenges of their daily lives.

The building blocks of theory, religious practices, and the role of churches discussed in this chapter provide a foundation for understanding lived religion for urban mothers in poverty. The next three chapters explore everyday religion in several key areas. Providing for and caring for their children are the central elements shaping the lives of low-income single mothers, marking these as two sites of everyday religion that merit special attention. Making meaning of difficult situations in their lives is a third important site where poor urban mothers "live" religion. The theoretical framework of religion, resilience, and harm provides a useful analytical map in navigating these areas. Religious practices such as prayer form the heart of everyday religion. Churches still exert influence, even among many mothers who do not attend services. With this foundation laid, it is time to explore lived religion.

THREE

"God Made Somebody Think of Welfare Reform": Religion, Welfare, and Work

The study of lived religion calls attention to the way spirituality and religious beliefs are experienced in the ordinary circumstances of people's daily lives. The ways in which people, including those who do not participate in organized religion, imbue the activities of their daily lives with religious meaning are varied and rich. Studying lived religion calls us to delve into areas that would not normally be considered "religious" in order to see how religion operates (Orsi 1985; Ammerman 2007).

In the United States, the issue of welfare is fraught with debates about morality. Working motherhood can still find mothers' motives and actions scrutinized, although most mothers now work. Because both welfare and working motherhood are "moral" issues in the United States, it is not surprising to find poor women of faith drawing on religion in framing and experiencing welfare and working motherhood. As for work itself, research reveals a large number of Americans wishing to integrate their faith lives with their work lives (Miller 2007). This issue has become a topic of interest in the academy and the workplace, yet most of the research and interest focuses on professionals, not on how people in low-wage jobs might integrate their faith and work lives.

Religion figures prominently in the post–welfare reform era, with the 1996 enactment of Charitable Choice legislation and the 2001 formation of the White House Office for Faith-Based and Community Initiatives. A 2004 study of welfare-to-work job programs in four major U.S. cities found 24 percent of welfare-to-work programs in those cities to be faith based. Of these, 40 percent were "faith-integrated," meaning they explicitly and actively integrate faith into the program. More than 95 percent of such programs indicate they use religious values to encourage clients to change their attitudes (Monsma 2004). These programs take varied forms. For example, some churches mentor individual women moving from welfare to work; other programs teach biblically inspired soft skills (such as attitudes, personal qualities and habits, and communication ability) to enhance work performance. These programs may use injunctions from the Bible, for example, "work heartily as unto the Lord,"[1] to encourage participants to work hard and be honest. These types of faith-integrated welfare-to-work programs view religion as a positive force in transitioning women from welfare dependence to work. Proponents see faith and religious teachings as helpful in aiding women to develop a strong work ethic and become self-sufficient. Public support for faith-based initiatives remains high, with almost 70 percent of the American public approving of faith-based social services (Pew Forum on Religion and Public Life and Pew Research Center for the People and the Press 2009). Surprisingly, however, few researchers have asked poor women themselves about any connection between religious beliefs and views on work and welfare. An understanding of these connections is important for several reasons. Practically, it points to assumptions of policy makers and proponents of faith-based welfare programs that need to be explored. Does religion really enhance the work ethic of low-income mothers, making them more eager to work "heartily" in the low-wage workplace? Second, it draws attention to what poor women believe about the veracity of American narratives of morality and work and how they connect such narratives to religious constructs. Finally, work and welfare are critical sites of lived religion, and it is important to understand religious imagery, symbolism, beliefs, and practices as related to this central part of everyday life.

The Morality of Welfare and Work

The Personal Responsibility and Work Opportunity Reconciliation Act (PRWORA) enacted welfare reform in 1996, and the name alone reflects the profound change in welfare policy the new law represented. The poor were now to take personal responsibility for themselves, as opposed to "irresponsibly" remaining dependent. They were to work as opposed to living off of welfare checks. The new welfare program's name, Temporary Assistance to Needy Families (TANF), underscored that welfare is now to be just that—temporary.

Under welfare reform, states have latitude to set their welfare benefit levels, eligibility requirements, and, to some degree, requirements to participate in work-related activities. The Deficit Reduction Act of 2005 reauthorized TANF but implemented much stricter work requirements by increasing effective work participation rates and hours of required work and limiting the activities that could be considered as work. The lifetime time limit for receiving welfare is five years, although states can establish shorter limits, as well as exempt up to 20 percent of their caseload from this limit due to severe barriers to employment. States can choose to provide post-time-limit assistance through state and locally funded programs, but most do not routinely allow such extensions. Across the board, the maximum welfare benefits are low, ranging from 12 percent of the national poverty line in Mississippi to 50 percent in Alaska. Welfare rolls have fallen dramatically since welfare reform, and a smaller percentage of poor families currently receive benefits than when welfare reform was enacted (from 44 percent of poor families with children in 1996 to 30 percent in 2008). States actively discourage people from entering welfare, with forty-two states establishing formal programs to divert people from the rolls; overall, the administrative process to receive welfare is complex and slow. There has been a 72 percent real decline in the amount of cash assistance between 1996 and 2008, and most TANF funding now goes for noncash assistance, such as child-care subsidies or short-term emergency needs. Sanctions for failing to meet participation requirements are strict and serve as one way of removing families from the rolls (Zedlewski and Golden 2010).[2]

The "Protestant work ethic" served as an underlying foundation for the formulation of welfare reform, both supporters and critics agree (Hudson and Coukos 2005; Olasky 1992; Hayes 2003). Max Weber (1930) argued that the Protestant ethic, as manifested by Calvinist Puritans, extolled hard work as a religious duty and condemned idleness. Calvin emphasized the notion of the calling, that is, people are called by God to a worldly vocation in which they must work diligently. Faithfulness in hard work is one's duty and is pleasing to God. Calvin's doctrine of predestination spurred on hard work, because success in one's worldly calling could be taken as a sign of one's salvation as one of the elect. Well beyond its effect on the behavior of early Puritans, the Protestant work ethic has come to have a profound impact on much of Western culture. Cohen (2002) explains how the Protestant work ethic moved from a Puritan religious idea to being part of mainstream culture, distinguishing between behavioral mechanisms of influence—how an early Calvinist's religion would impact his economic behavior—and a cultural mechanism of impact that operates long after the religious impetus is gone. The Protestant work ethic continues to be strongly manifested in modern American society, even more strongly in secular form than in its original religious form, as it is now shorn from the Puritan religious practices and obligations that limited work (Cohen 2002; Hudson and Coukos 2005).[3]

The Protestant work ethic's emphasis on hard work and disdain of idleness has impacted American attitudes toward those in poverty and toward programs designed to assist them (Hudson and Coukos 2005). Jennifer Hochschild (1995) writes that success is associated with virtue in the American dream. By this token, failure implies not only a lack of talent and will but also sin. Thus, "even the poor blame the poor for their condition" (31). The strong individualism often associated with the American dream leads to a focus on personal attributes and people's behaviors as causal explanations for success or failure. Critics of the welfare state, such as Charles Murray (1984), took this argument further, blaming social welfare programs for enabling and increasing bad behavior by keeping people from taking personal responsibility for their actions. Gertrude Himmelfarb (1995) argued that society lamentably had divorced welfare from moral sanctions, calling "illegitimacy" and "dependency" moral pathologies (243). Evangelical scholar Marvin Olasky's (1992) influential book *The Tragedy of American Compassion* touted alleviating poverty through morality. "Today, a single, family-based standard of morality, taught and communicated through every way possible and supported by state and private programs, remains the major antipoverty weapon" (204). Providing philosophical grounding for the faith-based initiatives of welfare reform, Olasky contended that government social service agencies lacked personal contact with the poor and ignored their moral and spiritual needs (224). Lawrence Mead, another influential conservative scholar, portrayed the nonworking adult poor as incompetent, immature, and undisciplined and in need of paternalistic oversight, much as strict fathers provide "morality for the wayward" (Bane and Mead 2003, 127).[4] For Mead, the nation's welfare laws (pre-reform) exacerbated the immoral culture of the poor, promoting illegitimacy and dependence (Hayes 2003).

Mothers on welfare are judged immoral in American society due to a combination of factors: lack of working, nonmarital childbearing, and reliance on taxpayer money to support their children (Jarrett 1996). By using welfare benefits, single mothers are viewed to have failed to live up to societal norms of responsibility and self-sufficiency. Yet most welfare mothers possess a work ethic, want to work, and have worked at different times in their lives (Hayes 2003). What makes up poor mothers' moral narratives of work, welfare, and economic independence? Do they view these as moral issues? Does religion play a role in their narratives?

Mothers in poverty, it turns out, indeed connect morality and work, with many of my study participants using religious language. They believe that religion extols hard work.[5] A number of women pointed out to me examples of people in the Bible who worked hard, including Jesus. Indicated Marilyn, "All the apostles, all the fishermen. Jesus was a carpenter." Instead of highlighting practical occupations such as fishing and carpentry as work, like Marilyn did, Carrie focused on Jesus' work carrying the cross, as well as the work of the people who helped him: "When Jesus carried the cross, people tried to help him, and it was work." Still another mother, LaToya, intertwined notions of self-sufficiency and serving others, noting that Jesus "worked for what he wanted" and that he "worked for us." For those who drew on images of biblical figures, the ways in which they remembered, interpreted, and emphasized them varied.

My respondents thus indicated that Jesus' occupation as a carpenter demonstrated hard work, as did the occupations of the apostles, such as being a fisherman. Jesus' carrying the cross, fulfilling his religious mission, demonstrated work. Mothers noted how Jesus worked hard not only for what he wanted but also to serve others. These themes point to several messages regarding work that mothers in poverty extract from their knowledge of biblical figures. People are to work hard in their occupations, they are to work in their religious lives, they must work hard themselves for what they want, but they are also called to work for others. In addition to drawing on biblical examples, mothers connected religion with the morality of work by emphasizing the responsibility to work. Marilyn stated, "Religion teaches work is a responsibility." She added, "It's necessary to work. Work is prayer." Jane commented, "My church believes that if you can work, you should work. You need to work to eat. I mean, that's what the Bible says." Lindsay (twenty-three-year-old African American who attends a black Protestant church weekly) said, "My religion teaches you to work for what you have to do for your family." The influence of the Protestant ethic is clear in all of these comments.

None of my respondents had been involved in faith-based welfare-to-work programs. However, poor mothers gain cultural knowledge of the connection between religion and work from various sources, beyond, of course, a general awareness that hard work is considered moral in American society. The Bible is one source, as women have knowledge of people in Bible stories, most of all Jesus. Women do not need to be deeply religious to have cultural knowledge of connections between religion and work. Marilyn, who never prays or attends religious services, holds a clear image of Jesus as a worker, a worker who models to his followers the value of working hard. Although Marilyn would show up as nonreligious on any survey, she describes work in terms of biblical figures, as a religious responsibility, and as prayer. Church involvement or even personal spiritual practices are not necessary to draw on religious narratives in formulating a morality of work. In addition to Jesus, other biblical figures, such as apostles, are known by poor women as hard workers. In the Catholic tradition, Joseph, Mary's husband, is called Joseph the worker. (Joseph is the patron saint of workers, with prayers, feast days, and novenas related to work.) The ways in which most mothers emphasize Bible figures and sayings align with the aims of welfare reform, most obviously, perhaps, in Jane's reference from the Second Letter of Paul to the Thessalonians: "In fact when we were with you, we instructed you that if anyone was unwilling to work, neither should that one eat" (2 Thess. 3:10). The logic of welfare reform resonates with women's religious conceptions of the morality of work.

The teachings of religious leaders provide religious cultural knowledge about the connection between religion and work for a considerable number of Americans. Survey data find that 40 percent of all church and synagogue members and 52 percent of weekly attendees had heard a sermon in the past year that inspired them to work harder (Wuthnow 1994a). Congregations, former or current, served as a source of religious knowledge about the morality of work for only a few of the mothers I studied. Although few women remembered pastors preaching about work, those who did recalled sermons exhorting congregants to work hard and try to be excellent for God in their work and to be upright and honest in work. Explained Peggy (age forty-three, white, nonattending evangelical) about the teachings of her former church, "You know, you should be the most outstanding of all workers if you were Christian, to stand out for God's sake. To be an example for him, so that people know that you are different. . . . It was often preached from the pulpit to the whole congregation." Religious leaders may reinforce the message that God calls people to be hard workers, which can become a lasting part of a religious cultural repertoire for women like Peggy who later become disengaged from organized religion.

Poor mothers believe hard and honest work pleases God, even if the jobs are bad. Theologian Miroslav Volf (1991) critiques a Reformation-based theology of work, which sees opportunity to glorify God in all work. Commenting on Calvin's statement that viewing work as a vocation can "give singular consolation" when people's occupations are "sordid and base" (107), Volf argues that this understanding of work suggests that all jobs are places to serve God, which acts only to "ennoble dehumanizing work" (108) when instead it should be improved through structural changes. Volf's critique applies to the vision of work and religion among low-income mothers because their views on religion and work primarily reflect values of individual hard work as opposed to a religious vision calling for structural change. Whether involved in congregations or not, the mothers lacked a concept of religious justice that might call for better jobs or working conditions. In fact, when directly asked what they thought religion/God might require of employers, almost all replied with some version of the supervisor treating them nicely and with respect. Only one mother mentioned decent wages and benefits.

The source of this religious cultural knowledge stems from a wider cultural norm of individualism, enhanced by the religious ideology of the Protestant work ethic. The poor particularly embrace the notion that hard work by self-reliant individuals yields economic success. Several earlier studies have found mothers on welfare to blame other welfare mothers' laziness and other negative personal behaviors for their situation (Seccombe 1999; Hayes 2003). The African American poor exhibit a strong individualist ethos and are more likely than middle-class African Americans to believe that everyone has equal opportunity to achieve and will succeed if they try hard enough (Hochschild 1995). Smith (2007) contends that the rampant individualism of the black urban poor stems from their defensiveness in the context of structural constraints.

If poor mothers consider hard work to be moral and desired by God, then what about welfare? The message of welfare reform has clearly taken root among poor women. In line with previous ethnographic studies of women on welfare (Seccombe 1999; Hayes 2003), many of the mothers I interviewed voiced support for welfare reform. Women positively contrasted people like themselves who use welfare in a "moral" fashion with people who abuse the system and would be weeded out by welfare reform. Furthermore, many connected the morality of welfare use and welfare reform to religious narratives. The majority of study participants held quite definite opinions on what they perceive "religion" (interpreted as their religious tradition, priest or pastor, the Bible, God, or some combination) to think about welfare. The largest number (45 percent) thought religion has a positive view of "proper" welfare use; a minority (15 percent) thought religion has a negative view of welfare use; and the rest thought religion has no opinion about welfare (20 percent) or did not know. Although numbers themselves must of course be interpreted cautiously in a small study, the categories prove theoretically and conceptually useful in understanding the various religious cultural interpretations of welfare among low-income mothers.

"God Would Not Have Made It if It Wasn't to Be Used"

Perhaps most surprising is the notion among some poor mothers, not even necessarily particularly religious, that God made the welfare system, brought about welfare reform, or both. As noted in the last chapter, Ann Marie, who has a three-year-old son and is pregnant with another child, is not deeply personally religious and rarely attends Mass. Having recently left her job (driving a van transporting the disabled) when the physical demands became too great for her pregnancy, she believes that God made welfare so that people in need would have something to fall back on: "Everybody's got a down point in life at one point. Do I think it should be right for me to be collecting right now? No. But am I getting anywhere? Am I looking for a job? Yes. Am I trying? Yes. But where I am seven months pregnant, nobody's taking me. I still have a family to support and if that [welfare] is the only way . . . God would not have made it if it wasn't to be used."

Mothers in poverty have absorbed the moral language surrounding welfare debates and know that women who use it find their morals questioned by the larger society. In the late stages of pregnancy with another young child to support and unable to find a job, Ann Marie demonstrates society's views of welfare mothers in stating that it is not right for her to be "collecting right now." Her religious interpretation of welfare, though, that "God would not have made" welfare if it were not to be used, provides some psychological protection against these broader social interpretations. In this understanding, God made welfare for a reason, and certainly a pregnant single mother "trying hard" and needing to support her older child would be worthy of using it for the purpose God intended.

While mothers in poverty may believe that God made the welfare system to be used in times of need, the hand of God is also seen in the welfare reform law. Rhonda had previously been on welfare and now holds a social service job; she spoke negatively of other women who kept having more babies, receiving welfare checks, and not working. Rhonda believes that God brought about welfare reform: "For those who want to better themselves, but just are stuck right now, just to do things to help yourself in a positive way, whether it be to go back to school, get a trade, look for work that's going to pay for you in your career. . . . But people not trying, I think the church would shun them. For people making welfare their career. He [God] made somebody think of welfare reform! And it helped because, I mean, you don't have people making a career out of the welfare system."

In this understanding, God has (a) brought about welfare reform, an interpretation that raises interesting issues to be considered, and (b) done a good thing in bringing about welfare reform because welfare reform stops immoral, lazy women from cheating the system. This view highlights in religious terms what other researchers have found to be common among mothers on welfare, the drawing of symbolic boundaries to distinguish between themselves (good, morally deserving welfare mothers) and "others" (the other bad, lazy welfare cheats) (Hayes 2003; Seccombe 1999). Sharon Hayes writes of the use of symbolic boundaries by welfare mothers to develop hierarchies of social worth by affirming their own moral values while drawing on negative societal images of women on welfare to cast blame on other women (2003, 220; Lamont 1992). In this case, the symbolic boundaries are drawn in starkly religious lines, with the view of God instigating welfare reform to stop the immoral "others."

Although women may not state this view in such graphic religious terms as God actually creating welfare and its reform, the combination of these two positions illustrates the most common way mothers in poverty make connections between religion and welfare. Religion (however women construe it) approves of a welfare system to support families in need, but religion also approves of welfare reform that enforces a work ethic and stops abuse. In this "positive" religious view of welfare, God or church's compassion for poor families is blended with a commitment to a strong work ethic as embodied in time limits. This frames God or a faith community as approving or accepting of mothers being on welfare for a relatively short time while staying home with a young baby, getting training or education, or looking for a job, but displeased with people who stay on welfare for a long time, "abusing the system." Brenda , who construes "religion" in terms how the Catholic Church might view welfare, illustrates this position clearly: "I think they [the Catholic Church] would be for it [welfare]. Anything to help out a disadvantaged family. I think they would be for the time thing too. That makes the people living off the system get off their butts. The Church wants to see people working. They don't want to see people living off welfare for the rest of their lives." This view points to an understanding of religious values embodied by welfare being not only compassionate toward people truly in need but also strict with regard to a work ethic of hard work, not idleness.

Problems arise when the ideal—using welfare "morally" for a short time for acceptable reasons—bumps up against reality. People's lives do not necessarily fit neatly into the timelines prescribed by welfare reform.[6] What happens when welfare time limits come around, yet physical health problems, mental health problems, and other issues persist? The majority of welfare clients cannot gain exemptions from time limits because the exemptions go only to those with multiple substantial barriers to employment. If religion calls for both compassion for those in need and the strictness embodied in time limits to promote work, then what happens when those who remain truly needy and are using welfare in a "morally" appropriate way hit their time limits? As noted in chapter 2, the welfare time limit created a crisis for Sally when she desperately and unsuccessfully searched for a job while welfare officials showed no mercy.[7] Off of welfare for several years at the time of the interview, Sally now sees other women in the same predicament, as part of her job in social services. Although she highly values working and says God does not want people on welfare long term, she does not put forth a positive religious formulation of welfare reform.

I think he [God] would pray for all of us; we're getting cut off of welfare, and we don't know what we are going to do. . . . I knew people that got thrown out of their apartments because they didn't have money. They had to look for shelter because they couldn't afford to pay their rent. They weren't getting the money. There wasn't food. They were stealing food, or changing their food stamps into cash, just to buy diapers. I've seen lots of that. It's getting worse and worse, actually, people trying to find jobs and child care and training.

Poor mothers' "positive" religious framing that highlights how God or church would support welfare reform (or even that God instigated welfare reform) is called into question by those who suffer as a consequence. Welfare reform is not viewed as an unalloyed moral good for women thrown into tremendous hardship by its sanctions and time limits, even if they share the value that work is a moral and religious good. Far from God "thinking up welfare reform" to "make the people living off the system get off their butts," this religious framing highlights God's concern for women thrown into crisis by welfare reform's time limits. Religion's compassion trumps its strictness encouraging work. These positions reflect the ambivalence of both low-income women and social workers about welfare reform (Hayes 2003). For most, trying to live out an ethic of self-reliance and providing for one's family is considered morally and religiously desirable. Yet the realities entangling women's lives bring more ambiguity than moral or religious clarity.

The Importance of Trying Hard

An ethic of trying hard is a key central determinant of religious morality for poor women. "Trying hard" usually brings mothers into God's good graces, according to their understanding, even if they are receiving welfare. Liz thinks the Catholic Church approves of welfare because it is a way of helping people in need. She believes God is pleased with her on welfare because she is trying hard to find a place to live, gain more education, and be a good mother. "I think he [God] is happy with it because the situation that I'm in, I'm in a shelter right now trying to get my own place for me and my daughter, and I'm doing everything I can. I'm trying to further my education and spending all of the time I possibly can with my daughter, just so I can be a good role model." Women think God is pleased when they try hard. Welfare may be part of the picture, but women contrast themselves to a stereotypical welfare recipient by underscoring their hard work. If they are trying hard, then most women believe God has compassion and understanding for them (temporarily) receiving welfare. It is by emphasizing how hard they try that mothers attempt to maintain their claim on being moral citizens or godly women, despite welfare receipt. The importance of trying hard is underscored by Rhonda's assertion that the black Baptist church she attends monthly would "shun" people who are "not trying." In addition to illustrating the scholarly contention that African American churches are sites of negative sanctions for those who violate church norms (Taylor, Chatters, and Levin 2004), this comment demonstrates church norms with regard to welfare. Religious sanctions are leveled not at those who receive welfare but at those who receive welfare "without trying." Long-term welfare recipients are scorned and shunned at church because they are assumed to not be trying. In doing so, they are considered to violate not only norms of American society but God's norms for moral behavior.

Most, though not all, of the mothers interviewed believe "religion" (by which they usually meant God, though for some it was their perception of church teaching) would rather see them working than on welfare, certainly in the long run. Those who do may also believe that God works in partnership with them to help them gain the necessary resources, such as child care, transportation, or training, so they can go to work. "He understands the reason why I'm not [working]," explained Magda, who stopped work after losing child care. "It was not under my control, as we understand it, but he's helping me through this to get a new day care. So, he's walking me through it. He'd rather see me work and have my own car and have my own apartment." Magda's way of drawing on religion in interpreting welfare raises and illuminates several important issues. In this framing, God understands temporary nonwork, especially when things happen beyond women's control that impact their ability to be self-sufficient. In a counter-interpretation to conservative religious understandings, God will enable women to find day care, which will allow them to work. Most revealing, however, is the connection between an individualistic ideal of self-sufficiency and what God desires for poor single mothers. God wants women to "do good," which here is interpreted to mean working and being financially self-sufficient, placing their children in day care, and having their own cars and apartments. Welfare may be a necessary and acceptable short-term source of assistance in working hard toward this version of the American dream, cloaked in religious understanding.

"God Would Be Disappointed in Me"

Although in the minority among the women interviewed for this study, some mothers believe their welfare use demonstrates that they have not tried hard enough and thus have disappointed God. If American ideology posits success as resulting from one's own efforts, actions, and willpower, then failure indicates insufficient effort (Hochschild 1995). In a society that emphasizes self-reliance and demonizes welfare recipients, turning to welfare constitutes "failure," a failure that can be understood and expressed in religious terms. In this "negative" religious interpretation of welfare, religion (be it God, church, or pastor) disapproves of any welfare use. Thirty-year-old Lisa, a white nonattending Catholic on welfare and in a job training program, thinks neither the Catholic Church nor God approve of people being on welfare:

I would say that the Catholic Church doesn't approve of it [welfare]. They would say that you have to get up, and you have to do what you have to do. You can't sit and wait on a check. . . . God tried to teach man to work hard for what you need. . . . I think God would be disappointed in me. Before I was coming here [job training] I was just sitting at home. . . . I think God was disappointed in me because I wasn't doing what I was supposed to be doing. [SCS: What do you think God would have been wanting you to do?] Work. [SCS: Even when you have a little baby?] Yes.

This framework shares elements of "positive" religious views of welfare in that both emphasize that God, church, or both want people to work hard. It differs in that even short-term welfare use is interpreted as not trying hard and thus displeasing to God. By using welfare, even short term, women believe they are not fulfilling God's will. Martina believes God saw her as "selfish" for "not trying" when she was receiving welfare on and off for two years before her new job in a self-service laundry. "I was being selfish by not trying. . . . Even if I got a measly job that paid a little bit of money, I still should've tried and taken it so that at least I had some kind of money coming in so that certain things could be paid. . . . One of the scriptures says that I will help everyone, but I will help you better if you help yourself. . . . I feel he [God] would think that it is a shame that I [wasn't] trying and doing better than he knows I can."

Again we see the reference to "God helps those who helps themselves," the supposed biblical saying that is actually found nowhere in the Bible. Mothers such as Martina and Lisa have appropriated moral narratives of welfare from the wider society. Here they apply these constructs to themselves (recall, though, that it is more common for welfare mothers to apply them to other mothers on welfare) (Hayes 2003; Seccombe 1999). They have embraced a moral and religious narrative of self-reliance and, in looking at their lives, find themselves deficient in the eyes of God. Claire, who thinks God views her welfare use negatively, put it succinctly: "He [God] just thinks that I can do better. And so that is what I think of myself. I have really gone the wrong way." Underlying this interpretation is an image of God as a disappointed father. The image of God as one who knows women "can do better" than being on welfare is the image of a disappointed human father who knows his child or adolescent can behave better. Women do not believe that God is actually angry with them for their welfare use. The imagery is always that of letting God down, disappointing God, and making God not proud of them. Much as children usually feel when they disappoint their parents, mothers on welfare perceiving themselves to have disappointed God feel guilty and desire to do better.

Why do some mothers find religion or God to be approving of short-term, "legitimate" welfare use while others do not? Women holding either view attend church or not, are personally religious or not, and are of all racial, ethnic, and religious backgrounds. A large quantitative study could perhaps tease out demographic differences. Differences do stem from the subtle interior processes of how women perceive and experience their time on welfare. Those who feel themselves to be working hard on welfare caring for children or disabled relatives or attending to other important things outside of paid employment have different interpretations than women who perceive themselves to be sitting around in their apartments "waiting on a check." Mothers scrutinize their reasons for being on welfare. Martina, for example, had a long work history, but stopped working after encountering a series of problems in her life, including having a child removed by the Department of Social Services. She explained, "I really did want to just stop and take a break from life in a way so I can heal myself. . . . I decided to just stop working and take some time off and then heal myself." In fact, she did not even stay consistently on welfare for the two years in which she used it, because she found the community service and training requirements too onerous. Having recently returned to work, she retrospectively regards her time out of the labor force seeking healing as "selfish." If mothers decide their reasons for going on welfare were not valid, they may formulate negative religious interpretations of welfare use. The connections mothers draw between religion and welfare are intimately connected with how they feel about themselves being on welfare. God is either supportive and compassionate or disappointed and wanting them to do better. Churches either shun them or understand.

Women's strong internal sense of guilt and shame about welfare use may even lead them to feel unworthy to be at church. Take the case of Rebecca, who has survived domestic violence, is separated from her abusive husband, and struggles with depression. She told me, "I feel like even if I go to church, I'm not doing anything for myself. I don't belong there—that's how I feel. . . . I mean I'm the parent, and I shouldn't be here [at church] not working. . . . God would think I'm a bum for not working." Mothers who believe themselves to have failed God for failing to support their families and relying on public assistance can feel a considerable sense of shame. This religious shame adds additional weight to the shame experienced from violating societal expectations about self-sufficiency.[8]

Religiously based condemnations of themselves on welfare reveal women's feelings of guilt, a sense of church disapproval, a sense of God's disappointment in them, or some combination of the three. In this less common way of religiously framing welfare, women draw a connection between religious values and popular negative stereotypes of welfare mothers.[9] These views correspond with religious views of welfare mothers put forth by conservative scholars such as Lawrence Mead. In his chapter titled "A Biblical Response to Poverty" in *Lifting Up the Poor* (Bane and Mead 2003), Mead contends, "In our day, as in biblical times, many of the poor have visibly failed to observe God's commandments" (77). This statement suggests that the poor are poor *because* of failing to observe

God's commandments. My interviews indicate that some poor mothers themselves agree. Mead appears to equate poverty with the fruit of sin, consonant with interpretations of Calvinist doctrine and the equating of success with virtue in American ideology. Mead writes that we must follow the example of Jesus in the gospels by holding the poor responsible for themselves and maintaining reasonable expectations about good behavior (78).

What about Children?

"Misuse" of welfare—and sometimes any use of welfare—is seen by most poor mothers as religiously and morally deficient. The conflation of religion and attitudes toward work and welfare among impoverished urban mothers reflects an internalization of American ideals of hard work and self-sufficiency. It also reflects a post–welfare reform era in which long-term dependency has become unacceptable.[10] Although often stereotyped as lazy, many mothers on welfare believe hard work pleases God. Indeed, a number of other studies have found that welfare recipients value work (Seccombe 1999; Hayes 2003). But it is religion in the abstract that connects hard work in the labor force with moral and religious good for mothers on welfare. When the ideal of the valued work ethic meets the reality of caretaking, things can get more complicated. What actually constitutes work? How does child rearing fit in?

Social norms linking morality with good motherhood call for mothers to put the needs of their children first, whether or not they are employed (Hayes 2003; Blair-Loy 2003). Low-income mothers providing solo care for their children are often without stable partners sharing either the child rearing or financial burdens (Edin and Kefalas 2005). Single mothers are thus simultaneously trying to fulfill traditional religious imperatives and roles for both men and women—to be both provider and caretaker, and in the case of low-income single mothers, doing so with comparatively few resources. In nonreligious terms, welfare reform reveals our nation "simultaneously celebrating the importance of children, holding high an ethic of care and commitment to others, while at the same time demanding that all Americans be completely self-reliant" (Hayes 2003, 232). My study participants had absorbed both moral messages—caretaker and provider—from religion, emphasizing the different messages to varying degrees. The religious message of hard work as something pleasing to God underscores the importance of the self-reliant provider role, leading a mother such as Rebecca to remark, "People are supposed to take pride in what they do, strive to take care of their families financially.

When I think about that I feel bad that I'm not." Religion in this understanding calls low-skilled single mothers of very young children, perhaps dealing with physical or mental health problems, domestic violence, or other hardships, to be the economic providers for their families. However, mothers in poverty also contend with traditional religious messages about women's domestic role as caregivers.

"They Would Probably Want Me to Stay Home": Working Mothers

Although women bring up Jesus as an example of a hard worker, Jesus was not a poor single mother with young children. Tellingly, the examples of biblical "hard workers" the mothers put forth in interviews are all unencumbered males. In the post–welfare reform era, low-income women find themselves pressed between the demands of the marketplace and the demands of parenting young children alone. Welfare originally came into being so that single mothers of young children could stay home and care for them. "Mothers' pensions," early twentieth-century state laws that were the forerunner of welfare, were instituted so that "worthy" women who were widowed would not have to go out to work.[11] Later, the Social Security Act of 1935 enacted Aid to Dependent Children (later called Aid to Families with Dependent Children [AFDC]), which instituted a nationwide program of financial support for mothers raising children alone. Public discontent with AFDC (commonly known as welfare) rose throughout the 1960s and 1970s, as recipients went from being widows to being mostly never-married mothers and as the number of African Americans on the rolls increased (Hayes 2003, 14). Politicians drew on negative stereotypes of welfare recipients, most notoriously Ronald Reagan's evoking of the lazy, Cadillac-driving, black "welfare queen" giving birth out of wedlock to many babies and committing welfare fraud to cheat the government out of money.[12] With increasing numbers of non-poor mothers entering the workforce, the notion of the state paying poor women to stay home and care for their children seemed outdated. In 1994, prior to welfare reform, a greater percentage of low-income women were full-time homemakers than in any other income group (Williams 2000).[13] Families struggling to get by on two paychecks found it galling to have the government subsidizing poor mothers to be at home. Joan Williams (2000) also notes that in successfully stirring up working-class anger against poor single mothers, political conservatives tapped into not only racism but envy.

Since its inception, welfare has been about children and who should care for them. Welfare has been about the role of mothers, what "good mothers" do, and what mothers should be expected to do. The debates cut to the heart of our values as a nation (Hayes 2003). Labor force participation among mothers of young children has increased substantially since the 1970s. In 2008 the labor force participation rate for all mothers of children under age eighteen was 71.4 percent; for mothers with children under age six it was 64 percent; and for mothers of infants it was 56.4 percent (U.S. Bureau of Labor Statistics 2009a, 2009b).[14] Despite the fact that the majority of mothers work, Americans remain ambivalent about working mothers. A survey by the Pew Research Center (2007) found that 41 percent of adults think the trend toward more mothers working outside of the home is bad for society. Forty-two percent of adults think an at-home mother is ideal for children. Among mothers of minor children, 44 percent of at-home mothers and 34 percent of working mothers believe the trend toward more working mothers is bad for society. Similarly, 44 percent of at-home mothers of minor children believe an at-home mother is ideal for children, as do 30 percent of working mothers. Only about 10 percent of mothers believe it is ideal for a child for a mother to work full-time, and only 16 percent of mothers of children age four and under desire to work full-time, down from 24 percent in 1997. Single mothers were much less likely to prefer working full-time in 2007 (26 percent) than they were in 1997 (49 percent). (Almost half of single mothers [46 percent] would prefer to work part-time, and 26 percent would not like to work outside of the home.) African American mothers are more likely than white or Hispanic mothers to consider mothers working, especially full-time, as ideal for children.

Amid ambivalent attitudes toward working mothers, pervasive ideologies about what constitutes a good mother continue to operate. In the contemporary American mores of mothering that constitute "intensive mothering," mothers are expected and advised to spend tremendous amounts of time, energy, and resources nurturing their children's development (Hayes 1996). Sociologist Pamela Stone (2007) reflects, "No mother, working or at home, whatever her class, race, or social position, is immune from the imperatives of this ever present ideology" (42). Stone contends that the norms of intensive mothering impact more affluent women to a greater extent (because they listen to parenting experts more and have more resources to expend on their children) but that women lower in socioeconomic status still feel the effect. Annette Lareau (2003) draws a sharper contrast between lower-income mothers and more affluent mothers, claiming that more affluent parents are more likely to parent in a style of "concerted cultivation," whereas lower-income parents engage in a "natural growth" style of parenting. For poor single mothers who must keep children fed, clothed, housed, and safe, survival plays a key role in child-rearing values (Edin and Kefalas 2005). However understood and enacted, being "a good mother" requires time and self-sacrifice. Domesticity remains an entrenched American norm, with child-rearing duties still falling disproportionately on women and workplaces structured around an "ideal worker" without caregiving responsibilities (Williams 2000). Studies, including mine, find that poor mothers believe that being a good mother is their most important responsibility. Moreover, they believe that not just their young children require substantial care but also that the older children need parental attention after school in dangerous neighborhoods (Seccombe 1999, 82; Hayes 2003).[15]

Religious institutions have been intimately connected to the development of ideals of family life in the United States. Penny Edgell (2006) contends that religious institutions foster a type of middle-class family life and that the 1950s model of family life centered around the nuclear family—a provider husband, homemaker wife, and children—continues to shape religious ideals of "the good family" to the present day. The dominant family ideal in congregations, she argues, remains a 1950s *Ozzie and Harriet* model, albeit somewhat updated. She notes that conservative Protestant denominations (about a third of American churchgoers), as well as many Catholic parishes, continue to support traditional notions of gender roles in some form. Both the cultural ideal of the 1950s traditional family as well as forms of church ministry organized around it have proved long lasting.

Churches have historically seen men's and women's roles as different, with men engaging in the public sphere and providing for their wives and children, and women tending to the private sphere of the home (Edgell and Docka 2007). Today, Protestant religious conservatives are most likely to promote traditional gender roles. A review of conservative Christian literature finds that women are encouraged to tend to the home. This literature blames mothers who work while their children are young for problems such as divorce, infidelity, juvenile delinquency, and teen pregnancy. Working mothers are portrayed as unhappy and unfulfilled (Sherkat 2000). In an August 2005 newsletter, James Dobson, founder of the influential conservative evangelical organization Focus on the Family, expounded at length about the deleterious consequences to children of day care. Why not, he suggests, reduce the tax burden on families so that mothers can do what most desperately want to do—stay home? Single mothers, he concedes, are in the unfortunate position of having no other alternative (Dobson 2005). Although competing and more egalitarian views of gender roles exist among Protestant evangelicals, the rhetoric among evangelical authors and leaders has been dominated by conservative traditionalist understandings of essentialism and separate spheres (Bartkowski 2001, 163). Thus, even though segments of religious conservatives have become open to mothers' employment outside of the home, sustained intensive engagement in the labor force for mothers of young children is still discouraged (Glass and Nash 2006, 616). Support for traditional family practices has a broad reach. Diverse congregations that might be expected to hold views far from traditional religious familism nonetheless exhibit surprising amounts of symbolic and actual affirmation of traditional gendered practices (Edgell and Docka 2007).

Quantitative studies indicate that conservative religion can impact labor force behavior for married white mothers of young children, although not mothers of older children or married women without children. White Protestant women in conservative Protestant denominations married to similarly religiously conservative men were found less likely to be employed (Lehrer 1995). A recent study found a large decrease in the labor supply for married white women affiliated with conservative denominations experiencing a marital first birth. Women did not necessarily leave the labor force completely, but, notably, almost no new mothers continued to work full-time if both spouses were religiously conservative (Glass and Nash 2006).[16]

Married women from conservative faiths who scale back or leave the labor force to remain at home with young children are presumably women with some choice to make about working, whereas under welfare reform's time limits, poor single mothers of young children are required to work. Yet some poor single mothers are also members of those conservative denominations that endorse traditional gender roles. Although single mothers in poverty face constrained choices after welfare reform regarding working versus caring for their children at home, religious beliefs and cultural norms can still shape attitudes and action.

"They Would Probably Want Me to Stay Home"

Mothers in poverty are aware of traditional views of religious familism. Among the women interviewed, almost one-third believe "religion" disapproves of mothers of young children working outside of the home (26 percent thought religion approved of mothers working, 23 percent thought religion was neutral, and the rest said they did not know). This is a powerful finding in a post-welfare reform environment where such mothers are expected to work. Women conceived of different sources of authority for their religious views on working motherhood, usually what they believed God thought or what they believed their churches or former churches taught. Perhaps disturbing to policy makers and others who would wish to draw on religion to help move women from welfare to work, more mothers thought "religion" would view them negatively for being working mothers than for being on welfare. Women who think religion disapproves of working mothers do not necessarily themselves agree that mothers of young children should not work outside of the home—about half do and half do not—but the fact that a substantial number believe "religion" wants them at home is compelling.

Low-income white women appear particularly likely to associate religion with traditional gender roles, as almost half of white respondents believe religion teaches that mothers of young children should not work out of the home. (This does not even include women who thought religion approves of mothers working but only with limiting caveats such as after an infant reaches one year of age or only in jobs with "mothers' hours.") Those who agree with this notion believe that because children are a precious gift from God, mothers should stay home and raise them. Mothers who hold these convictions emphasize that even if one has to go on welfare in order to stay home, it is the right thing to do. Peggy explained:

The Bible says that your children are a gift from God, and how we treat that gift, I think, yes, we'll be judged. . . . I would say to any woman, if you can stay home with your children for as long as you can, I would say do it. [*SCS: Even if they don't have a partner to help support them, and they are going on welfare to do it?*] If you have to do it, yes. I think your kids are more important, because your first responsibility is—like I've always seen it as I can have a career at any point in my life. But I only have one shot at being a mother, and if my kids need me, that's where I need to be—that's my first responsibility.

Peggy had worked hard for many years owning her own housecleaning business, until she went on welfare following an unexpected pregnancy in her late thirties. She attributes some of her fifteen-year-old son's problems to the fact that she had been working long hours building her business when he was young. Given another chance with a new child, now age five, she sees it as God's will for her to go on welfare for as long as possible to enable her as a single mother to stay home. After being employed for so long, Peggy finds being on welfare particularly stigmatizing and distasteful, but it is a sacrifice she feels called to make for the opportunity to provide the full-time, hands-on mothering she believes God desires for her children.

Peggy's experiences have several implications. Some women draw on the Bible in constructing their vision of appropriate roles for mothers, just as Peggy refers to the Bible saying that children are a gift of God. How does this notion that children are a gift from God get translated into the need for mothers of young children to be at home? The idea of God's judgment, presumably referring to an afterlife judgment of one's conduct on earth, connotes that there is a right way and a wrong way to choose between working and mothering, with God judging and being displeased with those who choose incorrectly. Peggy's interpretation of the Bible is likely shaped by the many years she was active in her conservative evangelical church before stopping all church participation after her divorce. Ironically, when married and an active congregant, Peggy was a working mother. Conservative churches may endorse traditional lifestyles, but many in practice accept and affirm the reality of mothers working (Edgell 2006; Edgell and Docka 2007; Bartkowski 2001). Yet the ideal of women's domesticity remains an available ideal religious construct to many conservative Protestants. Low-income single mothers from conservative religious traditions that value traditional notions of gender and motherhood can absorb and sometimes appropriate these constructs.

Religion intertwines with powerful cultural narratives shaping modern debates about motherhood. Peggy's story shows how the role of guilt, familiar at times to many working mothers, can become an important factor in how poor mothers frame decisions about work and welfare.[17] Maternal guilt, combined with religious ideology, can be a potent force. Scholars of gender and family, as well as media coverage of the "mommy wars," have noted how nonworking mothers and others may attribute bad behavior of working mothers' children to the fact that the mothers are working (Blair-Loy 2003). Mothers, more than fathers, tend to experience guilt when their children experience troubles such as mental health problems, behavioral problems, and problems at school (Francis 2008). Mothers, including low-income single mothers, may choose to scale back or withdraw from the labor force if their children's needs (troubles, but also other needs, such medical or academic needs) become too great (Blair-Loy 2003; Hayes 2003; Francis 2008). In Peggy's case, the framework of religiously based conservative gender role ideology intersects with guilt over her older son's problems. Had her older son not developed problems, would she draw so heavily on these religious ideologies? Women may fear they will be negatively judged by God for not treating the gift of their children properly, that is, by leaving them for long hours in the care of others. Conservative religion can thus be a powerful component in a cultural repertoire for framing moral narratives and decisions regarding appropriate gender roles. Not only might earthly consequences of maternal "failures" such as children's problems be manifested, but, women such as Peggy believe, the specter of eternal judgment looms.

The complex interaction of religious and societal messages about motherhood impacted my respondents in different ways. The perception that one's religion does not approve of mothers working can compound anxiety or guilt for working mothers of young children, even if women disagree with the perceived teaching or are not even themselves religious. As mentioned earlier, Marilyn was raised Catholic and currently practices no religion either in terms of personal prayer or church attendance. On welfare during her pregnancy and when her child was a baby, she now is a union painter. In addition to thinking the Catholic Church would probably not like her situation of being an unmarried mother, Marilyn believes it would not approve of her being a working mother. "The fact that she's in day care while I'm going to work . . . I really don't think they [the Catholic Church] would approve of that. They would probably want me to stay home with her until she's ready to go to school and then work at her schedule. I really think the Catholic Church is not up-to-date. I would prefer to stay home. You know, I have a lot of guilt over that. I probably would have preferred to stay home with her. I couldn't. That's probably where I feel my guilt from, not staying home, is from my religious background."

Marilyn is a success story in terms of welfare reform, having moved from welfare to a good job. Yet her guilt for being a working mother is evident, guilt fostered by norms of intensive mothering and fueled by perceptions of religious expectations. In addition to parenting alone while struggling to uphold societal norms about what constitutes a good mother, some women have internalized religious ideologies that can place them under a burden of guilt. Even for women who are not religious in their adult lives, religious traditions may retain influence and serve as part of an interpretative framework.

If women believe that religion (construed as God, the Bible, a religious tradition, or other manifestation) teaches that mothers should not work, it may shape their views of themselves as mothers and workers. For mothers who agree with and follow such "teaching," religion offers strong moral justification for their decision to stay home and rely on welfare as long as possible. This religious justification adds moral weight to societal approval of mothers expending considerable time and energy in rearing their children. Hayes (2003) notes that although welfare mothers know that most mothers now work, they can also "draw on a valid cultural claim that motherhood is work, and that stay-at-home motherhood is what is best for children" (192). Given the survey data above showing 42 percent of American adults agree with this view (including 30 percent of working mothers), this belief is certainly a valid cultural claim that would resonate with a substantial number in the wider society. One study of "highly qualified women" (surveying women with graduate degrees or high honors undergraduate degrees; these women are usually married to professionals) found that just under half (43 percent) had left the labor force for some period of time, usually to care for children or elderly parents (Stone 2007, 9).[18] That almost half of the well-educated, upper-middle-class women surveyed had stopped engaging in paid employment for some period of time to attend to caregiving underscores the availability of this cultural construct. When conservative religious ideology is included, poor mothers draw not only on a valid cultural claim that staying home is best for children but also on a moral and religious claim that stay-at-home motherhood is preferred by God.

Many mothers in poverty, like many Americans overall, act as their own interpreters and arbiters of church teaching and religious doctrine. When their own convictions are strong enough, they do not hesitate to contradict official religion. This is clearly seen in the case of Jane, whose former Assembly of God church supports the idea of mothers working. As she remarked, "I think that they believe that women should work . . . and provide for the family. . . . That's what my pastor preached, and they have a day care there now." Jane, however, does not accept the church's view of the role of mothers. "I don't agree with that. . . . God ordained it to be that the mother should be with the children, raising the children, not somebody else raising the children." Although Jane is married, she believes single mothers should go on welfare to enable them to stay home as well. "I still think that he [God] would rather have her be on welfare and stay home with her children, because that is the most important thing, the mother raising the child." Women's own interpretation of what they believe to be morally right is more authoritative than church teaching or a pastor's preaching.[19] Jane echoes one strain of conservative Protestant discourse, highlighting essential differences and "separate spheres" for men and women, with women's role at home caring for children (Bartkowski 2001). These roles and differences are, in this framework, "ordained by God," language Jane herself uses. A more progressive church interpretation of women's roles does not shake her own conviction that God has ordained that mothers, not other people, should raise their children.

What is striking for low-income women who hold such a belief is the degree of financial hardship it can impose. Mothers may linger as long as possible on meager welfare benefits or remain at home even if a partner's income leaves the family in severe poverty in order to fulfill "God's will" of providing full-time, hands-on mothering to their children.

The notion that "religion" disapproves of mothers working is not necessarily passively accepted. Marilyn, for example, says the Catholic Church is not up-to-date. Vicky stated that the church "still operates with the idea of the nuclear family" and complained that the church is "not on the same page as what the world is really like." However, even if women disagree, these perceptions still exist as part of their religious cultural repertoires and can contribute to conflicted feelings about working in the labor force. These ideologies are unrealistic and unhelpful for most low-income families, especially those living in expensive areas. Maria, who was no longer welcome to participate in her Pentecostal congregation after moving in with her children's father, nonetheless tries to uphold its gender role ideology as much as possible. She indicated, "Our religion is, the men should work, the wife should stay home with the kids, and that is exactly what I am doing. It's he works, I stay home with the kids, I cook, I do the dishes, and stuff like that." Maria, who had a solid work history prior to having her babies, went on to explain that although she will need to go to work (presumably for economic reasons), it makes her feel uncomfortable. Even though she is not currently involved with church, her internalization of its gender ideology affects her attitudes and actions toward paid employment. Religious norms that militate against mothers working can be detrimental for low-income mothers needing to help support their children. Women's perceptions of such norms where these perceptions are not correct can be detrimental as well. For people whose religious beliefs are particularly salient, religion comprises a significant part of their worldview and the cultural components on which they draw in creating strategies of action (Swidler 1986). It is more difficult for women to construct a strategy for action toward increased work and improved economic circumstances when they perceive that the cultural components making up their worldview discourage work.

Other women view religion as promoting mothers' employment and egalitarian gender roles. About a quarter of the women interviewed thought religion (construed as God or church) wanted mothers of young children to work once the mother has had a chance to bond with her baby or the baby was old enough to be safe in day care (women thought bonding time ranged from a few months to one or two years). About another quarter thought religion was neutral on the matter of mothers working, leaving the decision up to the individual. I encountered a number of mothers such as Elisa, who related that Pentecostals thought men and women should be the same with regard to working. On welfare with three children age three and under, she was herself looking for a job at the time of the interview. Women who see religion as wanting mothers of young children to work emphasize the importance of providing for their families and God's desire for them to work hard.

Unpacking how poor mothers' gender role attitudes may be impacted by religion is not necessarily straightforward. Women's own religious convictions with regard to working motherhood do not necessarily square with those of their churches. Women may be misinformed, attributing to religion what in fact is not there. Women's religious cultural repertoire regarding gender and work is broad, including messages from individuals' specific congregations, messages absorbed during childhood socialization, and beliefs of one's network of family and friends. This religious cultural repertoire exists within a wider and confusing framework of societal ambiguity about working mothers in a culture where most mothers work.

Low-income women's interpretations of religious teachings on combining work and motherhood differ by race. African Americans are much more likely than white or Hispanic women to perceive religion as supportive of mothers working. Maternal employment historically has been higher for African American women than for white women (Goldberg et al. 2008). Only one African American respondent in my study thought religion might not want mothers to work, and she voiced uncertainty based only on the fact that her religious grandmother thought mothers of young children should not work. For African American women, there appear to be few conflicts between religious values and being a working mother. They think churches either want mothers of young children to work or are neutral on the issue. They believe work honors God, and they do not express religious guilt over working. LaToya, who was about to put her two-month-old baby in day care to get a job, related how the minister of the Baptist church she used to attend would want mothers of very young children to work. When I asked her why she thought the minister would want that, she responded, "Because he works, you know, to help us. So why can't we work to help ourselves? . . . I think that God feels like the people who can work should work." In a different interpretation of the Catholic Church's views than provided by some white mothers, Jamila, a twenty-eight-year-old African American, thinks the Catholic Church wants mothers to work. Jamila is a single mother of two young children and occasionally attends Mass with her mother. She said, "Now it is time to be independent and get out and work and support your kids." Far from God or church calling for mothers to be home providing hands-on caretaking, this view of religion calls mothers to work to support their children. Broader research on the black church and maternal employment affirms this finding. Black Protestant churches are often conservative theologically but not necessarily conservative in terms of traditional gender roles. Affiliation with conservative religious denominations has been found to actually promote black women's employment, and black women affiliated with conservative religious denominations are less likely to decrease their employment levels after a marital birth (Glass and Nash 2006).

Few women who think "religion" (especially when construed as God) wants them to work disagree. Lenora, a twenty-two-year-old Latina single mother who occasionally attends an evangelical church, is an exception. Living in a long-term family shelter with her son, who is almost two years old, she is currently on welfare. "God would like it if I got a better job. He sees me doing nothing, but I do have a job. I have an awesome job taking care of my son. . . . It's a big responsibility, so in a way I am working." It is particularly telling that a mother on welfare feels compelled to defend herself against God's disapproval of her lack of paid employment by emphasizing how much work it is to care for her son well. In her eyes, not only does she have a job, but it is "an awesome job" and a "big responsibility" to raise her child. Lenora draws on a long-standing traditional claim that stay-at-home motherhood, providing hands-on, full-time caregiving to young children, is a lot of work (Hayes 2003). Most people (men or women) who have done so would agree with her. Somewhat oddly (because this is a traditional religious claim and she is at least loosely affiliated with a conservative religious tradition), she places God on the side of seeing women's caregiving as "doing nothing." This reveals her belief that God wants what the American public wants, as embodied in welfare reform laws: Single mothers of young children should work long hours to financially provide for them. Mothers providing full-time, hands-on caregiving are *doing nothing*, or at least welfare mothers doing so at taxpayer expense are doing nothing.[20] Hayes (2003) astutely describes the societal devaluation of caregiving as a whole, which, like many social trends, has disproportionately negatively affected the lower classes. "Under current conditions, both the state and the market operate as if children did not exist and as if there is no caregiving work left to be done" (236). Low-income single mothers, who often lack access to high-quality paid child care, face considerable challenges in a culture that devalues caregiving as work.

Congregational cultures vary in their support of mothers who are working, with most being supportive. Despite the persistence of traditional family ideals, in practice most congregations are open to and supportive of egalitarian gender roles and the reality of dual-earner households (Edgell 2006). Still, poor mothers in mixed-income, theologically conservative congregations may find themselves in an environment where some of the more affluent mothers of young children have chosen to scale back their labor force participation and engage in church activities. Aletta described the culture of her Seventh-Day Adventist church: "I really don't think they [the church] want mothers to work . . . because half the women in there don't work. . . . They attend church seven days a week. . . . I think they [the church] want them to volunteer for stuff and do community stuff . . . raffles and bake sales and all that good stuff." Aletta believes that mothers of young children should work, worked herself until moving to transitional housing and going on welfare, and plans to work again as soon as she gets an apartment. Yet the congregational culture she describes as primarily encouraging women to be church volunteers is unlikely to provide support to women as working mothers. Conservative congregations may encourage women in their roles as primary caretakers of their children and as volunteers at church, classic "private sphere" activities. Close-knit church communities make norms more widespread and compelling, and low-income mothers may experience little affirmation for their role as family provider.

My findings suggest that larger-scale statistical studies showing an effect of conservative religion on the labor supply of white married mothers of young children may conceptually extend to some low-income single mothers. They may not have the choice to remain out of the labor force indefinitely, but some poor mothers holding conservative religious beliefs may choose welfare when possible to "please God" by staying home for a while to care for their children. There were relatively few such women in my study (slightly less than one-sixth of participants), but they are a minority worth considering. Mothers in poverty who believe that "religion" would have women as children's primary caretakers have grounds for holding such perceptions. Religious messages that affirm traditional roles of mothers as primary caretakers of children have persisted despite the fact that most mothers now work outside of the home. Poor single mothers are often aware of these messages, whether or not they themselves are deeply religious. Single mothers, furthermore, may not appreciate religious conservatives' views of mothers such as themselves being the "unfortunate exceptions" who have no other alternatives. (Ironically, religious conservatives were strong proponents of welfare reform, which propelled low-income single mothers into the workplace.)

Amid a society of working mothers and welfare reform, certain cultural notions of motherhood can place women in conflict about how much commitment they should devote to the workplace versus raising young children (Blair-Loy 2003; Stone 2007). The fact that mothers are poor and single does not mean these conflicts necessarily go away and that mothers fully embrace a provider role necessitating long hours of child care; additional challenges such as child-care problems and transportation problems heighten the conflict. Mothers desiring to care for their children themselves, lacking good child-care options, or needing to care for children with medical or other special needs may view welfare as a valid choice. A number of earlier studies have found a subset of mothers on welfare to believe they are justified in using welfare to stay home to work as caretakers for their young children, as the 1935 Social Security Act originally intended for "worthy" widows (Hayes 2003). Some further subset of this group, I contend, draws on religious justification for believing so.

Most low-income single mothers of young children, however, want to balance work and their responsibilities for their children;[21] this would mean, at the least, access to safe, affordable child care and jobs with workable schedules. Whether mothers wish to work or not, an everyday religion perspective shows that religion plays a role in the ways some interpret and experience the dual demands of caretaking and providing. This relationship is more complex than promoters of faith-based job training programs would have it. Religious interpretations can either encourage or discourage women in the pursuit of jobs and economic independence. Faith-based welfare-to-work job training programs capitalize on religious cultural interpretations emphasizing hard work and self-sufficiency. Poor mothers appear to believe that religion calls them to work hard, without having ever attended a faith-based job training program. But the examples of workers from the Bible whom poor women extol are not single mothers of young children who must leave their children in substandard child care to toil in poorly paid jobs. While a religious cultural interpretation that emphasizes how working hard "pleases God" enhances women's work ethic, a religious interpretation that emphasizes the primacy of motherhood and caretaking discourages some from the labor force or adds a burden of guilt on some who work.

Lived Religion in the Workplace

Whatever poor mothers' religious views on welfare, work, and working motherhood, welfare reform means that the majority of them will work. How, then, do faith and religion enter into their lives as low-wage workers? Sociologists since Weber have sought to understand the connection between religion and work (Lenski 1961; Riccio 1979; Wuthnow and Scott 1997). Contemporary scholars find only a weak connection between religion and economic behavior but claim that religion plays a substantial role in the meaning people attach to their work. Robert Wuthnow (1994a) conducted the most comprehensive academic survey on the relationship between religion and economic behavior, surveying a nationally representative, randomly selected sample of the labor force. One-third of working Americans think about how to link their faith more directly with their work a great deal, and 60 percent of attendees of weekly religious service think about it a great or fair amount. Overall, the main function of faith with regard to work is to provide work with a sense of meaning and purpose, rather than to significantly influence workplace decisions and behavior. Faith plays some role in reducing burnout at work, evangelizing at work, and influencing workplace ethics. Wuthnow summarizes, "A tentative conclusion that can be drawn from considering the relationship between faith and work, therefore, is that religious commitment has come to play a kind of therapeutic role in relation to economic behavior in postindustrial society. . . . Rather than providing guidance, religious conviction contributes meaning—that is, work becomes more interesting . . . because it has cosmic significance" (77).

The relationship between faith and work has been a topic of growing academic and workplace interest in the past decade or so, especially as it relates to business occupations. David Miller (2007), a theologian, former business executive, and director of Princeton University's Faith and Work Initiative, presents some relevant evidence. For example, in 2001 *Fortune* magazine ran a cover story titled "God and Business: The Surprising Quest for Spiritual Renewal in the American Workplace"; universities have programs and centers studying spirituality in the workplace.[22] Books on faith and work have proliferated, too, with titles such as *Business by the Book: Complete Guide of Biblical Principles for the Workplace* (2006); *God Is My CEO: Following God's Principles in a Bottom Line World* (2001); and *Jesus CEO: Using Ancient Wisdom for Visionary Leadership* (1995).[23] A 2002 compilation of faith-work writing from an evangelical Christian perspective, *The Marketplace Annotated Bibliography: A Christian Guide to Books on Work,*

Business, and Vocation, catalogs more than seven hundred publications. Groups, websites, and blogs dedicated to connecting faith, spirituality, and work abound from a variety of religious traditions. Large corporations have workplace chaplains. Prayer groups, meditation groups, Torah classes, and Bible study groups meet at the workplace. Miller provides a typology for the integration of faith at work, highlighting four categories: ethics, evangelism, experience, and enrichment. Workers seeking to integrate their religious beliefs with their work do so in one or more of these ways. Workers in the ethics category highlight the relationship between their religious beliefs and ethical behavior in the workplace. Those located in the evangelism group emphasize the workplace as a mission field where they can witness to coworkers and others. People in the experience category integrate faith and work through issues of calling, meaning, and vocation. The enrichment group seeks personal transformation and self-actualization through meditation and other religious practices in connection with their work.

The increased attention to faith at work in the past ten or fifteen years has corresponded with people increasingly desiring to live a more integrated life in a busy, fast-paced world (Wuthnow 1994a; Miller 2007; Nash and McLennan 2001). This movement has arisen mostly outside of the institutional church, as businesspeople and other professionals have perceived the clergy to be uninterested in the workplace. The so-called Sunday-Monday gap indicates that workers feel unsupported by their religious organizations in their occupations (Miller 2007, 10). Yet as the place where most workers spend the majority of their waking hours, experience stress, face ethical dilemmas, and interact with a variety of people, the workplace emerges as a key social location in which to examine religion as lived (Wuthnow 1994a).

The burgeoning "faith at work" movement does not focus on the types of jobs available to mothers transitioning off of welfare. Low-skilled urban women who gain employment often work in frontline service-sector jobs. These jobs are characterized by poor wages and enforced deference to customers and managers. Service employees are expected to greet customers in a friendly, smiling manner and interact with them in a polite way, no matter how the customers are treating them. They have been described as the "emotional proletariat," frontline service workers who must defer to the customers and whose managers monitor and control their emotional interactions as part of the job (Macdonald and Sirianni 1996). In *The Managed Heart,* Arlie Hochschild (1983) analyzes the "emotional labor" involved in jobs that require workers to manage their emotions in particular required ways. Women are more likely to be in jobs in which niceness and deference are needed to perform the job. In addition to the gender component, race and class issues come into play. The indignities that service workers encounter in demonstrating deference to customers are particularly problematic for members of disadvantaged groups (Wharton 2009; Newman 1999).[24] Deference to management is another key piece of service-sector jobs. Workers experience little control. They can be fired and replaced easily. Some workplaces submit their employees to purse checks and urine drug testing. Ehrenreich (2001) argues that if overbearing managers or a myriad of informal rules constantly reminds poor women of their lowly social status, they begin to internalize and accept this status. This likely explains why the mothers I interviewed believe that religion's primary requirement of employers is that they treat them nicely and respectfully. Having experienced managers who have treated them or others with disrespect, poor women in low-wage jobs crave to be treated in a dignified, respectful manner. They may be doing low-status work, but they do not wish to be treated as low-status persons, either by customers or supervisors.

"Help Me Survive the Day"

For mothers in poverty, the workplace indeed proves to be a key social location for lived religion. In my study, two-thirds of the women somehow connect their faith with their daily work lives, either in current jobs (for those employed) or in previous jobs (for those not currently working). The primary way that low-income urban mothers "live religion" at work is by praying at work during times of job stress, which are numerous. More than half the mothers interviewed did so; I briefly recount some of their prayer narratives here.

Juliana spoke in great detail about the role of prayer in her former job as an assistant drugstore manager: "When I am stressed—as an assistant manager you can get really stressed, especially if cash comes out wrong or if a customer comes to you so mad and you have to deal with it. You have no choice but to deal with it. . . . I started saying, 'Okay, give me faith.' If I know I'm doing something wrong, he [God] will give me the strength to be better."

Peggy prayed for help during her former housecleaning work: "Sometimes you can get into a cleaning situation . . . and it can be frustrating. 'God please help me.' . . . 'God, you have to help me.'" Gabriella was shy and inarticulate when I first spoke with her. However, when the topic turned to faith and work, she became animated, explaining vividly how she used to pray during difficult times at her recent job at a toy store.

"'God, help me, this is too much.' Sometimes when you are at work and you just feel like you can't work, you're like, 'Oh please, God, I can't.' . . . He helps me a lot."

Attending to the language of these prayer narratives points to women's experiences of stress and feeling overwhelmed at work. The mothers' language and tone were fresh, vivid, and full of strong emotion, even though the majority of participants were on welfare at the time of the interview and talking about jobs they no longer held. Their prayers are those of beseeching God for assistance in seemingly desperate work moments. My questions were broad, merely asking women if they ever thought about religion or prayed in connection to their work. The frequency of prayer narratives of distress and cries for help suggests potentially many low-income single mothers turning to faith to help contend with difficult work situations. The immediacy of prayer narratives is telling. Prayer frequently takes place on the job itself. God is considered accessible and interested in being involved in these very ordinary daily experiences. Religion is lived in seemingly mundane locations, such as the fast-food counter or the cashier's station. Religious activity pertains to the transcendent, the sacred, and the divine, something not typically associated with such locations. Yet it is precisely in these locations that women seek to encounter the divine.

Mothers especially turn to prayer to help maintain self-control in difficult interactions with customers. Take the case of Jamila, who, unasked, narrated her frequent prayers from her previous jobs as a cashier: "Things like, 'Oh God, please help me. Help me through the day. Survive the day.' I usually work with customers, and that's not easy. You have to ask for help. When people have a bad day, they take it out on you." I was struck by the note of desperation in her language. "Help me *survive the day*." Given that employees must swallow their pride and dignity to defer to customers when the customers are obnoxious, insulting, and rude, the emotional labor involved in this kind of "surface acting" can be extremely draining (Newman 1999; Hochschild 1983). A recent review of research literature on such emotional labor cites numerous studies elaborating its deleterious effects to workers. Workers who have to suppress negative emotions and fake positive emotions report higher levels of emotional exhaustion, burnout, and job stress and lower levels of job satisfaction and sense of personal accomplishment at work (Wharton 2009). In prayer, poor women in service jobs that lead to emotional dissonance turn to a divine being to help them deal with the resulting stress and emotional exhaustion. Through prayer, they feel they are not alone in facing irate or abusive customers but rather that God is with them.

The sense of divine assistance helps them to smile and bite their tongues, emotional labor necessary to keep their jobs.

Mothers in poverty turn to prayer in seeking to gain self-control in dealing with difficult employers. As noted earlier, low-skilled workers need to defer to employers, even employers who try to control employee behavior and treat workers in a demeaning or disrespectful manner.[25] Brenda indicated, "I wanted to rip my boss's head off, but I would take some time out in the bathroom just saying, 'God, grant me the serenity to accept the things I cannot change.'" Martina had recently gotten into a confrontation with her boss, something she said would not have happened had she been praying and gaining strength from her faith. Faith, she explained, would have helped her understand the boss's point of view and kept the confrontation from escalating. Low-skilled women know they are easily disposable in high-turnover service-sector industries, and an outburst against the employer can quickly find them out of a job. They need jobs to support their children and satisfy the requirements of welfare reform. Maintaining self-control in the face of being spoken to disrespectfully or being subjected to dehumanizing workplace procedures is sometimes required to remain employed. Fellow employees, as well as customers and managers, can serve as sources of stress; mothers told me they also pray for self-control in difficult interactions with other workers.

Prayer, job stress, and resilience are intricately linked for mothers in poverty. Survey data find that 51 percent of Americans and 80 percent of attendees of weekly religious services agree that praying in the morning helps them have a better day at work. People with strong religious commitments are significantly less likely to experience burnout in their work. Robert Wuthnow writes, "God becomes a kind of sounding board, a partner in the internal conversations people have about their jobs while at work or before starting their day" (1994a, 67). Poor mothers believe that God wants them to work hard and will help them to do so. They turn to prayer when they are frustrated with work to the point of being tempted to quit. Quitting a job leads to sanctions under welfare reform, and women need to persevere to the best of their ability. Magda had previously worked as a cashier at McDonald's, as a certified nursing assistant in a nursing home, and as a receptionist, although she was on welfare at the time of the interview due to a day-care crisis and her son's illness. When working, Magda says, she thought about God "all the time" on the job: "If I get lazy or something, I pray to him to give me strength to go on, or if I feel like I want to quit, I pray to him to give me strength not to quit, and if I feel like I'm running into a fight with one of the employees, I pray I'll get some self-control." In prayer, women request divine assistance to work hard, keep going, and maintain control. Their belief that God helps them in these work-related challenges provides a source of strength and resilience. Mothers feel they are no longer alone in facing their work stresses in that God is there with them as a partner, walking with them throughout the day. Prayer allows them to step back mentally while in the midst of tense and stressful situations.

The Divine Physician in the Low-Wage Workplace

Although difficult physical labor is more commonly associated with jobs for low-skilled men, poor women encounter this same situation in some occupations. Physical pain plays no small role in certain low-wage jobs occupied primarily by women (Ehrenreich 2001). Rosalyn is a twenty-eight-year-old black/Hispanic single mother of a four-year-old. After work experience as a home health aide and two years of community college, she was receiving welfare, living in transitional housing, and working part-time as a hotel housekeeper when I met her. A Catholic who prays every day, she says religion is very important in her life although she does not attend any religious services. "I don't go to a church, but I'm believing. . . . I don't go because I don't have time to go. Sunday I work, so I never have time." Rosalyn frequently turns to prayer at work. Responsible for making beds quickly, she sees God as helping her both to finish making the beds early and to deal with the physical pain the work produces. "When I need to finish my job, I say, 'Oh my God, help me to finish early,'" When I asked if she thought God helped her in her job, she responded, "Yeah. . . . I say, 'God, help me to feel better.' Maybe when I go to lunch or when I come back I feel better. When I go back, I don't have pain. So he's helped me." Rosalyn experiences religion alone on the job, making hotel beds, not in a church with a congregation. Hotel maids and other women in physically demanding occupations engage in less frequent direct interaction with customers than frontline service workers. Instead of prayer narratives concerned with divine assistance for emotional self-control, these prayer narratives focus on the body and the bodily pain that their occupations induce. The biblical image of Jesus as Divine Physician is well known, and prayers for health are a common type of petitionary prayer (Baker 2008). My respondents believe that God cares deeply for their bodies, as well as their souls. As such, God is concerned with their complaints of bodily pain on the job. At work, personally religious women in pain-producing occupations believe that God helps either by healing them or by helping them to deal with work-induced pain that impedes their further job performance.

Being Honest, Doing Good

Religion is concerned with issues of morality and ethical living. Religion may encourage ethical behavior at work through people's desire to be pleasing to God, through the exhortations and perhaps examples of pastors, and through religious communities' norms encouraging honesty (Wuthnow 1994a, 86). "Thou shall not steal" is one of the Ten Commandments known to many Americans. Many books and articles connecting religion and workplace ethics have been written recently for a general audience. Intensity of religious commitment does appear to play some role in people's behavior in the workplace with regard to ethics. Survey data find that people for whom religion is very important are somewhat less likely than nonreligious people to say they have engaged in the past month in such behaviors as using office equipment for personal use, bending the rules, bending the truth, charging for nonlegitimate expenses, or coming to work late.[26]

Peggy explained how faith kept her honest in her previous housecleaning work: "You feel a lot of temptation to do bad things, you know, to help yourself to people's things, or just do a slipshod job in cleaning and grab the money and run. I never wanted to do that, because I always knew that God's eyes were watching me, and I wanted to certainly please him, you know, maybe because I feel that God's watching. I would never touch anybody's things or give them less than I had promised them to, because I think that maybe God put that in my head." Faith-based soft-skill job training programs draw heavily on religious norms when talking about the importance of workplace honesty. The notion that "God's eyes are always watching" is a religious idea that is carried over in such job training settings. Programs emphasize that employees are not just working for employers but also working for God (or as one program put it, working for the "Boss above"). I have interviewed employers hiring from faith-based job training programs who expressed preference for job candidates from these programs over other job training programs in their area. Given that some workplaces use such practices as checking employees' purses for stolen items or installing hidden cameras to watch maids cleaning houses (Ehrenreich 2001), it is unsurprising that employers might prefer candidates who believe that God's eyes are always on them.

Religion is lived at work in the ways in which people perceive their work to be expressions of their faith-fueled commitment to "do good" unto others. Most religious traditions teach people to reach out and help those around them. For women engaged in low-wage jobs, this may mean working in jobs that provide direct care to others. Lisa, as mentioned earlier, is currently on welfare, but she found ways to express her faith in her previous job as a kitchen worker and food server in a nursing home. She prayed on the job for residents who were very ill or who had been taken to the hospital. Health-care settings are particularly amenable for a work-faith connection of fulfilling religious obligations to help one's neighbor. A 2004 study of nurses found that 84 percent of them thought there was something spiritual in the nursing care they provided (Grant, O'Neil, and Stephens 2004). Health-care settings employ substantial numbers of low-skilled workers who have direct contact with patients. The cadres of women working as nursing assistants, food servers, and the like have opportunities to infuse their care with spirituality. They may talk with patients, express concern for them, and pray for them, thus bringing religion into their daily work lives.

This type of direct-care environment is one, but not the only, venue for embodying a lived religious commitment of doing good for others. Peggy thought faith called her to infuse housecleaning work with love for the home's inhabitants. "A lot of times in these homes that I cleaned, it was in my mind a way that I could give a gift back to somebody . . . to go in there and put everything and clean everything with a touch of love." Upper-middle-class home owners would likely be unaware that the maid from the cleaning company is considering her work as a gift to them and is trying to infuse their homes with love as she cleans.[27] Low-income women living their faith in and through their work point to the myriad of unexpected ways in which religion breaks into daily life. Lived religion takes place in unlikely circumstances.

Framing one's work activity as an act of faith in the sense of "doing good for others" thus comes in many guises. A minority of mothers interviewed consciously reframed work activity that might not be seen as directly "doing good" for others—scrubbing toilets, working on an assembly line—in order to see it as an expression of their religious faith. This religious framing gave women a sense of pride in their work, because they saw themselves as living out their faith and being pleasing to God by helping others. Aletta, for example, used to work for a medical equipment company making five thousand intravenous (IV) lines per day. "I know I was doing good because there are a lot of sick people out there, and if I wasn't making IVs, who was going to make them?" The repetitive, tedious work involved in making thousands of IVs each day is connected to faith and framed as a way of doing good for others. Such an interpretation reframes onerous work as fulfilling the commandment to "love thy neighbor," infusing the work with meaning.

As religion is experienced and understood in the social context in which it is lived, narratives of work and spirituality differ for low-income women in jobs that approximate middle-class professional jobs. Mothers who perhaps have had some college and are employed in human services positions, for example, are more likely to associate workplace faith or spirituality with doing good by helping people who are needy. Vicky spoke at length about how her spirituality kept her centered at work in her previous human service job at a homeless shelter for women. Prayer and spirituality, she said, allowed her to work there and try to help other people, despite the difficult situations encountered. "I prayed there a lot. . . . My belief in God and in what I was doing was right carried me through a lot of situations there." This type of interaction-intensive work, while draining and stressful, engages a different language of prayer than low-status jobs involved with direct customer service. These jobs are more similar to middle-class professional work without the constant reminders of one's low status provided by low-wage frontline service work. The status hierarchy between social service worker and client differs from that between service-sector employee and customer. Although both types of jobs can be stressful and require maintenance of emotional self-control, the constant deference that undermines the dignity of frontline service workers does not play a large role in these more middle-class occupations, because the social service worker is the one in the position of authority. This leads to different ways of religion being lived on the job.

Also of note, although there are numerous ways in which jobs can be stretched to encompass the notion of doing good for others, my respondents working in frontline direct-service jobs dealing with customers did not tend to frame their jobs in this way. Their dominant narrative for faith on the job centers on beseeching God for help, not in expressing their spirituality by caring for and doing good for others. There are two reasons, then, that make poor mothers' overall dominant faith-work narrative one of turning to faith to help survive the workplace. First, a considerable percentage of poor women are in frontline service jobs dealing with customers. Second, mothers in other types of low-wage jobs more conducive to expressing a spirituality of caring or doing good also encounter many stressful situations where they constantly turn to prayer for help.

Doing good for others may include concern for others' souls, and evangelism or "witnessing" is one of the ways in which people engage faith with regard to work. The workplace is regarded as a mission field where people can garner converts to their religion. In general, evangelical Christians and other religious conservatives, southerners, and women are more likely to engage in workplace witnessing. More than half of weekly church attendees and one-third of the labor force overall say they have discussed their faith with someone at work in the past year (Wuthnow 1994a). Low-income mothers sometimes seek to witness to or evangelize others at work. As noted earlier, Maria adheres to the Pentecostal tenets of not wearing makeup or jewelry and not dancing, drinking, or listening to nonreligious music. Coworkers in the jobs she had held prior to going on welfare had asked many questions about her noticeably different lifestyle. She welcomed such questions as an entrée and opportunity to share her faith with them. Workplace evangelism can have an impact, as evidenced by one of the mothers interviewed. Jane experienced a major religious conversion at a prior job after a coworker evangelized and prayed with her while they were working at their keypunch operator jobs. She recounted, "All of a sudden it was like burdens were lifted. . . . It was a welling in my chest, and that was, I believe, the Holy Spirit coming in me at the time. No one bothered us, and we were keying for a time. I mean, you had to keypunch like you were on time, and no one came near us. And that's the moment I got saved, that Jesus came into my heart, and I became saved, and I became born again."

Jane's experience is a profoundly illuminating illustration of the low-wage workplace as a site for lived religion. All the while keypunching on time so as to keep away suspicious managers, women speak intensely of religious beliefs, pray with one another, and pray to God for salvation. What would look like to an outside observer as women toiling away at a low-paid, repetitive job is, in fact, a deep spiritual experience. Here conversion, prayer for salvation, and becoming "born again" occur not in a church but in the workplace. The actual work is but a backdrop, an unlikely setting, for the spiritual experience.

Living Faith on the (Low-Wage) Job

Being "born again" while keypunching, trying to evangelize coworkers through adherence to religious codes of dress, praying for nursing home residents, praying for help in dealing with rude customers—religious faith enters into the work lives of poor mothers with surprising frequency. The finding that two-thirds of my respondents in some way try to integrate their faith and work lives suggests that a substantial percentage of women in poverty may be doing so. I interviewed an array of women from various social service agencies, few of whom were regular church attendees, with almost all eligible women at the agencies participating in the study. Nothing indicates that this group is more likely to connect faith with work than other low-income mothers would be.

For very poor women, previous findings on the role of faith or spirituality in the workplace do not fully hold. The primary role of faith in the workplace is not to imbue the work with meaning and purpose, although that is one role for a minority of women. Rather, it is to help deal with the stresses of low-wage service-sector work. These women find their faith to be a powerful resource that helps them maintain self-control and deal productively with demanding customers or difficult bosses or coworkers. Faith helps them carry out unpleasant tasks and complete the work that has to be accomplished. Whether or not they attend church frequently, they draw on the religious culture in their repertoire to help them in the workplace.

What is most interesting and disturbing is how many low-income mothers pray at work using the language of survival: "Help me get through the day"; "Help me survive this day"; "Help me persevere." More than any other area, mothers were eager to share their narratives of prayer, always unasked. Their language of prayer burst out, as if women were expressing strongly felt and bottled-up emotions, glad to have someone willing to listen. "Help me, God." It unnerves me to think that the cashier at the store might feel she has to pray like this in order to survive her job. The stresses, labor, indignities, and disrespect inherent in many low-wage service-sector jobs, combined with mounting pressures to support their families, lead women to turn to faith to help them survive the work day. For a considerable number of poor urban mothers, a theory of survival more appropriately describes the work-faith connection than Wuthnow's (1994a) finding of meaning and cosmic significance.

Faith often fosters resilience on the job. It can help low-income mothers to persevere, to not quit, to perform the job, and to maintain self-control instead of getting into confrontations with customers, managers, or coworkers. Religious faith can also help women in low-status, stressful jobs reframe their image of themselves, given that the enforced deference adds an additional psychological burden to the actual job stresses. Others also labor in stressful occupations—firefighters and emergency room personnel, for example—but not with the lack of respect many low-wage service jobs engender. Although the broader society may show poor women disrespect and look down on their jobs, seeing themselves as working with God's help and being loved by God allows some women a different image of self.

The notion of seeing one's daily work in the world as a calling or vocation, originally stemming from Reformation theologians, is an important one found in studies of higher-status occupations. Martin Luther understood all Christians, not just those in religious life, to have a vocation to serve God in daily life through their work. People are called to serve God through their professions. For Calvin, all occupations could function as a place to serve God, no matter how lowly the job. People's hard work in their jobs and resulting material success were viewed as ways to please God and as signs of God's favor.[28] In the United States, 30 percent of the labor force feels called to their occupations by God, as do 40 percent of church members and 46 percent of weekly religious service attendees (Wuthnow 1994a). Intrinsically religious people who are well rewarded at work in terms of pay, benefits, or status are more likely than others to view their work as a calling or ministry as opposed to a career or job (Davidson and Caddell 1990).

Women working in low-skilled service-sector jobs do not usually view these jobs as a vocation. Few see ringing up french fries as a calling. If poor women feel a sense of God's calling or purpose for their lives (as more than 80 percent of those I asked did), it is usually in motherhood. Work may fit in because it helps them to support their children, but most believe God's calling, their vocation, God's purpose for their lives, lies in being good mothers. Given the jobs available to most low-skilled women in the labor force, it is little wonder that the profound responsibilities and joys involved in raising children embody mothers' sense of vocation and calling as opposed to jobs making hotel beds or getting chastised by customers.[29]

Poor women's experiences of spirituality and work have some resonance with those of higher-income workers. Faith helps higher-income workers by alleviating stress, thus reducing burnout and increasing job satisfaction. A minority of poor mothers link their work with a higher purpose like higher-income workers do, such as fulfilling the religious mandate to help others. Framing low-status and often difficult jobs as part of a transcendent purpose imbues such work with a greater sense of meaning. Some mothers connect faith with workplace ethics, and some evangelize, both practices found in studies of nonpoor workers. Yet there is also a significant disconnect. Miller's (2007) typology for the integration of faith at work (ethics, evangelism, experience, and enrichment) bypasses the most important way faith enters the workplace for women in service-sector jobs—helping them to get through the day.[30] Questions of vocation, meaning, self-actualization, and the like, prominent in studies of nonpoor workers, do not play the major part of poor women's faith-work integration.

Thus far this chapter has focused on religion as a source of resilience in the face of stress and as an interpretive lens that can reframe low-wage jobs as serving a higher purpose. Yet as chapter 2 discusses, religion can be engaged in deleterious ways as well as helpful ways. Overall, poor women perceive religion to be helpful in dealing with the immediate stressful situations of their jobs. As an interpretive lens, religion also seems to serve a positive role for mothers in dealing with their immediate circumstances. That is, framing jobs as ways to express their religious commitments is experienced as positive by women who do so. With regard to work, there appears to be little negative religious rumination, feeling punished by God or abandoned by God. As one unpacks the language of their narratives, one sees that work almost seems too busy, too immediate, and too provoking of women's need for prayer on the spot for them to engage in despairing religious thoughts. Churches seem to be most often absent, not harmful, in terms of women's work concerns. For example, one mother interviewed had sought congregational help for work but had no response, which made her feel let down by the church. Overall, the mothers' stories do not point to churches causing harm with regard to their daily work lives. One could construct scenarios where religion would be engaged harmfully in mothers' daily work experiences, for example, if their work makes them despair and feel abandoned by God or if they overzealously evangelize and alienate coworkers. These scenarios could, and probably do, occur in workplaces across the United States; they were just not situations I encountered. Given that previous research finds religion to serve more often as a source of resilience than a source of distress, and low-wage work seems particularly conducive to people drawing on religion for strength, this finding does not seem unreasonable.

This chapter, however, has examined the connection between religion and low-wage jobs from the perspectives of mothers in poverty, a micro perspective rather than a macro perspective of religion and work. It is undeniable that work conditions in many low-wage jobs are bad and that this should be a matter of religious concern, in a larger sense. Decent working conditions, pay, and benefits for low-skilled workers are fundamental moral issues and connect directly to religious values of social justice.[31] Many religious organizations are concerned with issues of worker justice. Religious organizations, for example, supported the farmworkers' movement in the 1960s and 1970s and continue to advocate for justice for farmworkers today. Religious organizations have been actively involved in recent living-wage campaigns. In the early twentieth century, social-gospel reformers crusaded for labor reforms ending child labor and limiting work hours. Religious people and organizations have also stood on the other side of worker justice. Bethany Moreton's (2009) *To Serve God and Wal-Mart: The Making of Christian Free Enterprise* portrays Wal-Mart's founders drawing on the fundamentalist Christianity of the conservative Ozarks region where the business began, using the Christian value of "servant leadership" to help the early Wal-Mart workers embrace servile and low-paid retail work.

Without denying that religion should play an important role in bringing about justice for workers and larger-scale changes, my focus is on the day-to-day experiences of the actual women whose lives are lived within current social structures. The "religion as the opiate of the masses" point of view would contend that women's drawing on faith to help survive the workplace is detrimental because it keeps them pacified. It is unclear, however, that nonreligious women would have any better alternatives within the low-skilled service-sector jobs available to them or would be any more likely to successfully protest and improve their working conditions. Within difficult situations, poor mothers draw on faith to forge productive lives (Frederick 2003) and gain strength to persevere and move forward. As isolated women in non-unionized jobs and disconnected from congregations or any organizations that might engage in action aimed at social change, none of the mothers studied is likely alone to be able to impact her working conditions dramatically. Single mothers also feel pressure to support their children in a post–welfare reform era. Hopefully sooner rather than later, they will become connected with congregations, unions, political organizations, or community organizations that might help involve them in efforts toward improving work opportunities and environments. In day-to-day existence, the religious narratives of poor women about work reveal strength in the midst of hardship and forging meaning in difficult work environments. This fortitude itself is an act of agency (Frederick 2003). This is everyday religion.

FOUR

"I Send Him to Church with My Mother": Religion and Parenting

Sarah, a thirty-one-year-old African American, is a single mother on welfare. She has intense personal religious practices but left the Pentecostal church as a teenager. Although she no longer attends religious services, she prays many times a day, reads the Bible daily, and devotes Saturdays to prayer. "On Saturdays for me, I just keep that day holy. I look at it as a Sabbath day. I don't do anything. I just pray. No housework, nothing. That day is just to pray and just for him." Her interview was filled with religious language. "I always try to talk about the word of God. . . . In everything I do, I always talk about God." Despite her devout personal religious beliefs and practices, Sarah says she fell "off the track" when she stopped attending church. She believes that leaving church led to her current problems. Now raising a three-year-old daughter, she wants to imbue her child with a strong faith. "I want her to know about God, and I try to teach her that." And although she does not participate in organized religion herself, Sarah sends her daughter to church regularly with her sister. "I send her to church. She goes to my sister's church, the Pentecostal. I was raised that way. So I want to do the same for her. When you don't do that, they depart from it, and it's awful. . . . I want her to know about God. I want her to know about God, and I want her to know about the Bible and that she didn't come here alone. [Church] will give her balance, hope. She would try to stay focused and keep that straight way."

If a majority of the low-income mothers interviewed believe that their life's purpose lies most of all in being good mothers, then parenting is a central site for their experience of lived religion. Parenting is likely a primary site for lived religion for any parent who is religious. Annette Mahoney and collaborators (2001) note that religions privilege the sanctity of relationships within families, and many Americans view family relationships in a sacred light. Religious rituals surrounding birth exist across many religious traditions, and child rearing is imbued with spiritual significance. "Part of the power of religion lies in its ability to infuse spiritual character and significance into a broad range of worldly concerns. . . . Judeo-Christian religions portray the burdens and pleasures of parenting as opportunities to model and deepen one's understanding of God's love, patience, and commitment, and frame the parental role as a sacred calling that requires personal sacrifices" (221, 223). The sheer awe and wonder that many parents experience on the birth of a child are connected to a higher meaning, as evidence of God's power and goodness. Children are seen as blessings and gifts from God. On top of this, poor, young, single mothers often view their children as their only source of identity, meaning, connectedness, and purpose (Edin and Kefalas 2005, 184), making parenting an especially important potential site for everyday religion. In my research, mothering was viewed by many as a calling from God and a sacred duty that they were called to fulfill well.

Parenting can be challenging under the best of circumstances, and mothers on or transitioning off welfare face similar challenges to their middle-class counterparts in balancing working with caring for one's family, yet they do so with far fewer marketable skills and resources (Hayes 2003). Low-income single mothers often face daunting situations. Many find it very challenging to fulfill even their children's most basic needs for food, shelter, and a safe environment (Holloway et al. 1997). Much of their stress stems from worry about their children. The majority of these women desire to be good mothers, although they often lack support in their parenting role. Poor mothers raising children on their own are more likely to live in dangerous neighborhoods, have jobs with inflexible schedules, experience difficulties finding reliable and safe child care, and have troubles with transportation and housing. Not surprisingly, many experience high levels of parenting stress (Hayes 2003; Edin and Lein 1997; Holloway et al. 1997; Kim 2003). But although scholars have examined a number of ways that poor single mothers try to manage parenting—from Carol Stack's (1974) seminal work on the intentional communities mothers construct to help raise their children to Holloway et al.'s (1997) work on cultural models of child rearing—very little research has directly examined how low-income single mothers engage religion in parenting.[1]

Religion and Parenting: An Overview

Popular titles about religion and parenting abound. Examples include *10 Principles for Spiritual Parenting; Jewish Parenting Wisdom; Talking to Your Children about God; The Tao of Parenting;* and *Keys to Interfaith Parenting.* Conservative Protestants in particular produce substantial amounts of literature on Christian parenting. The conservative evangelical Focus on the Family organization generates an extensive array of parenting resources. Wanting a religious upbringing for children is not, however, confined to subscribers of conservative evangelical philosophies.

The importance of religion increases for families once they have children, including those families who are not particularly religious. This is especially true of mothers (Fay 1993; Edgell 2006). Parents look to churches, synagogues, and other religious institutions to teach children traditions, reinforce morals and values, and provide a community. Nancy Ammerman (1997) describes "Golden Rule Christians," who do not necessarily hold traditional religious beliefs or attend church every week yet want the contribution of churches in raising their children. "Parents have persistently, throughout much of American history, sought the protection of faith and the good graces of the church for their children—even when they themselves were less than enthusiastic believers" (102).[2] These "Golden Rule Christians" describe stresses in family life as one of their most pressing concerns and say that the main criterion for choosing a church is a place that is good for their children. Although these parents have social networks and resources through other organizations to which they belong, they believe churches offer something unique for their children that other community or civic groups cannot. Penny Edgell (2006), studying working-class and middle-class congregations, found that regardless of the salience of their own religious beliefs, mothers wanted to engage children, particularly school-age children, in church ministries. Mothers desired to pass on their religious traditions or equip children to make informed decisions about religion.

A body of quantitative research has found religion to be linked to good parenting practices. Parental religiosity is correlated with closer parent-child relationships, greater warmth in family relationships, more frequent hugging and praising of children, less frequent yelling and less likelihood of abuse, and greater overall parenting functioning (Dollahite and Thatcher 2007).[3] Specifically regarding lower-income mothers, maternal religiosity is linked with more effective child-rearing practices. Among predominantly low-income African American mothers in the urban South, mothers with high levels of religious belief and personal religious practices were more responsive to their infants (Cain 2007).[4] Another study of low-income African American families found that mothers who were more religious used child-rearing practices that were more cooperative and interactive and less hostile (Strayhorn, Weidman, and Larson 1990). These studies prove nothing causal, but religion might positively impact parenting through several avenues. Religious norms place great value on children and encourage parental attention to children (Bartkowski 2001; Bartkowski and Wilcox 2000). Personal prayer might help parents feel a greater sense of agency and self-confidence in parenting and help them to deal with stressors in their lives. Churches provide social support and parenting resources. Adding another dimension to this line of research are recent studies assessing the impact of parental religiosity on child outcomes. In a study of more than sixteen thousand first-grade children, Bartkowski, Xu, and Levin (2008) found, controlling for demographic background variables, that religious participation of parents is associated with better behavioral, emotional, and cognitive development in children. Children of parents who attended services frequently and talked about religion with their children at home were rated by both parents and teachers as having better self-control, social skills, and learning approaches than did children of nonattending parents.[5] A recent longitudinal study indicated that children from disadvantaged families were less affected by childhood disadvantage and had better young adult outcomes if their parents were involved in religious organizations (Dehejia et al. 2009).[6]

Although statistical associations between religiosity and parenting are useful, we still know little about how and why low-income mothers actually engage religion in the daily raising of their children. Consequently, everyday religion remains little understood. Taking into account earlier research on religion and parenting, this chapter takes a close-up "everyday religion" look at parenting for low-income women. How does their faith play a role in parenting? What do they want their children to learn about religion and why, and how is this lived in practice? Is religion helpful to them in parenting? Is religion ever engaged harmfully?

The vast majority of mothers I interviewed engage religion as part of their parenting. Thirty-seven of the forty-five women want their children to have strong personal religious faith. Thirty-two women also want their children involved in churches, including 70 percent of those who infrequently or never attend themselves. Given the great importance that low-income mothers place on motherhood, parenting deserves special notice for scholars seeking to understand these mothers' lived religion.

Children as Catalysts

Similar to nonpoor women, low-income women often see religion as more important once they have children. Poor mothers often perceive their children as blessings or gifts from God.[7] Having a child marks a dramatic turning point for young unmarried mothers, and the responsibilities are immense. The combination of feeling responsible for a new baby, sometimes solely, and perceiving the child as a gift from God can turn mothers toward religion. Almost half of the mothers I interviewed said religion became more important to them once they had a child; this was especially true of those who were not particularly religious to begin with.[8] Women frequently see religious training of children as another responsibility for a good mother to undertake.

Mothers may choose to have their babies baptized, christened, or presented to the church, in keeping with their religious traditions, even if they have been distant from those traditions for years. For some, this is a symbolic occasion, undertaken as a cultural and family celebration more than as a religious ritual. For others, though, choosing to have one's infant formally recognized and welcomed into the church provokes a rethinking of the mother's own relationship with faith and church. Annie, a nineteen-year-old white single mother of an eight-month-old baby, was raised Catholic but had not attended church since she was sixteen and had found religion unimportant before having her child. She stated: "I think it's very important now. . . . I've never paid too much attention to religion, but if I'm going to have her christened, it will mean that I'm obviously doing it for a reason, so I'm responsible to follow through. . . . I want to bring her to church. . . . If I'm not going to follow through with religion, I don't think there's a point in my having her christened."

Undertaking the religious ritual of christening is believed here to entail a responsibility to raise the child in church. A baby's birth and subsequently planned christening have caused a young mother previously uninterested in religion to reconsider church participation. Some women disengaged from churches take christening or baptism very seriously, like Annie, and they believe it should not be done unless they are going to take the responsibility of continuing to integrate the child into church life. Otherwise, such women perceive it as an empty ritual. In these cases, the birth of a child instills in mothers a greater desire for connection to religion and churches. On the other hand, a baby's baptism may present opportunities for low-income single mothers to experience church rejection and serve to further distance them from churches. Adrienne, a twenty-one-year-old white woman in a social service program for GED and job training, had attended Catholic school through the eighth grade. She had not attended Mass regularly since about that time but wanted to have her baby baptized. She related her negative experience: "I think sometimes they look down at single mothers. Because I know at my church to get your child baptized there, you have to be married. . . . You have to be married to have children. . . . So I had to go outside of my parish [to another Catholic parish], because I wasn't married." Adrienne's experience does not accord with Catholic teaching, as mothers certainly do not have to be married in order to have their babies baptized. She had the baby baptized in a neighboring parish. Understandably, however, encountering or perceiving this prejudice in her home parish made her feel rejected and angry. Religion in a personal sense did become more important to Adrienne after having children, and she says she wants to find a church she feels comfortable with and return. She sends her now three-year-old son to Mass every week with her mother, ironically to the very parish that had refused to baptize him. But baptism in this instance did not serve as an opening for greater involvement with church; it served quite the opposite role. Moreover, Adrienne was not the only mother to relate an experience of a baby's baptism provoking an incident of church rejection and alienation.

Although mothers may view religion as unimportant in their own lives, they generally regard it as important in the life of their children. As their children get older, some mothers end up becoming more interested in religion as they try to provide religious training for the good of their growing children. Rebecca experienced this when she began to read a children's Bible at night to her three-year-old daughter. She noted, "I used to think [religion] was not very important at all, but when I started reading the children's Bible with my daughter it became more important." Annie's and Rebecca's scenarios illustrate a common finding in my research. In general, either the birth of a baby, which is a transformational time, or around the time a child turns three, when women think children can understand more about religion, often functions as a catalyst for low-income urban mothers to become more interested in and engaged with issues of faith and religion.

The mothers interviewed note that it is difficult to teach children about faith if they are themselves unknowledgeable or nonpracticing. Lisa, for example, stopped attending services in the Catholic parish in which she was raised when she perceived a priest to make negative comments to her about single mothers. Recalling her church upbringing that she hopes to pass on to her children, she states that she needs to find a new church in which she feels comfortable and return to church. "I need to go back to church. I need peace. I think it would help me feel better about a lot of things. When I was a kid, I was faithful. I always went to church, followed the rules. Always did what we were taught. . . . I want my kids to go to church. I want them to learn what I was taught by the church and by my grandmother. I can't teach them if I don't do it myself." Despite her negative interaction with the priest over single motherhood, Lisa recalls the positive structure that church gave her life as a child. In order to teach her children, and desiring to pass on the faith of her grandmother and of her childhood to her children (as well as gain peace in her own life), she wants to return to church.

In growing more interested in matters of faith in order to teach their children, mothers learn with and from their children. Tamika, one might recall, is personally very religious but was not raised in any church and does not attend as an adult. She describes how she has tried to teach her older son, a nine-year-old, about faith by encouraging him to pray, yet she lets her son know that she, too, is learning right along with him: "Well, I have my son pray. I mean, I don't pressure him. I feel like he is a child of God, and God listens. . . . I know he has faith. . . . It feels good that he comes to me and can ask me about those [religious] questions, and if I can answer them I tell him. [If not], I'm like, 'Honey, how about we pray, or we ask God about that question that I don't understand and that you don't understand, and we can figure it out together.'" Tamika, who hopes eventually to pursue a college degree in child development, is also clearly fascinated by the innate spirituality she sees in her children, a spirituality she says that she herself learns from:

[When] my nine-year-old was young, I thought that I had to go out and get these Bible movies, like animated cartoons. I want to know where kids' minds are reacting, and I never had to say anything. "Mommy, that's Jesus right there." "Yes, it is." It shocked me. It's just good to know that they know in their hearts; they feel it anyway. It's like you bring it out of them if you want, or you can just see where they're at with it, and it's amazing what you find. They know so much more than you thought, and they can help teach you.

In addition to trying to teach her children about religion, Tamika learns about faith both with and from them.

Faith Practices in the Home

Nearly two-thirds of the women studied engaged in faith practices at home in connection with their parenting role, including more than half the mothers who rarely or never attend church. There are relatively few qualitative studies exploring religious practices between parents and children in the home. Several studies of highly religious two-parent families who attend services regularly find family religious practices in the home to play a significant role in family life (Loser et al. 2009; Marks 2004). In a recent study of Mormon families, more than 80 percent of the families reported a family religious ritual as one of their most important daily activities, including family scripture study (67 percent) and family prayer (65 percent). Family members thought these rituals strengthened their beliefs, brought them closer to God, gave them a happier daily life, gave them more focus and direction, bettered their personal behavior, strengthened their family relationships, and created family unity (Loser et al. 2009). Another study of highly religious Christian, Jewish, Mormon, and Muslim families found families to engage in regular family prayer, sacred rituals such as the Shabbat meal, and the study of sacred texts. Parents highlighted the importance of "practicing what you preach," and most valued the family closeness and unity engendered by religious practices based in the home (Marks 2004). These studies indicate a variety of reasons for families to engage in religious practices at home. For Mormons, for example, faith and family are intricately linked, and family religious practices play a central role in their faith and worship (Loser et al. 2009). For highly religious families of several different faiths, the primary reason and main benefit associated with family religious practices is to promote a sense of family cohesion, meaning, and closeness. Other reasons include transmitting religious and moral beliefs to children, being a good example to children, providing children with a resource for times of stress, and growing in connection to God. Further benefits cited by families include relaxation, a sense of structure, better quality of life, improved parent-child communication, and a stronger marriage (Marks 2004).

These processes have been little studied, however, through careful qualitative research of families that are not so highly religious, may not attend services, or are headed by low-income single parents. The majority of my respondents, whether they attended church or not, were personally highly religious themselves or not, or were of Catholic, Protestant, or no religious background, fostered religion in daily life through some type of religious practices at home with their children. The most frequent family religious practice was prayer, followed by Bible reading with children. Prayer and religious reading content were simple for children, often a children's Bible or children's prayer book for reading. (Because mothers needed to have at least one child age six or under to participate in the study, I spoke disproportionately with mothers who had only young children, and our conversations focused on young children. The findings thus primarily speak to the religious concerns and practices of mothers parenting young children.[9])

Poor mothers' spiritual practices of prayer and Bible reading with children at home are similar in practice to those found in studies of religious two-parent families with higher incomes. However, lived religion cannot be considered apart from its social context, and struggling single mothers see some different reasons for engaging in family religious practices than wealthier two-parent families. One overarching reason common to both demographics is to help their children learn more about faith, but even here divergent themes emerge.

First and foremost, poor single mothers pray and read the Bible with their children to imbue them with a belief in God and consequent knowledge that they are never alone. This idea of never being alone recurs in the interviews, belying perhaps the mothers' own sense of isolation. As noted in chapter 2, Aletta used to take her three children to church twice a week to a Seventh-Day Adventist church but stopped all participation after moving into a long-term shelter. The children's religious education continues with Aletta spending time each day praying with them and teaching them about religion. "I just want them to learn that there is somebody out there watching over us and there is somebody to pray to. . . . I want them to know that there will be somebody there for them and they're not going to be alone. . . . God is always there for you, and if you pray to him and you follow him, he is going to help you, and everything is going to be all right."

Isolated from her religious community after the move to the shelter, Aletta herself relies on prayer and a sense that God is with her. She wishes to instill this same sense in her children. Mothers desire for their children to know that God is always there for them so that they never feel alone or abandoned and to know that God will help them and that all will be well. Mothers seek to comfort their children in disruptive circumstances and draw on religion in doing so. Jane says she prays and speaks scripture verses to her four children age three to fifteen when "a situation" is going on in order to try to comfort them. Because the children themselves do not necessarily read the Bible, she believes that speaking verses to them will help them imbibe the teachings. In her family, as in the families of most of the mothers studied and the broader population of low-income single mothers who are struggling, "situations" occur frequently. As described earlier, Jane's four children are victims of family homelessness and live in a shelter. Children believe their parents are all-powerful, yet their parents cannot stop poverty, hunger, and homelessness. In these dire social circumstances, mothers believe it is very important for children to know that God will never abandon them to face their problems alone. Because many children of low-income single mothers have been effectively abandoned by their own fathers, the image of God as a father who will never leave them alone is particularly potent.

Poor mothers believe that religious faith engendered by engaging with religious practices at home with their children will provide their children with a sense of self-esteem and self-efficacy. They posit that giving children knowledge of the power of a loving divine being will make the children themselves feel powerful. Thus Rebecca, who reads the children's Bible with her three-year-old nightly, indicated, "I never grew up having faith in anything. I'd like her to have faith in the belief that there is a higher power. I would like for her ideally to have faith to help her to have faith in herself, for her to believe that there is somebody there to guide her or help her." Rebecca believes that giving her daughter knowledge of a higher power that provides help and guidance will give her daughter self-confidence and faith in herself. Similarly, Claire prays with her toddler daughter every night. When I asked her why she did this—what she thought religious faith would give her child—she replied, "Faith, a lot of courage, and I think a lot of pride in herself. . . . She would know that he loves her. He gave her this world. She is breathing every day because of him. She can go out and do anything."

Rebecca's and Claire's responses, as examples of a prominent narrative, reveal mothers who want to help their children access a source of divine power that will imbue them with self-confidence. Poor mothers know that their children face many challenges in growing up safely in dangerous neighborhoods, getting good educations in failing urban schools, and generally beating the odds that militate against them succeeding. Mothers believe that their children need courage and pride in themselves in order to overcome their circumstances. Claire's language is particularly revealing. If her daughter knows God loves her, has given her breath and the world, then she can go out and do *anything*. Claire's little girl is only eighteen months old, yet she already faces daunting odds by being born to a low-income single mother with a high school education. Claire, by praying with her nightly in their apartment in the family shelter, hopes to instill the religious faith she believes will help her daughter beat those odds.

These narratives show mothers wishing for their children what they do not have themselves. Rebecca says she never had faith in anything growing up and suffers from depression; she wants her daughter to have faith in a higher power to provide self-confidence and faith in herself. Claire, homeless and struggling on welfare, wants faith to enable her daughter to go out and do anything. The mothers here also seem to see a different-acting God for their children than for themselves, as both women believe that God views their own actions with disappointment. Rebecca believes God would think she was a "bum" for not working; Claire states that God thinks she can "do better" than being on welfare. This disappointed God sounds different from the God who will infuse their children with self-confidence to go out and do anything. Not only do women wish for children's religious faith to help the children live a different life than theirs but sometimes even seem to envision a different concept of God for their children.

Self-confidence stemming from faith, mothers think, will also give their children strength to resist peer pressure, as part of the path to a better life. In this view, children's awareness that "God is watching them" will help them turn away from harmful behaviors. As Isabella put it, "I want my son and my daughter to believe in God. When you believe in God, you don't do a lot of things bad, because you think somebody else sees you." Religious parents in general might hope that the notion of God's watchful eyes would help their children or adolescents refrain from negative behavior. Poor mothers place especially high value on this idea because the consequences may mean the chance for a better life is squandered.

Parenting "in Partnership with God"

More than 90 percent of the women I studied are single mothers, often raised in troubled family circumstances. Perceiving themselves as lacking resources and skills needed to effectively parent, women petition God to help them be better parents. This phenomenon is most vividly illustrated by the case of Vicky. Although she does not attend church, she relies on her high level of personal religiosity and knowledge of religious culture in helping her to parent. She says she wants to raise her four-year-old son in a happy, well-balanced home, which she did not have growing up with two alcoholic parents.

I ask God for help a lot. I don't know the right way to parent. I know the wrong way. I've seen the wrong way, so it's hard for me sometimes. I second-guess myself a lot. I'm very insecure sometimes about it, but I just do what's right in my heart, and I think that God is guiding me so that I can give this child what he needs. I want to have the strength to give him the support and love to nurture him. I ask God for a lot of help in the way I discipline him, like the amount of time we spend together and the things we do when we're together. I have depression, and sometimes it's hard for me to get out of bed. I ask God to help me get up, get dressed, take him to the zoo or somewhere.

Vicky says that parenting her son well is God's calling for her life, and she believes that God is walking with her as a partner in doing so. Because Vicky is a single mother whose child's father is not involved in their lives, the image of God as a coparent is symbolically powerful. She sees herself not as alone in raising her son but doing it with the assistance of God.

Do Vicky's prayers for help in parenting help her to parent more effectively? A number of the quantitative studies mentioned earlier link measures of religiousness such as church attendance and frequency of prayer with better parenting skills for both higher-income and low-income individuals. Highly religious parents in nonpoor two-parent families believe prayer and family religious practices in the home help them to be better, kinder, and more nurturing parents in that they try to model God's love to their children (Loser et al. 2009). Several scholars have posited mechanisms through which personal religious practices could influence parenting. A sense of connection with a "divine other" may enhance a parent's self-esteem and sense of self-efficacy. Certain Bible passages may be interpreted as providing parental guidance, perhaps leading to better parenting. Prayer may help people construct positive perceptions of family life.[10] It seems plausible that Vicky's framing of her mothering role in a transcendent light and envisioning a powerful divine being as a parenting partner could help her to parent more effectively.

Poor single mothers face considerable life stresses that affect their parenting. In general, mothers facing major life stressors engage in more coercive parenting techniques. Abusive mothers are more likely to be very poor and socially isolated and experiencing major life stress.[11] Indeed, a notable number of my respondents had had children removed from them by the Department of Social Services at some point. More than five of the mothers volunteered this information during the course of the interview, and they were likely not the only ones to have had this occur. Some mothers had also experienced domestic abuse themselves at the hands of male partners. Maternal depression, with its negative consequences to children, was common among my respondents, as it is among mothers on welfare and other very poor single mothers in general. As noted at the beginning of this chapter, parenting is challenging even under the best of circumstances, which then becomes even more difficult when parenting without a partner's help, being destitute, having little education or access to good jobs, and possibly struggling with issues such as homelessness, depression, or domestic violence. In light of these obstacles working against good parenting, it would follow that mothers who are personally religious might seek divine assistance.

In turning to prayer, mothers seek insight and help. More than one mother, like Vicky, frequently prayed for help to just get up despite debilitating depression and attend to caring well for their children. Although women may have lacked effective models of parenting in their own lives, they believe God will help guide them to be better parents. In doing so, they feel themselves not to be parenting alone as single mothers but parenting "in partnership with God."

Part of parenting "in partnership with God" includes mothers, of course, praying for their children. Prayer concerns for their young children revolve around issues of providing protection and safety and meeting children's needs. Children's health is a primary concern for those with children with health issues, such as asthma, common in poor urban areas. Mothers without permanent housing pray for housing on behalf of their children. Mothers pray to be able to find safe child care. (Concerns about safety in day care came up frequently in interviews, probably indicating the kinds of options available.) Women pray that their children will be protected from the streets as they grow older and face temptations. All parents face some degree of helplessness in the knowledge that they cannot protect their children from every possible danger. Yet low-income single mothers feel considerably less agency in their role as protector. Their children lack homes or live in dangerous neighborhoods. Child-care options are often inadequate. Feeling helpless in the face of daunting child-rearing challenges, women turn to prayer to beseech God for assistance. Orsi's (1996) description of mid-twentieth-century Catholic women applies aptly here: "They had come to the end of their own abilities to help and protect the people they love, whom they were supposed to protect and help" (64). This expresses the driving force behind poor mothers' prayers for their children. Their circumstances place them beyond their ability to care for and protect their children as needed, and in prayer they cry out for a divine source of power to help them.

The social location of low-income mothers leads them to emphasize somewhat different issues in terms of what they seek from engaging in parenting-related personal prayer and religious practices at home with their children when compared to more affluent parents. For example, family unity, the most common reason given by more affluent parents for engaging in home-based religious practices with their children, was not mentioned at all by my respondents.[12] The issues of children's self-esteem and "never feeling alone," which dominate poor urban mothers' discourse, do not find a prominent place in existing studies of nonpoor families. Although one study of nonpoor two-parent families lists giving children "coping resources for stress" as one of the reasons for engaging in family sacred practices at home, it is not highlighted as a main reason (Marks 2004). More affluent families certainly would want their children to have self-esteem and resist peer pressure, but these concerns press much more heavily on impoverished single mothers. Because their children live in environments more likely to challenge their sense of self-efficacy and more likely to present them with difficult situations, low-income mothers stress the importance of their children knowing that God is always with them and that they can do anything with God's help. Nonpoor parents may perceive prayer and family religious practices to help them parent better, but poor mothers have far fewer resources to help them with good parenting and are more likely to have had poorer parenting themselves. This combination of background, environment, and access to resources shapes the context in which some poor urban mothers come to regard faith as an important part of their child rearing.

"They Would Learn the Right Way of Life"

Clearly, many poor mothers place a high value on instilling religious beliefs in children. However, most of the mothers in the study believe it is not enough for their children to just engage in prayer or Bible reading apart from church participation, as they themselves generally do. Whether or not they themselves attend church, poor single mothers often desire church communities for their children. Thirty-two of the forty-five women interviewed wanted their children involved in churches, including more than two-thirds of those who infrequently or never attend church themselves.

Mothers in poverty seek many of the same things more affluent families seek for their children in churches, and they see churches as having a unique role to play in their children's character formation. Poor mothers note several valuable things churches provide that assist them in raising their children, including one very basic reason common to families across the socioeconomic spectrum: teaching their children about faith. Aletta plans to take her children back to church once they leave the transitional housing shelter so they can learn about faith. "They need somebody to sit there and teach them, because I can't tell them everything. It's good, because Sunday school is excellent for kids. They go, they learn about God." Annie, who believes baptism entails a responsibility for bringing her child up in the Church, elaborated, "Otherwise she won't know anything. It will be, 'I'm Catholic, and I've been baptized.' And that will be it. This way she'll know more about her religion; she'll know more about God." Parents, particularly those who themselves have returned to church only after having children, desire the assistance of churches to pass on knowledge of faith and religion.

However, as in personal religious practices, the context of poor mothers' lives shapes what they wish for their children in churches, leading them to stress reasons for desiring churches that diverge somewhat from those of affluent families. Mothers raising their children in low-income urban areas are often raising children in dangerous and difficult environments and are all too aware of the violence, drugs, and teen pregnancy endemic in their neighborhoods. In addition to their personal prayers for their children's protection, mothers think churches will play a protective role.[13] Protection from negative influences and behavior is the most common reason poor mothers want their children in churches. This desire was most pronounced in my study among the African American mothers, who tended to be living in neighborhoods with higher levels of street crime and drugs. Shantelle, whose youngest three children are ages five, seven, and nine, said:

I want them to know right from wrong. I want them to know what is good and what is bad as far as being out in the world. What they should be doing, and church is a good way to let them get into the gates of heaven. Because there's a lot of kids that get mixed up on the street, young ages. They got kids my daughter's age out there in the wrong stuff. Little boys, nine years old, ten years old. I do not want my girls going that way. [SCS: And why do you think church would help keep them from that?] Because they teach the Word of God. They do teach you what is right and what is wrong. You don't hear them preaching, saying, "I want to go rob me a bank." . . . I want them to know God and believe in God.

LaToya said, "Because I think if I was to bring my kids up into the church, that they would learn the way of life, they would learn the right way . . . that they wouldn't get into any crime, and, you know, they would go to school and get an education." Lindsay brings her three children, ages three to seven, to her Protestant church every week. She said, "It will give them a better understanding about life around them. Let them understand more about peer pressure, the drugs around. There are sinners everywhere. I mean it's going to be really hard to keep them away from it. But if they deal with it face-to-face, knowing what they believe in, it will be a snap." All of these African American single mothers believe church involvement will help protect their children from harmful influences and behaviors. Church, they believe, will teach their children to go down the right path of life, avoid peer pressure and crime, and stay in school.

Although the notion of protection from the street is strong among African American mothers, it is not limited to them. Mothers draw on their own adolescence in highlighting the protective benefits of church for their children. Some credit church involvement for keeping them away from some negative behaviors, while those who had been involved with many negative behaviors as youth think that church involvement might keep their children from repeating their mistakes. Juliana thinks that raising her children, who are age one and two, with belief in God will give them "hopefully a better life. . . . I want them to be guided through the right path. I am hoping he would guide them. . . . There's peer pressure out there." One might recall that although Juliana prays frequently, she was not raised with religion and does not attend church services except as an occasional guest of her boyfriend's mother at a Pentecostal church. She states that had her mother raised her with religion, she might not have succumbed to adolescent peer pressure and become involved in the negative behaviors she believes have led to her current situation of homelessness and welfare. She explained: "If my mother was into a religion, then maybe I would have had a better head on my shoulders. . . . . Look where I am now. . . . I think if I would have been to church, then I probably would have had a better head on my shoulders. I would have known not to play hooky from school. I would have known not to try marijuana. . . . I probably would have never touched alcohol. If I would have had church in life, maybe I wouldn't have done those certain things." Juliana's understanding again illustrates the theme of mothers wanting to infuse their children with religion, in this case church involvement, in order to provide them with something they themselves lacked. Mothers desperately want their children—their very young children, whose futures are still open—to have better lives than theirs, and they view religion as a way to help ensure it.

All around them, mothers see teenagers who have taken the path of drugs and crime; some perhaps have older children who have already gone that route. They strongly desire to protect their young children from this fate, and they turn to churches as one of few possible alternative social environments to shape and protect their children. Mothers' high hopes that church involvement will readily keep their children from negative behaviors seem somewhat naively optimistic, because even for the most churched youth, resisting peer pressure is unlikely to be "a snap" as Lindsay described. Neighborhood environments pose considerable obstacles, and problems often carry over into urban public schools, making schools unable to function as alternate social locations to protect adolescents from the street culture. Mothers' hopes for the churches are necessarily high because there are few other places to which they can turn.

Research indicates that the mothers may be correct in stressing the benefits of religious involvement for their children, particularly in keeping clear of negative adolescent behaviors. Using a nationally representative sample of more than three thousand youth age thirteen to seventeen, Christian Smith and Melissa Denton (2005) found, controlling for demographic variables, that more religiously involved teens are much less likely to smoke cigarettes and drink alcohol regularly, get drunk, smoke marijuana, cut class, view pornography, be sexually active, and feel sad and depressed. They are also significantly more likely to feel close to their parents and siblings and have a greater number of other supportive adults they can turn to. Smith and Denton posit a constellation of factors to account for religion's beneficial impact on adolescents. The first group of factors deals with dimensions of cultural moral order, including moral directives of self-control and personal virtue, spiritual experiences that may help solidify moral commitments and positive behaviors, and adult role models. The second group of factors deals with competencies and knowledge that enhance youth well-being that religion can provide, such as leadership skills, coping skills for difficult times, and increased cultural capital. The third and final group of factors is the social and organizational ties available via religious participation, such as social capital and ties with people of different age groups, network closure, and links beyond the local community (2005, 241–49). Religious involvement, although by no means a panacea against countervailing social structures, can help youth overcome disadvantage by providing boundaries, guidance, structures, and social relationships that help influence positive life outcomes (257).

Equipping their children with conceptual frameworks through which to make sense of life's hardships is another role for religious participation that poor mothers emphasize, one that is also not prominent in earlier studies of more affluent families. Because very poor urban families face considerable challenges, children often find themselves at a young age in the midst of difficult circumstances that are hard for them to understand. Some women think church participation will give both mothers and children spiritual resources to help them frame situations in ways that foster understanding. Lindsay explained, "If something happens, my children ask, 'Mommy, why did God let this happen?' I try to teach them more about that. It's pretty hard, but they're learning." Because Lindsay is currently homeless and living with her three children in a shelter, her children might well have questions about why negative events have befallen them. As the following chapter details, women draw on religious narratives of suffering and perseverance through trials to frame their many hardships in ways that bring them spiritual coherence. Those doing so also try to help their children religiously reframe difficult events in a more positive light. Ann Marie states that raising her children as Catholics will help them understand the difficulties of life. "Life is not easy for my son. There are nos. . . . It's like trying to explain when you're in a store, sorry, I got no money. That's life." It is difficult for low-income mothers to raise children in a more affluent, broader culture that celebrates consumer goods. Mothers believe that raising their children with religion will teach them beliefs that will help them interpret and contend with their circumstances.

Churches, poor mothers believe, will give their children good values and place them into a broader community that supports good values, in addition to possibly providing support for themselves as parents. These views are shared by affluent parents in earlier studies, but the circumstances surrounding poor mothers' lives make such concerns even more pressing. In churches, poor women seek for their children community and adult role models, that is, social capital. They perceive churches to reinforce the values that they are trying to instill in their children, often through the actions of other adults who are modeling desirable values and behaviors. Sheila prays and reads the Bible with her two-year-old son each night. She says she wants to attend church services with her son when he is older because she believes that churches aid in child rearing by reinforcing values. "I think [church] helps everything. It's not only mom saying you should respect her, and you should do this, and you should do that. It's other people too." Women appreciate that other adults in the church reinforce lessons of respect, discipline, hard work, and gratitude. Given that disadvantaged mothers may feel themselves in an uphill battle against destructive values posed by popular culture, the media, and their neighborhoods, the appeal of churches providing a source of social capital that supports positive values cannot be underestimated.

Churches may provide their members with resources to help them guide their children. For example, Maggie received a prayer book for mothers and a children's Bible from her parish, which she reads with her daughter. As noted earlier, she also participates, along her daughter, in a weekly Bible study run by her parish for parents and children. She says raising her children with the support of her church community increases her confidence in her parenting skills. "[The parish] has that support, anything I want and need, and I know I'm doing the right thing." Despite her troubled circumstances as a single mother on welfare battling severe depression, the social capital and resources in her supportive congregation help Maggie in raising her children.

Getting Children to Church

Mothers in poverty elucidate clear reasons for wanting their children in church communities. This desire poses a problem for the many who do not themselves attend. In my study, a significant minority of those women who themselves rarely or never attended sent their young children to church regularly with others. These mothers want their children to be part of a church community, although they themselves are not. Adrienne, the mother who sends her three-year-old weekly with her mother to the Catholic parish that had refused to baptize him, said, "Church is important. I want to start going. . . . My mother brings my son, but I just don't go." Shantelle, whose sense of being a "sinner" prevents her from returning to church, sends her children to church with relatives. She has also signed her children up for a church summer camp, another strategy that mothers use for involving children in churches. Prior to moving to the shelter where she currently lives, she sent her children to church with relatives every week. Gabriella sends her son to Pentecostal services with her mother. "I send him to church with my mother. . . . I'm not in church, but I like church. . . . I want him to learn about God just like I learned about God."

These and other women see church participation as so valuable for their children that they make the effort to find other people with whom to send them. Some feel unwelcome at church; some say logistical problems impede their attendance. Yet they perceive church participation, not just religious practices at home, to be important in teaching their children right from wrong, protecting them from the street, and placing them into a community of other adults who will reinforce values they want instilled in their children. These women make very careful efforts to arrange for their children's church participation, despite the many competing and overwhelming demands in their lives. Although the issue of low-income urban children attending church without their parents has not been carefully examined by scholars, urban pastors confirm the phenomenon. In my study, the children are young and thus are usually sent to church with relatives rather than sent alone. However, pastors relate how mothers often send their older children to church alone (and some even send young children alone). In a study of churches near a low-income housing project in Chicago, one pastor estimated that only about one-third of the fifty to sixty children at church services come with their parents, and the rest are not related to the adults who are there (Laudarji and Livezey 2000).

What remains somewhat unclear is why those mothers who feel unwelcome in churches are eager for their children to be involved with organizations they perceive as rejecting of them and perhaps hypocritical. Sometimes, like Adrienne, they send their child to the actual church they perceive to have rejected them. A surprising number of my respondents who clearly feel unwelcome or uncomfortable at church—either because of overt negative incidents with churches or because of their lifestyles or perceived past transgressions—still want their children to be in church. Mothers see their children, particularly the young children who were the focus of the study, as people with a clean slate who have a future ahead of them. Thus mothers such as Sarah, who left church as a teenager, may believe they have already fallen too far off "the right path" to be comfortable in church, but they do not want these barriers to keep their children from churches. Mothers see the benefits of church involvement for their children as very strong, with the hope, ironically, of preventing their children from taking a life path that has led the mother herself to feel distanced from church.

Despite the substantial minority of respondents who send their children to church with others, most of the children do not currently attend. Although women provide detailed reasons why they want their children to be involved with a church, most do not actually take or send them. Getting children involved in organized religion is something they say they will do in the future, when job, housing, and general life circumstances are more stable. Some see school as the way to involve their children in organized religion and say they will send their children to parochial schools. Most of the children of these women are still young and are not actively confronting the temptations of the street. Perhaps their mothers do not thus perceive church involvement as an immediate and pressing issue. In spite of the mothers' stated desires, it is unclear whether these children will end up involved in congregations.

Religion, Parenting, and Child Well-Being

Parenting forms a key part of how impoverished mothers live out their everyday religion. In general, many parents across the socioeconomic spectrum want their children to learn religious tradition and faith, but the additional benefits emphasized depend in part on their social locations. Poor women draw heavily on personal faith and prayer in parenting, and for most in this study, it is the primary way they engage religion as a parenting resource. But my interviews reveal the surprising degree to which low-income mothers also want their children involved in organized religion, even though they do not always put this desire into practice. In this regard, parenting appears unique from other challenging areas of their lives. While discussing areas such as work, housing, or mental health, I only infrequently heard personally religious women who were not involved in congregations say that being involved in a church would help them with a particular challenge they were facing. Yet child rearing is different. More comfortably situated families have other networks and organizations that help meet parenting-related needs. They may think churches have a unique role to play in raising their children, but they do not depend on churches as their only resource. Poor single mothers simultaneously have greater parenting needs than nonpoor two-parent families and access to fewer resources to help them.

The findings of this chapter contribute to explaining studies connecting religion with more effective parenting techniques for low-income mothers and better outcomes for child well-being. Prayer and scripture reading provide some mothers with a sense of strength and comfort that may allow them to respond more patiently and effectively to their children. Those aware of the challenges posed to effective parenting by their own upbringing or mental illnesses and who address these challenges in part by drawing on faith find prayer to be helpful. Mothers in a helpful church community find support for their parenting through pastors, other church members, and church resources.

Women who draw on religious concepts and practices to help instill a sense of self-efficacy in their children may help their children gain resilience. Reading children Bible stories every night, teaching children they can do anything with God's help—these practices seem likely to equip children with religious cultural resources that will provide greater self-efficacy, hope, and perseverance. Women who integrate children into church networks can provide children the beneficial social support associated with church participation. Studies linking religion with higher levels of life satisfaction and happiness, greater levels of hope and meaning, and higher levels of social support have been conducted on adults and adolescents, and children may benefit from religion in similar ways. Religious resources can play an important role for children from disadvantaged families whose other resources are limited.

Parenting, Religion, and Harm

Although most research finds religion to play an overall positive role in parenting, several previous studies give some indications of how aspects of religion can be engaged or interpreted harmfully. Parental arguments about religion were found to be deleterious to first-grade children's development (Bartkowski, Xu, and Levin 2008). Compulsory family worship in the home is associated with some negative adolescent outcomes (Lee, Rice, and Gillespie 1997). Unmarried adolescents participating in religious activities in conservative denominations experienced higher levels of depression after giving birth, and those who were cohabitating experienced even higher levels of depression. Instead of gaining social support that could help in adjusting to parenting, adolescents whose behavior violated church norms yet continued to participate in church activities experienced increased distress (Sorenson, Grindstaff, and Turner 1995).[14] In general, church participation may compound or exacerbate certain family-related stressors, such as marital or parenting problems, because of church ideals of family unity and harmony (Ellison 1994). Imbuing family relationships with sacred meaning can lead to denial when problems occur and make conflict more difficult to deal with (Mahoney et al. 2001). Then, of course, there are the obvious and extreme ways in which abuses of religion can be harmful in parenting; examples include parents who use religion to humiliate or shame children or administer severe corporal punishment connected to religious beliefs and pastors who sexually abuse children.

It is difficult for parents who engage religion in parenting to find or verbalize possible downsides. For example, when directly asked in a recent study how their family religious activities in the home might be harmful, the highly religious parents interviewed were unable to think of any reasons (Loser et al. 2009). Parents who incorporate religion into parenting and family life do so because they believe it is good for their children and for family unity, and they would be unlikely to continue if they thought it deleterious. I did not ask my respondents whether they saw anything detrimental in the ways in which they involved religion as part of parenting. They mentioned nothing but benefits for their children, and from my limited role as an observer, the ways in which they engaged religion with their children seemed likely to be beneficial. For themselves as parents, personal religious beliefs provided emotional support in their parenting role, but organized religion sometimes proved a source of distress. When their nontraditional family form conflicted with church norms, some mothers felt rebuffed and excluded.

Mothers, however, sometimes drew on religious interpretations that compounded their guilt over maternal failure in unhealthy ways. A number of mothers perceived themselves to have at some point tremendously failed in their roles as mothers; this was certainly true of women who had had children removed by the Department of Social Services. These women experienced enormous guilt, pain, and loss. One mother said there was not a night that went by in the shelter that she did not cry herself to sleep because her older daughter had been removed from her by child protective services. Another mother spoke of the guilt she felt for harming her children through her involvement with drugs, crime, and jail. Even women with less egregious situations felt themselves to fail as good mothers at times, such as when they had a hard time getting out of bed due to depression or had to leave their children in inadequate child care. Sometimes women's guilt over maternal failure led them to believe they had also failed in the eyes of God, making them feel unworthy. These narratives parallel to a surprising degree the narratives of maternal failure Marie Griffith (1997) found among middle-class evangelical women. Griffith notes that American women have often felt shame for failing to live up to an idealized standard of motherhood. For religious women, she claims, "such feelings of shame are heightened by a sense of sin, burdening them with the guilty feeling that they are not fulfilling God's plan for their lives" (119). Religious guilt compounding guilt over parenting failures hits women with a "double burden" of guilt and shame. The fact that these narratives are found across such different social situations attests to their potency in American religious culture.

Several lingering questions remain. The few large-scale studies of religion and child well-being that exist focus on parental religious attendance.[15] It follows from social capital theory that placing low-income parents and children in an environment of increased social support available in a congregation could benefit children. However, many extremely disadvantaged mothers do not attend church even if they are strong religious believers, instead engaging their children in home-based religious practices such as prayer and Bible reading. Are the children of poor single mothers buffered from disadvantage by their mothers' integrating personal religious beliefs and home-based religious practices in child rearing? The focus on parental church attendance also obscures the fact that a considerable number of poor mothers may be sending their children to church without attending themselves.

By engaging with existing studies of religion and parenting and their focus on reasons, outcomes, and benefits, this chapter veers to more of a utilitarian bent than the rest of the book. In part this reflects the mothers' discourse around religion and child rearing. More than in any other area of daily life, women were very clear about why they engaged in particular religious practices and what benefits they wished to gain from religion for their children. Mothers did not calculatedly access religion in a utilitarian way, and they genuinely seemed to want to provide their children with deep faith and a church community. But they did emphasize the desired benefits, providing a much more instrumental view of religion than in other areas of their lives. This seems no different from nonpoor families, particularly those who put their children into religious activities despite having relatively little interest in religion themselves. These families too are quite clear about the benefits they believe religion provides to their children. Impoverished women raising their children alone in adverse conditions have comparatively few resources to support their parenting efforts. That they would wish to engage religion as part of the parenting role most value so highly speaks to their desire to provide their children with all that they can. Personal prayer, shared faith practices in the home, and participation in churches do serve as important parenting resources for them. Although not claiming to be representative of all low-income urban mothers, the findings of this chapter suggest that many such women may be actively engaging religion to some degree in raising their children. By providing a careful close-up look at why and how mothers incorporate personal religious practices and churches in parenting, these findings extend existing theory and research.

Their bonds with their children are for many poor single mothers their deepest, most meaningful, and most enduring social connections. Some researchers claim that people living in family systems that deviate from traditionally prescribed sacred family structures, such as single-mother families, may have difficulty imbuing these relationships with sacred meaning or believing that God is present in them.[16] Why, though, would poor mothers of faith not see their most important family relationships as sacred or believe that God is absent from them? Low-income single mothers do sanctify their relationships with their children, imbuing them with transcendence, seeing their children as gifts from God, and seeing their maternal roles as God's calling. Mothers and presumably their children live out their spirituality in their most intimate of family relationships. Scholars seeking to understand lived religion must understand and appreciate both the primary nature of the sacred bond mothers feel with their children and the many secondary benefits they believe religion to provide. Both constitute everyday religion for women who are parenting in a social context of extreme stress and deprivation.

FIVE

"God Has a Plan": Making Meaning

Peggy, introduced earlier in this book, stopped attending the evangelical church where she had been heavily involved after it was unsupportive during her divorce. No longer attending any church, Peggy views both her unplanned pregnancy later in life and having then to go on welfare as part of God's plan:

I see how my second child was of God's planning, because I was never planning a pregnancy at that point in my life, but I see how much joy he brought, and how God knew I was going to lose my mother, and I think he [God] gave me my son to kind of—not to fill the void, but certainly to keep me going, and to keep, you know, perspective on his plan for my life. . . .

I've seen how the world views women on welfare, and maybe someday I can come back, and when I'm successful, and I plan on that, come back and talk to them [women on welfare], and say, "Don't ever let them beat you down. You get what you need, whether it be emotional, or training, or you make yourself whole, because it's not hopeless. You can do it. It's hard, but you women are tough—you're tougher than the majority, the ones who are doing it with their spouses and have never had a lot of struggle and strife; they don't have the same kind of character that you have, and that's a treasure, too." So, I mean, I don't know, I guess there's a plan or vision, through my journey, my path that God gave us and wanted.

Peggy's story illustrates the subject of this chapter—how low-income women draw on religion in appraising situations and creating meaning. Very poor urban mothers, like most other humans, seek meaning and understanding. They try to make sense of their lives, especially negative events. In Peggy's case, viewing her troubles—an unplanned pregnancy, going on welfare—through the interpretative lens of her faith leads her to draw quite different conclusions about the events than an outside observer might predict. The unplanned pregnancy was part of God's plan, to provide comfort and keep her going on her mother's death. Being on welfare will give her a platform through which she can come back once she has left welfare and encourage other women in similar situations. Struggle provides character, a treasure not accorded to those wealthier married mothers who struggle less. Far from being disasters derailing her life, these events are part of the journey given to her by God. The process of religious "meaning making" illuminated by Peggy marks one of the most important ways that poor single mothers live their everyday religion.

Theology has long been concerned with the problem of suffering.[1] Why does a just and almighty God allow suffering in the world? Does God desire human suffering? If not, why does it exist? Does suffering serve any purpose? Old Testament writings show God inflicting suffering as punishment for sin, but the story of Job provides an example of a just man suffering despite being innocent of sin. Traditional Christian answers to the problem of suffering point to the redemptive suffering of Jesus on the cross. In this theological framework, an all-powerful God allowed his innocent son to suffer and die on the cross. Out of Jesus' suffering on behalf of the world, humankind was redeemed, and Christians are called to share in Jesus' suffering. Although painful, suffering has many benefits, and God uses suffering to bring about good ends in the lives of believers, both in this world and in the afterlife. Questions of theodicy, of course, exist within social contexts. Situated within particular social structures, black, feminist, womanist, and mujerista theology and liberation theology critique these traditional notions of redemptive suffering.

Theodicy has been an important question for classic social theorists as well as theologians. For Weber ([1922] 1963), theodicy addressed "the problem of meaning" (125). Religion has to reconcile the problems in the world with a conception of divine power. Religion functions to provide an interpretive framework for making meaning out of suffering, creating an ordered world that has both meaning and significance.[2] Drawing from Weber's conceptualizations, Peter Berger, in his seminal *The Sacred Canopy*, emphasizes the "centrality of the problem of theodicy for any religious effort at world-maintenance" (1967, 80). In the chapter titled "The Problem of Theodicy," Berger states that the sacred order of the cosmos must be maintained in the face of chaos, "despite the recurrent intrusion into individual and collective experience of the anomic . . . phenomena of suffering, evil, and death" (53). Berger calls our attention to the fact that theodicy need not involve a complex theoretical system; illiterate peasants explaining negative events as God's will engage in theodicy as much as academic theologians writing treatises (53). Following Weber, Berger claims that societies may establish two different theodicies—a theodicy of suffering for the poor and a theodicy of happiness for the rich. These theodicies serve to legitimate the institutional order, providing the poor with a meaning for their poverty and the rich with a meaning for their wealth. The dissolution of theodicies that legitimate social inequality has potentially revolutionary outcomes. Like Weber, Berger believes that explaining human suffering is central to any religious enterprise. Theodicy provides not happiness, but *meaning*. Painful events are painful, but they have meaning.

Mark Scott (2008) calls for a turn from "macro" theodicy to "micro" theodicy. Acknowledging that creating a sense of meaning occurs only in particular historical and social contexts, he argues for a vision of "theodicy as navigation" that attends to individual narratives of suffering and meaning (10). Narrative "fixes our gaze on the person doing theodicy and alerts us to the complex internal and external factors that inform the construction of theodicy" (35). By focusing on individual people's unique social location and life experiences, we come to understand how they construct theodicy. In addition to calling attention to the significance of individual narratives, Scott further notes that archetypal stories or "meta-narratives" serve an important role. Metanarratives such as the story of Job "function as a lens through which religious persons insert themselves into maps that become the territory within which they journey from crisis to resolution through the reinscription of meaning" (Scott 2009, 18).

Notions of narrative and metanarrative provide an excellent framework for analyzing how poor single mothers try to make coherent religious meaning in the lives. Many poor women are people of faith, and they experience considerable suffering. How do they make sense of their suffering in ways that are spiritually coherent? Poor mothers of faith believe that God is intimately involved in the world and in the details of their daily lives. How do they manage the contradictions inherent in their image of God as a loving and all-powerful father and the profound hardships they experience? What elements of their religious culture do they access in weaving a spiritually consistent moral narrative that integrates their suffering? By attending to women's experiences and narratives of meaning making, we can come to understand their theodicy "from the ground up." In interviews the women—unasked—offered theological interpretations for their suffering and hardship. From Christian backgrounds, they drew on metanarratives of divine will and redemptive suffering. None of the religious explanations offered by my respondents are limited to people in their social situations and are in fact common religious ways of interpreting suffering.[3] Listening carefully to women's narratives allows a window into how this theodicy is lived and experienced in a social context of family homelessness, severe urban poverty, and single motherhood.

"God Has a Plan"

First and foremost, poor mothers believe their suffering is part of God's larger plan to bring about good things for them. Traditional Judeo-Christian theology posits that humans cannot understand God's ways. As the Old Testament states in the book of Isaiah, "'For my thoughts are not your thoughts, nor are your ways my ways,' says the LORD. 'As high as the heavens are above the earth, so high are my ways above your ways and my thoughts above your thoughts'" (Isa. 55:8–9). This theology indicates that God sees a bigger picture than can be seen in limited human understanding. Furthermore, women believe that God not only sees a bigger picture but has a plan for them that is good, drawing on Judeo-Christian precepts such as found in the Old Testament book of Jeremiah: "'For I know well the plans I have in mind for you,' says the LORD, 'plans for your welfare, not for woe! plans to give you a future full of hope'" (Jer. 29:11). A number of studies show that people are more likely to attribute negative events to a divine plan or will than chance, themselves, nature, or others (Pargament 1997). Considering negative events as part of an overall divine plan confers meaning on difficult situations that may on the surface seem inexplicable. Attributing events to the will of a loving God reframes them so they are interpreted and experienced in a very different light.

When viewed through the interpretive lens of a loving God with an overall plan for good in their lives, then becoming homeless and having to move to a shelter can become for poor mothers part of God's plan to bring about good for them. For example, Aletta, despite having bounced around many months from shelter to hotel to shelter, construed her family's homelessness as part of God's plan to ultimately lead her to better housing. She said, "I know that when things happen, they happen for a reason. Because I lost my place where I was living, but that happened for a reason. Because now I'm moving into a bigger, more cleaner, more better place." In Aletta's interpretation, God knew that losing housing would eventually lead her family to a shelter where social workers helped people find apartments, and they would end up getting an apartment better than the one lost. Their homelessness was merely part of God's larger plan for their greater good. Jane also believed that homelessness was part of God's plan, in this case because it provided her new opportunities to evangelize. Sitting in the living room of her dimly lit shelter apartment, Jane told me how being in a long-term family shelter provided her with many opportunities to share her faith that she had not previously had. She was excited by the new opportunities to witness about her faith in Jesus to other residents, the shelter staff, and even me as I interviewed her. "For whatever reason, I am here [in the shelter]. I believe a lot of times it is to minister to people. Like even now, I am talking to you, it's no accident." Jane is not merely "making lemonade from lemons" but instead has profoundly reconstructed and reinterpreted the traumatic event of family homelessness as a special calling and opportunity for her to serve as God's minister to others. Constructing events through a religious vision that underscores God's omniscience and goodness allows poor single mothers to re-envision hardships so as to confer them with meaning. Difficult life circumstances thus make up coherent parts of women's religious worldviews as people loved by God.

Low-income women from Protestant, Catholic, or no formal religious backgrounds, devout or nonpracticing, believe that both good and bad things happen for a reason, as part of God's plan for good. These narratives reveal an image of a God whose ways cannot be known but who loves them deeply and must be trusted. This view belies a somewhat paradoxical image of God, as God is both mysterious with ways unable to be known, yet intimate and loving. Although God's ways cannot be fully understood, mothers believe, God abounds in unfailing love for them and is compassionate and merciful. Secure in their knowledge of God's great love, they trust that their trials are part of a divine plan even when events are undesired.

Because many of my respondents lived in shelters, awaiting stable permanent housing, the theme of patiently waiting on a loving but mysterious God recurred throughout the interviews. Poor mothers reiterate that God's timing is not their timing, and thus they need to be patient and wait and trust. Elisa, living with her children in a shelter while searching for housing, said, "He gives me the things that I need whenever he wants, not when I want it. So I have to understand that. . . . When he wants, not

when I want. Everything is not going to be right there when I want it. . . .
It's like he has something for me, and I'm going to get it soon, but I have
to wait." Women who focus on trusting in God's plan and God's timing
draw on this belief to sustain them in situations where positive changes
are not immediately on the horizon. The sense that God will help things
fall into place bit by bit keeps hope alive. These religious assumptions
emphasize God's power over that of humans; God does things when
God wants them done, not when humans do, and things will get better in time. As discussed in detail in chapter 2, this does not mean that
women sit passively and do nothing. They wait on God while filling out
housing forms or taking part in job training programs. But because results are not always immediately forthcoming even when they are taking
necessary actions, these mothers perceive waiting both as a test of their
faith (a theme found in the Bible, e.g., "These [trials] have come so that
your faith . . . may be proved genuine" [1 Pet. 1:7, New International
Version]) and as an opportunity to strengthen their faith. The Old Testament abounds with images of waiting on and trusting in God. "Wait for
the LORD, take courage, be stouthearted, wait for the LORD!" (Ps. 27:14).
"Trust in the LORD with all your heart, on your own intelligence rely not;
In all your ways be mindful of him, and he will make straight your paths"
(Prov. 3:5–6). These passages from the Bible exhort believers to wait on
God's timing and trust in God's goodness, constructs familiar to many
of my respondents.

By and large, mothers in poverty believe the good promised by God
will come in the here and now. They believe God will sustain them in
their suffering and walk with them through it to ultimately bring them
the things they need. These needs seem relatively straightforward (at least
as how the women described their needs): decent shelter, decent jobs,
and safe environments for their children. Manifestations of the prosperity gospel in the sense of thinking that prayer will bring worldly riches
do not appear prevalent, at least not among the mothers in this study.[4]
However, God will, the women believe, bring them the things they need.
A focus on heavenly rewards for human suffering, the "compensation"
theory, is also not prevalent. Poor mothers' theodicy does not primarily
focus on heavenly rewards. God's plan for their lives includes joy in the
afterlife, but their primary explanations for suffering connect it with the
good it will bring in this life. Although research in this area is limited,
Helen Black's study of African American women over age seventy indicates that even when poverty is lifelong, women believe that their lives
are part of "a divine plan that will bring rewards both in this life and the
next" (1999, 364). Despite long-term urban poverty, abandonment by

men, loss of children to drugs and violence, dangerous neighborhoods, and problems with physical health, these elderly women viewed their lives on earth as blessed and rewarded by God.

Some situations allow low-income mothers of young children to see a divine plan for good out of suffering manifested relatively quickly, such as Aletta's story of the better apartment. Unplanned pregnancies can provide a particularly quick manifestation of God's good plan, as many mothers in poverty view their children as precious blessings in their lives. Brenda is an exuberant young woman who eagerly and generously pressed on me her three-year-old's outgrown children's videos. Brenda had given birth as a teenager after a previous abortion, but far from a problematic event, she saw the unplanned teen pregnancy as part of God's beneficial plan for her life. "I didn't do it on purpose. I was on the pill. I was protecting myself, and it happened again. I felt like God would not have made this happen again if I wasn't meant to have a baby. I had to have the baby." Having a baby at age eighteen provided Brenda with a sense of purpose and meaning in life. Becoming a mother led her to pursue her education with the goal of becoming a social worker, further validating her understanding that the unmarried adolescent pregnancy was part of God's design for her good. The joy that poor young mothers find in their children, along with the positive life transformations some women undertake at becoming mothers (Edin and Kefalas 2005), make unplanned pregnancies an understandable site for seeing God's hand at work for good in what an outside middle-class observer might view as an undesirable event.

Such situations as prolonged homelessness, where women cannot readily find God's good purpose, are more challenging for mothers in their effort to maintain their trust. Sometimes women despair, lose faith, and become angry at God. Isabella, who is on welfare and living with her children in a shelter, recounted how she sometimes feels angry with God in trying to make sense of her situation. "Sometimes I be mad at him. . . . Sometimes I try to think what he thinks, but I don't know. Because a lot of things happen to me, sometimes I say 'why?'" However, most of the women, including Isabella, seem to persevere in faith, working through times of doubt and anger to continue trusting that God has a good plan for their lives.

Survey data indicate that most Americans believe in an engaged God who is directly involved with their personal affairs. Poorer people are more likely overall to believe in divine control, but this effect is moderated by church participation. People who report high levels of involvement in religious activities hold similar levels of belief in divine control and involvement, whatever their socioeconomic status. On the other hand, for those with low levels of church participation, people of low socioeconomic status are more likely than their more advantaged counterparts to have high levels of belief in divine involvement and control (Schieman 2010). Methodist minister and seminary professor Tex Sample (1993) writes about his work with what he calls "hard-living people" on the margins of society—the homeless, alcoholics, and drug addicts. He finds this group commonly believes that everything happens according to God's will and within God's providence. Sample argues that the belief that God is in control allows people whose lives are out of control to feel a sense of control, because they believe they can approach God in prayer, perhaps effecting change. This sense of ultimate security and safety stemming from the notion that God is in control provides hope and helps people to take action. These same processes seem to be at work among many of the mothers I studied, who consciously or unconsciously seem to draw on the notion from the New Testament book of Romans: "We know that all things work for good, for those who love God, who are called according to his purpose" (8:28).

Suffering as an Opportunity for Growth

One facet of the Christian notion of redemptive suffering entails God using suffering for people's good, to help believers become more holy and more conformed to the image of Jesus. In suffering, writes Pope John Paul II in his 1984 document "On the Christian Meaning of Human Suffering," "*there is concealed* a particular *power that draws a person interiorly close to Christ*, a special grace. . . . Not only [does] the individual discover the salvific meaning of suffering but above all he becomes a completely new person. He discovers a new dimension, as it were, of *his entire life and vocation*" (John Paul II 1984). Pope John Paul II contends that suffering entails a special call to the virtue of perseverance, which gives hope and allows human dignity. The apostle Paul wrote to his followers about his suffering, extolling the benefits that suffering produced and encouraging them not only to persevere but to rejoice in their sufferings: "Not only that, but we even boast of our afflictions, knowing that affliction produces endurance, and endurance, proven character, and proven character, hope, and hope does not disappoint, because the love of God has been poured out into our hearts through the holy Spirit, that has been given to us" (Rom. 5:3–5).

The history of black theological thought is rife with explanations of redemptive suffering that conceive of God using suffering caused by evil to bring about good. Anthony Pinn (1995) lays out several classic scenarios beyond personal salvation that black theologians and ministers have been using since the time of slavery. In these scenarios, God manipulates the moral evil of the oppression of African Americans for a variety of good ends: correcting character flaws, imparting some type of lesson, obtaining particular skills, benefiting American society as a whole, or bringing about some mysterious good whose end will become clear later. Black suffering in this framework is inherently evil and not desired or sent by God, but God can nonetheless turn it around to be used for good.[5]

Looking at it from the viewpoint of the psychology of religion, re-interpreting trauma as an opportunity for spiritual growth is a common religious attribution for suffering. Difficult events that seem to make no sense are transformed into opportunities—to more deeply appreciate life, to grow closer to God, to help others more (Pargament 1997). Thus, elderly African American women who are poor view their lives as victorious because their hardships have made them into strong, compassionate people who know God more deeply (Black 1999).

Some low-income mothers hence believe that God's good plan for them includes not only the concrete things they seek in their lives—jobs, housing, and health—but also the development of their character. This interpretation allows mothers to recast their situations as opportunities and challenges. Peggy draws on her faith in framing her many struggles as opportunities for character development and personal growth. She explained, "You know, it's really difficult times when your character is being shaped and strengthened. . . . I always try to approach it with God many times . . . just what do I need to know, and what does it mean? How does it apply to me? How can I be better through this? . . . I think it [faith] is the only thing that gets you through on the other side."

Peggy found herself unexpectedly pregnant by a man no longer in the picture, resulting in her relying on welfare after years of owning her own successful housecleaning business, dealing with her older son's problems, navigating job training programs and the welfare bureaucracy, and feeling scorned as an unproductive member of society. This confluence of events could well have shaken Peggy's faith and left her questioning God. Instead, she views them as part of the journey given to her by God, indeed as an integral part of God's beneficial plan for her. Framing suffering as opportunity for character development moves a stance of questioning God from "why me?" to "what do I need to learn from this?" Difficult times are actually the times in which strong character is forged. Thus, "waiting on God" when a bad situation is slow in resolving develops the virtue of patience. Drawing on faith to continue in the face of struggle develops the virtue of perseverance. Experiencing suffering develops empathy for others in similar circumstances, enabling women to comfort others with the comfort they have received from God (Pargament 1997).[6] Women walk closely with God in trying to discern what it is they need to learn from various situations. Interpreting suffering as a God-given opportunity to develop and grow and become a stronger, better, and more mature and compassionate person provides some with a meaning for their suffering.

"We Have to Suffer Like Jesus"

Identifying human suffering with sharing in the redemptive suffering of Jesus on the cross is the classic Christian interpretation of suffering. Pope John Paul II (1984) explains:

With these and similar words the witnesses of the New Covenant speak of the greatness of the Redemption, accomplished through the suffering of Christ. The Redeemer suffered in place of man and for man. Every man has *his own share in the Redemption*. Each one is also *called to share in that suffering* through which the Redemption was accomplished. He is called to share in that suffering through which all human suffering has also been redeemed. In bringing about the Redemption through suffering, Christ *has* also *raised human suffering to the level of the Redemption*. Thus each man, in his suffering, can also become a sharer in the redemptive suffering of Christ.

In the New Testament, the apostle Paul writes, "We are afflicted in every way, but not constrained; perplexed, but not driven to despair; persecuted, but not abandoned; struck down, but not destroyed; always carrying about in the body the dying of Jesus, so that the life of Jesus may also be manifested in our body" (2 Cor. 4:8–11). In suffering, a Christian believer draws closer to Jesus, whose suffering has redeemed the world.

Drawing on a religious cultural repertoire that includes a focus on Christ's suffering, some devout poor mothers of deep Christian faith imbue the suffering associated with poverty and homelessness with a higher meaning. Followers of Jesus are meant to share in his suffering, they believe, and the Christian life is not meant to be an easy one. Because trouble in life is to be expected, women can look to the suffering of Jesus and his disciples to provide inspiration to endure and rise above it. In my interviews, Jane very eloquently illustrated this way of interpreting suffering.

God says you have to deal with all trials and tribulations, and so things happen, and you do have to suffer. I believe you suffer, that God suffered for us. He came here for us, and died for us, and that's part of walking the Christian walk. . . . It's not easy. It's not an easy life to live.

And you read the Bible, and then it is like, wow, okay. You read about the witnesses that went before you, the people, the saints that went before you, that went through the hard times, Paul, the apostle, and Jesus, what he did for you on the cross, and how he suffered and died, and he came from heaven, and became a man, you know? I mean, he came from glory. You can't even imagine what it's like. He came here and suffered and died for us. He was mocked and ridiculed, and everything, for us.

Jane draws on her understanding of Jesus' suffering to suffuse her own hardships with meaning. Seeing her suffering as part of her Christian call to share in Christ's suffering gives her a sense of transcendent meaning. Poor mothers sharing in the suffering of Jesus believe that Jesus' suffering on the cross far surpasses their own struggles with the travails of urban poverty. Furthermore, they reiterate that Jesus was innocent, unlike humankind, and sacrificially suffered to offer the opportunity of redemption to the world. They believe that sharing in Jesus' suffering draws them closer to him and to holiness.

Women such as Jane look to the suffering of Jesus and the early disciples to try to put their own suffering into perspective. The apostle Paul offers a litany of the suffering he experienced in the name of his Christian discipleship, including beatings, imprisonment, and shipwrecks. Because Christ's early disciples suffered and struggled, some mothers think, modern followers should expect no different. Being homeless and living in a shelter with young children become in this view a way of sharing in the sufferings of Christ and suffering like the early Christians. Interpreting suffering as uniting them to Christ does not seem to inhibit action for women but often gives them strength for action, because they believe that in sharing in Christ's suffering they also share in the power of his resurrection.

Does God Punish?

Among some Old Testament narratives, one finds images of an angry, punitive God; suffering comes about as punishment for human sin. Survey data indicate that the poor are more likely to pray for forgiveness of sin compared to the nonpoor and suggest that poor women may be more likely than nonpoor women to believe that God is punishing them for their sins or has abandoned them. Yet even though these views of God are more prevalent among poor women, they are held only by a minority.[7] Some of my respondents believed that God at times sent suffering, but they viewed this much like a loving human father might discipline his children in helping them to become mature adults. (This notion can be found in the New Testament, e.g., "God disciplines us for our good, that we may share in his holiness" [Heb. 12:10, New International Version]). If this is the case, women feel they must be especially attuned to trying to figure out what God wants to teach them through struggles. Said Peggy, "Because if you don't go through a difficult experience without your faith in God and without knowing what perhaps he's trying to teach you, you're going to have that same lesson hit you in the face again." Women believe it is not a punitive, vindictive God sending hardships but rather a God who loves them and is trying to teach them through struggle. One mother told me how a bad drug trip was a punishment from God, waking her up and turning her away from drugs. These women believe that walking with God through suffering, alert to the lessons God is imparting, will strengthen their characters and allow them to learn what it is God wants to teach.

The Christianity popular in modern American culture downplays the existence of suffering with its insistence that God wants people to be positive, happy, healthy, successful, and well-off. A 2006 poll found that more than 60 percent of Americans believed that God wanted people to be prosperous (Ehrenreich 2009). The culture of the prosperity gospel has spread beyond the large megachurches and televangelists that are its most visible manifestation, affecting elements throughout much of American Christianity. Barbara Ehrenreich writes, "Gone is the threat of hell and the promise of salvation, along with the grim story of Jesus' torment on the cross. . . . Instead of harsh judgments and harrowing tales of suffering and redemption, the new positive theology offered at megachurches (and many smaller churches) offers promises of wealth, success, and health in this life now, or at least very soon" (2009, 124). People such as disenfranchised single mothers who experience poverty and considerable suffering may feel themselves to be further marginalized and rejected from mainstream culture and, perhaps, abandoned by God. Thus, Elisa, a single mother in a shelter, can say, "Sometimes when I am stressed out, I don't have no faith at all. I'm like, 'God, why are you doing this to me? Why is this happening to me?' I think he's not there for me." Analysis of poor mothers' interpretations of redemptive suffering should not downplay the fact that many women have times of despair, doubt, and loss of faith in the midst of difficult circumstances. However, narratives emphasizing God's plan or redemptive good from suffering are by far the most prominent narratives in the mothers' discourse. Times of despair and doubt, even though they occur, seem to be more transitory.[8]

Although popular Christianity in the United States may downplay suffering, religious explanations for suffering that do not suggest abandonment by God are available constructs. American culture's religious metanarratives include images of God as a close and loving friend, not a distant, angry, or punitive God. Poor women draw on metanarratives and narratives of redemptive suffering as resources in trying to make spiritually coherent sense of difficult lives, reconciling their image of a loving God with their experiences of deprivation. In my research, black, white, and Hispanic women, of Catholic and Protestant backgrounds and of varying degrees of religious belief and practice, invoked such religious responses to suffering. In particular, women from backgrounds across the spectrum emphasized that "God has a plan" and that one needed to trust in God's timing. The fact that similar themes emerge from women's narratives across a variety of denominational backgrounds and levels of belief and practice suggests that these common religious interpretations of suffering are available in American culture. These explanations are not limited to those suffering in poverty, as research finds them to be common among more affluent believers facing such challenges as illness and losses.[9]

One source that certainly impacts the ways in which low-income mothers religiously frame situations is an individualistic American culture. Women interpret their suffering, the reasons behind it, and the outcome desired by God in highly individualistic ways. Women believe they became homeless because God allowed or willed it for their lives—be it to ultimately get them better housing or to test and strengthen their characters by hardship—not because they lived in an expensive city that lacks enough affordable housing for low-income residents. Women personalized and justified problems on religious grounds. The negative events befalling them result not as unfortunate consequences of being on the losing end of capitalism without strong safety nets but as part of an overall plan orchestrated by God with the women's greater well-being in mind.[10]

Feminist, black, and liberation theologians have strongly critiqued the notions of redemptive suffering from which poor mothers draw. African American theologians writing in the womanist tradition critique traditional Christian theological explanations for suffering, as do Latina mujerista theologians. They contend that traditional theological explanations glorify suffering in ways that are especially unhelpful to black and Latina women.[11] Theologian Emilie Townes (1993) writes that a womanist ethic rejects the idea that suffering is God's will. She notes the historic association in the black church with the sufferings of the Israelites in Exodus and argues that the notion of the inevitability and desirability of suffering must be challenged. A womanist theological ethic of suffering calls for pain to be transformed into action to end oppression, to change unjust situations and make them better. A theology that accepts suffering as a positive good is disempowering. Similarly, Latina theologian Nancy Pineda-Madrid (2001) criticizes the idealization of women's passive response to suffering found in some Christian reflections on suffering. For her, a theology of suffering, "Latinamente," calls for courage and struggle, transforming suffering in service of the greater good of the whole community. Pineda-Madrid looks at how Latinas can transform their suffering for the greater good of the community; "those who have known suffering become the agents of redemption, the agents of liberation for others" (199).

For very poor single mothers, however—feeling overwhelmed with daily concerns, lacking stable housing, struggling to care for their children, and feeling disconnected from churches and other civic organizations—the transformation of suffering they seek and experience is in the realm of immediate personal concerns and not in social action. Furthermore, the views of suffering held by feminist theologians are not a part of these mothers' religious cultural repertoire. In this regard, their traditional interpretations of finding good out of suffering often seem to serve as an empowering part of their religious cultural repertoire, strengthening them in the midst of oppressive circumstances. That is, their theodicies are, on the whole, helpful to them in dealing with their immediate problems. Women draw strength from believing that God will work through their circumstances to a good end or, for the particularly devout, consciously uniting their sufferings to those of Jesus and the early Christian believers. These beliefs can provide them with hope and the ability to persevere and take action in dealing with difficult situations. This is not at all to suggest that my respondents' explanations for suffering are unproblematic or that social change is unimportant but rather to highlight that many marginalized women themselves perceive and experience the theodicy of redemptive suffering as a positive framework in the immediate circumstances of their lives.[12] The mothers' interpretations for suffering, while they do provide a sense of comfort, cannot be categorized as mere "compensation." The actions engendered by their beliefs for the most part show women proactively engaging faith. Poor mothers emphasizing divine providence are not denying that hardship exists, but their religious beliefs help them live with a sense of spiritual coherence and human dignity while they work toward and hope for better times (Frederick 2003; Mooney 2009).

Religion and the Self

Mothers on welfare are stigmatized in American society, stereotyped as lazy, dependent, sexually irresponsible, and wanting to live off government handouts. Seccombe (1999) cites a number of ways in which welfare mothers try to manage their stigma, including denying the stereotype, distancing themselves from other welfare recipients, blaming external forces, and extolling the importance of motherhood. Religion was not among the strategies her respondents drew on in salvaging their self-esteem and sense of self in the face of widespread societal disapproval. However, several other scholars studying disenfranchised groups have commented on the role religion plays in structuring a reinterpretation of the self. Snow and Anderson's (1993) study of homeless street people describes how some choose to frame a personal identity around an ideology or alternative reality, including religious beliefs. Mooney (2009) found Haitian immigrants relying on their self-interpretation as "children of God" to keep negative stereotypes of Haitians from affecting them. By viewing themselves through God's eyes and respecting themselves, no matter what others think of them, Haitian immigrants felt a sense of personal dignity that helped them relate differently to the larger society.

Religion plays a role in reimagining oneself, even among those who do not suffer abject societal stigma and discrimination. Robert Orsi's mid-twentieth-century Catholic women, conflicted by societal expectations and changing women's roles, experienced transformation in their devotions to St. Jude. In petitions and devotion that allowed the "re-experiencing of everyday life in a new way," these women felt themselves transformed to be whole people. They "crafted accounts of themselves as women in their narratives of grace" (1998, 186). Similarly, Marie Griffith's middle-class evangelical women, although not scorned or despised by American society, nonetheless experienced significant family strife, marital discord, and abuse. Experiencing themselves as transformed in Christ led to new ways of perceiving themselves, entailing "feelings of ecstatic freedom, of victory over all previous afflictions and obstacles, and of invincible strength and unfailing courage in the face of future misfortune" (1997, 109).

Religion perhaps has a particularly powerful role, however, in allowing members of stigmatized groups to re-envision themselves. Thus mothers on welfare may draw on religion in shaping a sense of self that contrasts with the dominant society's negative view of them. Peggy imagines what she wants to say when she gets off of welfare, is successful, and comes back to encourage women still on welfare or living in long-term shelters. Peggy reiterates that she knows how the world views women on welfare, but she insists that such women have a "treasure" borne of struggle and endurance, which wealthier women lack. Peggy, who believes that God develops character through struggle, has fashioned an image of welfare mothers as women with stronger characters than wealthier women with spouses. She has taken the image of herself as a daughter of a loving God and refuses to accept and internalize the way that the broader society sees her. Underscoring her strong faith-fueled self-image, she emphasizes, "I had to ask for help, but I'm not going to be treated like I'm a second class citizen." Rather than believing that she and other welfare mothers are lazy, she turns the stereotype on its head to emphasize their character and strength. Marla Frederick (2003) found poor rural African American women to engage in similar reframing work. The process of spiritual salvation transforms not only their spiritual status but also their social status. Women experience their stigmatized social status as "temporary," as compared to their eternal status with God, and consequently view themselves differently. Women's spiritual transformation "gives precedence to what women consider to be God's vision of their life versus anyone else's vision" (217). For marginalized mothers on welfare, viewing themselves as women loved by God gives them a potent alternative self-image and narrative to the negative images of the wider society.

Believing that God has a special calling or purpose for one's life further contributes to a positive religious sense of self that contradicts negative societal images. Seccombe (1999) claims that welfare mothers adopt a primary social identity of motherhood as one of the strategies for managing welfare stigma. The women she studied extolled the amount of time they spent caring directly for their children, which welfare facilitated, as evidence that they were good mothers. As intensive motherhood and being a good mother are highly valued in the dominant society, welfare mothers gained a positive sense of self from adopting this identity. Translated into religious terms, most mothers I interviewed thought God had a special calling or purpose for their lives in motherhood. Explained Vicky: "I think that the situations I was in when I was an alcoholic, then the situations with the depression, that I would probably be dead if God didn't have a plan for me. I wouldn't be here if there wasn't a reason, and maybe that reason is to have my son and do it the right way, nurture him and show him love." God, Vicky speculates, has rescued her from death due to alcoholism and depression for the special reason of mothering her son well. Jobs sometimes enter the picture when poor mothers try to articulate God's purpose for their lives, but not often. For most women, even if they are working, raising their children well forms the central part of what they see as their life's purpose, with work secondary. Maggie illustrates this view as she says of God's calling for her life, "To live my life the best I can live and do what I can. . . . Right now it's my kids and doing what I'm doing. You know, the job will come, but not like right this moment. But it will come." A sense that God has a special purpose for their lives in good motherhood helps mothers on welfare push back mentally against social stigma. Furthermore, a sense that God has entrusted them with the important job of raising their children well, no matter how difficult their circumstances, provides women with a sense of purpose. "Underlying the search for religious purpose is the belief that life has an ultimate goal. . . . Each of us has a reason for being, no matter how terrible our situation may be" (Pargament 1997, 237).

A few respondents interpreted God's calling for their lives in ways outside of the primary realm of motherhood. Shantelle, for example, is struggling to pull her life together, as she is a domestic violence survivor and has been homeless for ten years. She thinks she is called to serve God by living well, getting situated, and figuring out where she is going.

He would want me serving him. [SCS: How do you serve him?] All you do is just you praise God. You don't do things that you know you're not supposed to do. Like you know you're not supposed to do drugs, drink, have sex without being married, curse, run out to bars and meet men, sleep with them, shoot somebody in the head, rob a bank, all the wrong stuff. I'm not doing none of that stuff. It's just that I'm just not—I have so much on my mind. I'm trying to get my life situated so that I can know where I'm going, you know. I think God is trying to help me. I know he is.

Tamika viewed her aspirations to become a child psychologist as God's calling: "He wants me to definitely give all the love that I have in my heart to everyone. He wants me to share that. He wants me to listen to people clearly. He wants me to understand them. He wants me to have a good influence on people, affect their future. . . . He definitely wants me to work on the children." Although conclusions about ways of construing "God's calling" have been heretofore drawn from studies of higher-income individuals, very poor mothers often have a sense of God's calling or purpose for their lives that serves as another force toward a positive view of self.

Yet people's identities are complicated, and many mothers on welfare suffer from depression, guilt, and low-self-esteem. Although a sense of God's love and calling can shape their identities as women loved by God and trying to fulfill a calling to raise their children well, women still struggle with guilt over life events. Suffering is most often interpreted as part of a loving God's larger plan, but women sometimes also see suffering as resulting from their own poor decisions (and sometimes individuals combine elements of both interpretations). Religion is also complicated, and along with its potential for creating alternative positive self-interpretations, it can be interpreted in ways that promote negative feelings of guilt and self-castigation.

Personally religious poor mothers disconnected from organized religion may experience guilt about lack of church participation. This guilt manifests itself in women's belief that had they participated (or continued to participate) in churches, they would not have made the choices that landed them in their current situations. Sarah, whose personal religious beliefs and practices are unusually rich and deep, is a good example. She related that as a teenager heavily involved in her Pentecostal church, she was happy and not involved in negative behaviors; she believes that had she stayed with church, she would not have experienced the problems she has encountered. "I don't think I would have fallen. Instead of keeping that straight road, I went and made a turn. . . . I am not going to blame God. I will never ever do that. I blame myself." Rebecca mused how church participation might have helped save her marriage to a violent, abusive gambler: "My ex-husband, he's had a problem with gambling. . . . Maybe if I had more faith, maybe if we were going to church, maybe if there were a pastor or somebody to talk to, somebody that meant something as a mentor, like a teacher, religious individual, leader. . . . Maybe that would have had an impact on him. And maybe have had an impact on me, on how to guide him." Regretting her lack of church involvement, Rebecca constructs a scenario in which pastors or other church mentors could have straightened out her husband. Reflecting the self-blame often found among domestic violence survivors (Nason-Clark 2001), she surmises that having deeper faith and participating in church could have also helped her change her husband. Her guilt over her self-described lack of faith, in conjunction with lack of churchgoing, is palpable. Juliana, who had expressed disappointment with her mother for not raising her in a church, believes her poor choices have led to her current situation: "If you put yourself in a certain position, then I think that basically you get what you deserve."[13]

"I blame myself." "You get what you deserve." Note that women are not blaming God or feeling punished by God. Their image of God as a loving father remains intact. Instead, women fault themselves for lack of involvement in church, a community where had they been involved, they believe, they might have made better decisions and avoided the hardship they currently experience. Feeling guilt and regret both over not going to church and some of their poor choices, some personally religious poor mothers intertwine these to try to forge a coherent explanatory narrative. This narrative emphasizes personal responsibility and reflects a self-image as women who have not lived up to their responsibilities. It fits neatly with societal narratives of women on welfare, as it reflects society's perception of welfare mothers as women who have ended up in their situations due to poor personal behavior. Here ideas about religion play into, rather than challenge, the dominant negative view of mothers on welfare.

Personally religious women are vulnerable to this interpretation unless they consciously draw on other elements of their religious cultural repertoire to forge alternate positive identities. However, this type of self-blaming and religious guilt also surfaces in women who are not personally religious at all. Take the case of Maribel, a thirty-five-year-old Hispanic single mother of three girls, who ended up on welfare after a fifteen-year career with the government. (She lost her job when the computer system was upgraded.) Raised nominally Catholic, she stopped attending church at sixteen, does not engage in any personal religious practices such as private prayer, and says religion is not at all important in her life. Yet Maribel thinks that if she were religious, then things would be better. "Maybe I wouldn't be in the situation I am in now. I have talked to a lot of people that have God in their life. Their life seems so together. Not like mine now." Martina expressed similar sentiments. Although she does not pray privately, never attends church, and says religion is unimportant to her, she ties her job-related problems to her lack of religious faith: "I haven't been faithful to my faith, but if I did, I might have better control of how I handle my job." Martina related how she had been fired from several jobs for lack of organization and poor performance, something she thinks would not have happened had she been getting "support and self-confidence" from reading the scriptures. Although on standard religious questionnaire items Martina would appear to be non-religious, clearly religion plays a role in how she interprets and tries to make sense of her failures. Some women with low levels of personal beliefs and practices, who perhaps have never been involved in churches, look at religion and wonder what they are missing. They see friends who they think benefit from faith or church participation and surmise that perhaps they could have prevented bad outcomes had they had faith or gone to church. These women blame themselves for the negative outcomes, thinking that perhaps religion would have helped them to be "better" people, more able to fulfill their obligations and responsibilities. Thus, even for women for whom religion seems to have little salience in their lives, religious guilt can contribute toward a negative self-concept reinforcing negative stereotypes of poor single mothers.

Profound religious guilt can lead women to place emphasis on being a sinner. While most religious believers would acknowledge themselves to have fallen short of the standards of their faith (and, indeed, 61 percent of people say that one of the things they prayed for the last time they prayed was for forgiveness of sins), poor people are more likely to pray for forgiveness of sin (Baker 2008). Pinhey and Perez (2000) describe "self-appraised sinfulness" as a form of stigma resulting from religious involvement and internalization of religious doctrine (1). As internalized negative self-evaluations, sinful self-appraisals are significantly associated with greater levels of psychological distress, guilt, and frustration, particularly for people who have engaged in deviant behavior such as drug use. My most eloquent interview on this topic was with LaToya. LaToya was introduced briefly earlier in the book, but here her self-image as a sinner desiring forgiveness and transformation can be fully seen:

I feel that I need God in my life, you know. Maybe by going to church and praying, and praying more to have Section 8 [government-subsidized vouchers for private housing], maybe I'll get an apartment. Maybe, you know, God will forgive me for my sins. I just got out of jail and all, some things that I did that I am not proud of, and I need to go back to church and ask God for forgiveness. I went to jail for selling drugs, and I am not proud of it. . . . I want to get saved, you know, and just ask God for forgiveness. For hurting other people and my kids. . . . I think if I give myself to God, and I turn my life over to God, that things will get better. . . . Being saved means take away all your sins, that I would be clean again. . . . I want to turn my life over to God, I want to change my way of life. I want to be a better person. Because I never want to go back to jail. I never want to hurt anybody anymore. . . . Because my soul would be clean, and I know that God would have forgiven me for all my wrongdoings. And I know I would never do no wrong anymore.

These comments reveal a wounded woman's strong desire for inner transformation that would result in outward transformation in her life actions and decisions. Religious women perceiving themselves to have profoundly failed God desire God's salvation, which they believe will help them to become better people. LaToya's story brings up many questions. Raised Catholic, she had previously regularly attended a Baptist church before being sent to prison for selling drugs. She attended weekly church services in prison. Did she have experiences of spiritual salvation and transformation in her Baptist church or the prison church services? She connects needing to pray more and go to church with perhaps finally getting a government-subsidized apartment. Does she believe that God is withholding an apartment from her because of her sin or lack of devotion?

Women experiencing religious guilt who hold a strong self-conception as sinners desire cleansing from their sins. They use the language of rebirth, of new starts, of transformed beings. "My soul would be clean." "I would be clean again." This language indicates the belief that these newly cleansed souls will gain a new chance at life, a chance to live life with God, where they will abide by the straight and narrow path and "never do no wrong anymore." Once cleansed and forgiven, LaToya told me, she will feel good about herself and her life, as well as be able to accomplish her dreams. She seems particularly haunted by her failure as a mother, for hurting her children by her involvement with the drug trade and for losing custody of some of them. Women such as LaToya seeking transformation look to shed their past lives and walk in a new life with Jesus. Griffith (1997) describes spiritual transformations experienced by middle-class evangelical women: "Suddenly, an old way of viewing the world, of actually being in the world, gives way to a revised perspective and mode of living, as she who is transformed realizes herself to be a 'new creature,' her former self discarded and her sins forgotten. Newly in love with God, the transformed person interprets the world afresh. . . . Healed, forgiven, purified, and strengthened by the power of God, she feels reborn" (103). It is not surprising that poor mothers with rocky life histories desire this profound spiritual and personal transformation. To leave behind a life of jail, drugs, welfare, and failures in mothering—to be reborn into new chances and fresh starts—is strongly appealing. Along with the inner transformation and cleansing, mothers believe, will come a new outer person better able to tackle her challenges. Accompanying this premise is perhaps the notion that a transformed self may also merit more of God's favor, in the form of finding housing or jobs, for example.

Because people's deep-seated religious feelings, as well as their identities, are complicated, elements of positive and negative religious identities often coexist. A woman who strongly views herself as a sinner, which indicates a more negative sense of self, may also see God as having a good plan for her, deriving a sense of being loved despite a sense of sinfulness. While 60 percent of my respondents offered positive religious interpretations for their situations, a quarter expressed religious guilt, and about a quarter expressed guilt over life events, with sometimes these expressions overlapping.[14] Negative stereotypes about women on welfare, depression, and guilt over past choices and actions combine to provide powerful challenges to low-income mothers' sense of selves as whole and valued members of society. Those with the deepest ability to see themselves as loved in the eyes of the divine and the greatest ability to consequently shrug off perceptions of the wider society can best draw on faith to maintain a strong and positive sense of self.

Everyday Religion and Making Meaning Out of Difficulties

Like other religious believers, mothers in poverty turn to religion to help make sense of difficult lives. There are perhaps few other cultural resources that poor women can use as a lens in trying to interpret difficult situations. Why am I here? Why is this happening to me? The mothers I spoke with explored big questions of meaning when faced with life's challenges, as likely do many other poor women. For more comfortably situated people, major challenges are often more episodic in nature, such as job loss, illness, or bereavement. For impoverished single mothers, much of their daily lives can be extremely challenging. The cultural resources they bring to bear in interpreting their situations provide a repertoire of actions from which they can choose (Swidler 2001). Understanding the interpretations that both motivate and constrain these actions is thus crucial.

In their chapter on how homeless people "salvage the self," Snow and Anderson (1993) comment on how puzzling it is that research on the homeless has focused almost exclusively on their demographics to the exclusion of understanding their inner lives. The same question might be raised for mothers in poverty. Snow and Anderson attribute the lack of sociological attention to the inner lives of marginalized people to an overemphasis on a perceived hierarchy of needs whereby needs for physical security must be satisfied before higher-level needs such as identity and self-worth can be considered (Maslow 1943). In fact, the need for meaning likely often coexists with physical needs. How poor mothers understand and interpret their experiences and who they are as members of the human community form an essential part of understanding their lives and their lived religion. Religion may contribute to creating an inherent sense of dignity and self-worth; religion may also be interpreted in ways that contribute to feelings of guilt and failure. Both form an integral part of understanding how religion is lived and experienced in the daily lives of mothers in poverty.

SIX

"I Don't Get to Church Anymore": Capacity, Stigma and Exit, and Religious Individualism

The last several chapters of this book examined how poor mothers' "live religion" in several key areas of daily life. These next two chapters focus on the paradox of high personal religiosity and low levels of church participation, as well as broader issues about churches and the urban poor. Why do highly religious, low-income single mothers with many needs, who likely could benefit substantially from the social capital and resources available in supportive congregations, live out their often deep faith without participation in organized religion?

Sounding different from the middle-class "spiritual seekers" of previous studies (e.g., Roof 1999; Bellah et al. 1985), the mothers in my study spoke of difficulties in transportation or work schedules, housing problems and geographical transience uprooting them from their previous churches, challenges in controlling very young children in church services as a single mother, disappointment or disillusionment with church leaders or members, and a sense of stigma or feeling unwelcome in churches. Although low-income women share some reasons for nonparticipation in churches with more affluent "unchurched believers," some factors are particularly pertinent for single mothers in severe poverty.

Capacity

To participate in organized religion requires a certain capacity: to know about a church, to have the Sunday morning available, to have transportation to the church, and to deal with your young children while there. Most of my respondents had local family members or friends involved in churches, so social isolation leading to lack of interaction with churchgoers does not appear to be a primary cause of their noninvolvement.[1] However, a substantial percentage did have impaired capacity to participate due to chaotic and disrupted life circumstances, as would be true for a number of low-income single mothers.[2]

Transportation issues and housing instability leading to geographic dislocation can significantly impede the capacity to participate in organized religion. Elisa, one might recall, used to attend Pentecostal church services regularly until a few years ago, when her church stopped providing her family with a ride. "We used to get transportation, but they stopped, and it was too far. We couldn't find a church like that around our area, so we had to stop." Nine months before the interview, Elisa and her children had moved away from her prior community to live in a long-term family shelter. To complicate matters, since then her church has also moved. Elisa does not know whether she could call on anyone from her church anymore for assistance if needed, because she doesn't know where to find the church. "Right now? I don't know. They moved the church, and I don't know where they are." A highly religious woman who prays every day, Elisa does not currently participate in organized religion. Although Elisa had many good friends in church, she hasn't seen them now in over a year. Rebecca attends Mass only in good weather, because she has no transportation and has to walk there with young children. "I would take them to church on Sundays, but I haven't done that since November. When the weather got bad we didn't go anymore. I know this sounds awful, but if the weather is conducive, I bring my children. If it's really cold, wet, or rainy, I don't go."

Related to transportation issues, housing problems can inhibit the capacity of women to attend church. Aletta cites shelter rules as an impediment to attending the Seventh-Day Adventist services she had attended twice weekly prior to living in the shelter. "Once I get my apartment, we will attend church. But in the shelters it's kind of hard. You've got to do a lot of things, follow the rules. So I don't really attend church right now." Long-term family shelter housing or supported-housing social service programs, with their rules and curfews, can make it feel difficult for residents to regularly participate in church life. More generally, when a family experiences a housing crisis, it substantially disrupts their lives. For women regularly involved in a church, a move to long-term family shelter housing or a supported housing program usually means a move away from the proximity of their church and church community. Lacking transportation, most neither continue attending their previous church nor readily seek out church communities near their new location. Perhaps women perceive their situations in transitional housing to be temporary, and for some lucky individuals this is the case. However, it can take years for eligible residents to find subsidized or otherwise affordable housing; in expensive urban areas, waiting lists for Section 8 housing run to thousands of households. Where I conducted the interviews, 87 percent of welfare recipients, 86 percent of those recently off welfare, and 91 percent of people entering welfare live in some type of government-subsidized housing. I met mothers who had been living in "transitional" family housing shelters and waiting for permanent housing for several years.

In general, mothers in poverty often experience considerable geographical mobility due to housing crises, changes in domestic relationships, job loss, neighborhood crime, and family crises. Studies of low-income children find high levels of mobility; a researcher interviewing mothers in homeless shelters noted that some children had moved as many as ten times during their first five years of life (Weissbourd 2000).[3] Women receiving long-awaited subsidized housing may be placed in communities some distance away from their home community. When they become uprooted from their previous communities, they can become disengaged from formal religion altogether or at least for substantial periods of time. Moving from place to place, living in a long-term shelter far from one's church community, staying with relatives after losing housing—these all-too-common scenarios substantially disrupt lives and often cause a severance with organized religion for those participating. I found women to be uncomfortable leaving familiar environments, and those moving away due to housing dislocation did not seek out new churches.

Low-income women face unpredictable job schedules that may limit their capacity to go to church. Many service-sector jobs have fluctuating job schedules and can require work on weekends. Furthermore, women may lack power in their jobs to request and receive schedules that would accommodate their needs. Sally, who previously attended Catholic mass regularly, has not attended in three years. The social service job that she has held since then requires her to work on weekends. Rosalyn, as noted earlier, is highly personally religious but does not attend church due to her job schedule as a part-time hotel housekeeper. Even without a job schedule actually impeding church participation, single mothers juggling school or jobs with raising children can feel too overwhelmed and busy to attend church. Busyness, of course, does not just afflict mothers in poverty; affluent suburban parents face competition for Sunday morning with youth sports schedules and other commitments. However, single mothers responsible for caring and providing for young children feel particularly stretched.

Obstacles that might not seem insurmountable to families with access to more resources can prove daunting to families with few resources. If a more affluent family moves thirty minutes from their former church community, they can choose to commute and remain members. Facing transportation challenges, women in poverty may lack this option. If a more affluent person has to work Sunday morning, that person can likely find services with a more convenient schedule. A common practice among contemporary Americans is a consumer-based model where people "shop around" until they find a church that meets their needs (Wuthnow 2007). However, chaotic lives, coupled with care of small children, leave little time for single mothers on welfare to shop around for the right church to meet their needs or fit their schedules.

Dealing with young children can further limit church attendance. Single mothers of very young children can find it difficult to get their children to church and to control them once they are there. If they have nobody with whom to leave their infants and toddlers on Sunday morning or if the church does not provide child care during the services, they may opt not to go. Ann Marie noted, "I go to church every so often. I was going all the time, and then Matthew started getting older and running around the church. The priest didn't mind it, but other people did, and I did." Sheila tried to take her young child to a church but found he couldn't sit still. "I want to start going to church. I haven't because of my son's age right now. Last time he was in church he was running and very busy. I am waiting till he calms down—around age four or five." The problem of dealing with young children in church exists only when children are very young and are unable to sit still for church and the church does not provide child care during services. But because many mothers on welfare have young children, a considerable number may encounter this obstacle. Furthermore, depending on how many children one has and how far apart they are spaced, this critical and challenging phase of child rearing can last a while.

Stigma and Exit

Impaired capacity to participate regularly in churches due to logistical challenges provides one piece of the puzzle of why some highly religious poor mothers are distanced from organized religion. But capacity does not tell the whole story. Some women also feel stigmatized by churches and unwelcome in church. In my study, one-third of the mothers felt stigmatized by churches due to being on welfare, being single mothers, or otherwise having a lifestyle not in accordance with church norms. In his classic work on stigma, Goffman relates how the term originated with the Greeks to refer to signs they cut or burned into the bodies of criminals, slaves, traitors, and other morally inferior "blemished" persons to be avoided (1963, 1). Goffman divides stigma into three categories: "abominations of the body," "blemishes of individual character," and "tribal stigma of race, nation, and religion."[4] Society places demands and expectations on individuals, and those who fail to live up to societal norms are stigmatized. Most stigmatized people, however, hold the same social norms as the rest of society and thus struggle with issues of shame and self-acceptance. Individuals use several strategies for reconciling their "differentness" from "norms of identity." In some cases, "the individual who cannot maintain an identity norm alienate[s] himself from the community which upholds the norm, or refrain[s] from developing an attachment to the community in the first place" (1963, 129).[5] In keeping with this logic, almost all of the women who perceived stigma at church did not attend.

Welfare and Poverty

American society stigmatizes mothers on welfare for failing to live up to economic and family societal norms. Since the passage of welfare reform, welfare receipt has become more stigmatized; welfare mothers are "perhaps the most stigmatized subset of the poor" (Seccombe, James, and Walters 1998, 851).[6] Mothers on welfare are quite aware of their stigmatized status, with most in one study having had criticism personally directed at them. Women feel embarrassed to be poor and living off of welfare and experience discrimination in a variety of arenas, including welfare offices, grocery stores, places of potential employment when applying for a job, and health clinics (Seccombe 1999). Women I interviewed confirm the stigma associated with public assistance. Mothers who had previously lived up to societal norms of supporting themselves and their families find welfare particularly stigmatizing. Said Peggy, "People think that anyone who's on welfare is no good. . . . You're just a lowlife scum bag. It's terrible." Maribel stated, "I hate going to a store and pulling out my card, and people see me, and I get embarrassed. . . . Living off the system, it's just embarrassing. When you have a job, you feel good about yourself." Gwen, a twenty-two-year-old white mother on welfare, summarized the feelings of many respondents by stating, "Everyone looks down on those who need help, who need assistance."

While feeling generally stigmatized in society due to welfare and poverty, some women receiving welfare may feel stigmatized in churches as well.[7] As briefly mentioned in chapter 2, Rebecca feels unwelcome in her church because she receives public assistance and does not work (she receives disability for depression and previously received welfare): "I feel guilty when I think about religion and taking, you know, like having the Sunday, the Sabbath day at rest for prayer, for thankfulness, and then working and not doing that. I feel bad. I even feel like if, if I even go to church, I'm not doing anything for myself. I don't belong there. That's how I feel. I wish that I did have a job. I wish that I was self-sufficient. I wish my children had a positive role model."

According to Rebecca, seeing "other parishioners who are functioning, self-sufficient, unified, respectful" makes her feel like she does not belong at church, but she continues to attend when the weather is good. Rebecca knows no one at church, including the pastor, nor does she make any effort to meet anyone. When she goes, she stays in the back, tries to keep her children quiet, and leaves quickly when it is over. Despite the fact that no one in her church has rejected her or likely even knows she is on welfare, Rebecca's strong internal sense of guilt and stigma makes her feel unwelcome. For those who attend church despite the perceived stigma, it could limit their involvement with the church community. Even women who think their religion approves of short-term "legitimate" welfare use might still feel some sense of stigma. Women on welfare are, in Goffman's (1963) terms, "discreditable"—their stigma is not readily apparent. Were pastors or church members to learn of their welfare use, women might feel pressed to prove they are not in the morally unsuitable category of those who "misuse" welfare. Shantelle, one of the few respondents who was a long-term welfare recipient, says her church would think she was a sinner for a variety of reasons. She does not believe receiving welfare would make her unwelcome at a church, but she equates norms of church behavior with working. "Growing up in church, most of the people there were working people. They wasn't on welfare." Nelson (2005) describes how the congregants of a low-income black church he studied differed from other residents of the surrounding neighborhood; although the church members also resided in the neighborhood, most held jobs, and few collected public assistance.

Chapter 3 explored in detail how social norms of work and self-sufficiency come to be understood by poor mothers in religious terms. In terms of impact on church participation, societal expectations of economic self-sufficiency can lead poor mothers to conclude that they are unworthy in the eyes of God or a church congregation for being on welfare. Rebecca actually uses the term "self-sufficient" to describe the other "worthy" congregants, none of whom, she has assumed, themselves need assistance. Although fear of stigma due to welfare receipt, at least among my respondents, did not actually keep anyone from attending church, welfare use marked some as women who disappointed God. Poor women see churches as places of respectability. They do not believe that being on welfare would literally prevent their attendance, but some feel keenly aware that they have not lived up to their social responsibilities as church people should.

Welfare aside, women may experience the stigma of poverty itself as a barrier to attending church. In one study, half the women in a shelter-based social service program said they would be uncomfortable approaching a minister, feeling that the minister would judge them for their clothes not being nice enough (Sakalas 1999). Other scholars have also highlighted the importance that low-income people attach to clothes as a barrier to church attendance.[8] Rhonda spoke of the "hypocritical" people in the black Baptist church she attends monthly, who are unwelcoming to those who come to church not dressed well.

Those members that I told you they're very hypocritical? They make certain comments, like you're supposed to be able to go to church in whatever you have, because you're there to serve the Lord. And I remember one time a family—I don't know where they came from, but they didn't have the nice suit and tie and Talbots' dress, and they came in what they had on. . . . But that was the nicest thing she had in her closet. and she put it on. . . . I think they [some church members] would pretty much shun them. I know a lot of Christian families that are like that, that if you don't live up to their expectations, they don't have nothing to do with you, and that's terrible.

Rhonda's church is located in a poor neighborhood and attracts neighborhood residents and others. Yet the norm of dressing up for Sunday services is important, so much so that she believes certain church members would shun those who attend not nicely attired. Whether this is merely Rhonda's assumption or actually occurs in her congregation is unknown;

it may be the case that the congregation members would not be as unwelcoming as Rhonda assumes. Urban pastors I interviewed confirmed that some low-income women feel they are unwelcome in church because they lack nice clothing. They point out, however, that self-consciousness over their attire can lead to people fearing lack of welcome when that fear is unwarranted.

Feeling like they lack money for the collection basket may deter poor women from church, another reason confirmed by urban pastors. Certain churches call for tithing, or giving 10 percent of one's income, to the church. Tithing is viewed as giving back to God what is rightfully due and is considered to result in blessings on the giver (Frederick 2003). In some churches, the collection is orchestrated by congregants walking to the front to put their donation in the basket, and then the amount each family contributes is published. Those unable to contribute may have to walk to the front nonetheless to be acknowledged in prayer. Financial expectations associated with church involvement are intimidating for poor single mothers. The ways in which monetary contributions are expected and expressed present the possibility for stigmatization of very poor women with consistent difficulty in giving, with the stigmatization either by church members and leaders or through self-imposed embarrassment and stigma.[9]

Single Motherhood, Cohabitation, and Other "Lifestyle" Issues

Norms accepting of unwed motherhood are highly prevalent in poor communities, and women of low socioeconomic status are more likely to give birth without being married. Births to unmarried women have risen dramatically in recent decades, from 5.3 percent of births in 1960 to 39.7 percent of births in 2007. Statistics vary by race and ethnicity; in 2007, 71.6 percent of births to African American women, 51.3 percent of births to Hispanic women, and 27.8 percent of births to non-Hispanic white women occurred outside of marriage (Hamilton, Martin, and Ventura 2009). Scholars posit a number of reasons for the decline in marriage, including economic and cultural factors. Conservatives such as Charles Murray (1984) have blamed the old welfare system for subsidizing and thus encouraging single motherhood. William Julius Wilson (1987), on the other hand, has pointed to the decreased availability of jobs for low-skilled black men, diminishing the pool of marriageable men.[10] Drawing on ethnographic data, Kathryn Edin and Maria Kefalas (2005) argue that Wilson is only in part right, claiming that a culture-wide redefinition of marriage is the primary reason behind decreased marriage among the poor. With American attitudes increasingly accepting of premarital sex, cohabitation, and nonmarital childbearing, expectations for marriage have risen across all social classes. Poor mothers hold high expectations for marriage, and many do hope to get married, but they want marriage in the context of a strong couple relationship and a solid economic foundation. Though poor and nonpoor women alike have increased expectations compared to previous generations, poor women are much less likely to find their desired stable marriage partner and situation. Given that poor women highly value children and do not believe having children while young will affect their economic opportunities, they bear and raise children while continuing to hope someday for marriage (135–36, 210). However, nonmarital fertility goes against the norms and values of a number of churches, especially conservative ones, which prescribe sexual abstinence for unmarried individuals.

Despite the low marriage rates in their neighborhoods, the majority of black Protestant, conservative Protestant, and Catholic congregations in urban America extol marriage as an ideal for family life. Churchgoing is most common in urban America for married families (as well as for African Americans), and congregations serving urban neighborhoods disproportionately draw married families. Seeing marriage as sacred, religious institutions highlight values such as permanence and faithfulness. The norms of religious institutions help keep the belief and practice of marriage alive in low-income urban neighborhoods where nonmarital childbearing is now standard. Urban women who give birth to a child out of wedlock are significantly more likely to get married within a year of the birth if they attend church regularly (Wilcox and Wolfinger 2007).

Given the pro-marriage stance of many churches, it is realistic to expect that single mothers may feel stigmatized in some churches. Indeed, seven of the forty-five women in my study either had personally experienced incidents they perceived as stigmatizing at church due to their single motherhood or otherwise believe churches stigmatize unwed mothers. Several stopped attending services after negative church interactions due to their status as single mothers. Vicky decided to try returning to church after experiencing a long stretch of difficult years and recovering from drug and alcohol addiction. However, the priest's sermon made her feel stigmatized and unwelcome: "I made a stab at becoming a practicing Catholic a couple of years ago, and I went to church. There was a visiting priest, and he denigrated drug addicts, single mothers, and people having sex out of wedlock and nullified me. Every single thing I've ever done he talked about that day." Vicky said she left church that day feeling very small.

Vicky later spoke to the regular priest at the church, who told her that

God forgave her and that she needed to forgive herself. She still thinks single mothers are looked down on and does not feel welcome to attend, despite very high levels of private religiosity. Ironically, Vicky knows a number of congregants because she goes weekly to a food bank run by the church. Although she likes the church members she interacts with at the food bank, she feels unwanted in the congregation, lending credence to the claim that churches engage poor people more as social service clients than as congregants (Laudarji and Livezey 2000). Lisa wanted to have her sister and a female cousin serve as godparents at her daughter's baptism. In perhaps a sad testament to the retreat of urban men from family life, there were no men she wanted to choose as a godfather. Lisa perceived the priest's refusal as an indictment against single motherhood, which led her to stop attending church.

The church I grew up in disappointed me, so I don't want to go to that church no more. The priest told me that it takes a man and a woman to conceive a child and it takes a man and a woman to raise a child. That's the first time I swore at somebody of the cloth. I feel bad for it, because I do believe in God, and I do believe in what I was taught. But don't tell me that it takes a man and a woman to raise a child because it doesn't. . . . I told him that's where he was wrong, because my mother raised three daughters by herself. We came out pretty damn good. . . . I need to find a church that I am comfortable with going back to before I go back.

Lisa sees the pastor's telling her that it takes a man and a woman to raise a child as a pointed criticism of her status as a single mother. However, many poor single mothers (particularly those, such as Lisa, who were themselves raised by single mothers) do not see marriage as necessary to bear and raise children (Edin and Kefalas 2005). A more general stance of churches supporting marriage as the right environment for sexual activity and child rearing can either devolve into or be perceived as outright personal criticism directed at single mothers, alienating them from churches.

Even with no outright negative experiences such as the examples just cited, some women think churches look down on them nonetheless and view churches as hypocritical and unsupportive of single mothers. Furthermore, despite increased societal acceptance of single motherhood, some women feel churches view having a baby out of wedlock as a sin. Both Catholic and Protestant mothers used the term "sin" in discussing with me their perception of church views on out-of-wedlock childbearing. Having a child out of wedlock makes it visible to the congregation that women have engaged in sexual activity while unmarried. Although research finds congregational social support to be helpful to people in stressful situations, this is not the case if the congregation disapproves of unwed pregnancy.[11]

Paradoxically, African Americans have both the lowest levels of marriage and the highest rates of church attendance of any racial and ethnic group (Wilcox and Wolfinger 2007). A report on promoting healthy marriages in African American churches highlighted practices within the culture of black churches affecting attitudes toward single mothers. Many black churches deal with the gap between their theological teachings and members' behavior by maintaining a "conspiracy of silence" around issues of sexual activity and cohabitation. This indicates that although church doctrine affirms marriage as the place for sexual activity and childbearing, breaking these norms does not necessarily incur stigma (Franklin 2004). My research supports the idea that black churches are accepting of single motherhood, because none of the African American respondents experienced negative incidents due to single motherhood or otherwise believe churches look down on unwed mothers. High rates of church attendance and low rates of marriage among African Americans in general mean that single mothers are a regular presence in the black church. However, not all black churches turn a blind eye. Unwed mothers (but not the fathers) are often required to publicly apologize before the congregation for moral failure and ask for church membership to be reinstated (Franklin 2004). One study of a black African Methodist Episcopal (AME) church where most of the members were working class or close to poverty found that single-mother households were still highly stigmatized (Edgell and Docka 2007). Overall, however, stigma due to single motherhood is significantly less in the black church than among other churches.

Although single, never-married motherhood is much more common in low-income urban neighborhoods, single motherhood due to divorce can incur church disapproval. Divorce, despite being highly prevalent in American society, still violates church ideals of marriage and family life. Peggy found her evangelical church controlling and unsupportive when she was going through a divorce.

In the later years of the church . . . they wanted to keep control of everybody. . . . You [were] told that you can't think that way; you are not a good Christian; you can't do that, or you won't be a good Christian. . . . Even God gives you the freedom to make the mistakes. . . . When I was going through a very ugly divorce and asked the church if they could assist me with the legal fees, they were real hesitant. I was a little disappointed. "All that I've contributed to this church in the nine years that I've been a member, and when I need to ask for help. . . . I mean, I wouldn't ask if I wasn't in need."

Peggy, whose references to God pepper her conversation, had previously been deeply involved with her congregation, but she has not attended this church or any other since her divorce. Her church's response to her divorce stands in sharp contrast to the support church members provided when she was married and having her first child. Peggy recalled, "When I had my baby—my first child—you know, one of the women came over, and she helped with my housework and ironed and tried to cook—and they all brought over foods and something to eat day to day—and those wonderful things—those acts of life were there." With the congregation clearly more comfortable in supporting her role as a married new mother than a woman experiencing divorce, Peggy's story substantiates Edgell's (2006) contention that many churches still operate with the ideal of the nuclear family. Of course, many churches do support divorced members, and Edgell shows that while churches put forth the ideal of a traditional nuclear family, in practice some have adapted to provide acceptance and support for those in situations outside of that convention. Yet where this has not occurred, those standing outside of traditional nuclear family structures may feel unwelcome in church.

Closely related to single motherhood is another source of possible church stigmatization for poor women: their "lifestyles," including cohabitation. Like unwed motherhood, cohabitation has increased substantially in the United States during the last several decades; similarly, cohabitation does not carry the social stigma it once did. Because low-income urban women are less likely to marry, cohabitation or other nonmarital sexual behavior is common. However, due to prohibitions against nonmarital sexual activity, cohabitation remains in conflict with the teachings of many churches. In the working-class and poor black AME church Edgell and Docka (2007) studied, cohabitation met with great disapproval, and church leaders and members worked to persuade those members who were cohabiting to stop, and sometimes they were successful. Maria discussed with me her church's views on cohabitation. As recounted in chapter 1, after she moved in with the father of her three children, she was no longer welcome to attend church. When she lived alone with her children before she moved in with her partner, Maria received substantial material support from her church, such as food and temporary housing, in addition to spiritual and emotional support. At that point, she was an active and engaged congregant, attending weekly, with many friends in the congregation. However, when she began living out of wedlock with her children's father, the church became censorious and did not want her to attend until they married.

Why does a church support a single mother on welfare so generously, yet cut her off from the congregation once she begins cohabitating? In this case, nonmarital sexual behavior not in accordance with church norms had clearly begun prior to moving in with her partner—Maria already had three children by him. Yet the church embraced her then deeply, as a full member. However, cohabitation marks a public display of nonmarital sexual behavior, highlighting lack of adherence to certain church standards. Longitudinal research shows cohabitation to decrease religious service attendance. Because religious leaders or other church members may subtly or explicitly negatively sanction those who are cohabiting, people who are cohabiting may decrease their participation in church.[12] The low marriage rate in poor urban neighborhoods makes this an issue particularly relevant for pastors and residents of these areas, and for members of churches with strict norms, as in the case of Maria, it can impact church participation.

Because people with strong personal religious beliefs do not necessarily follow church teachings on various norms of behavior, the disjuncture between beliefs and lifestyles leaves low-income single mothers wondering whether they would be accepted at church. Jennifer indicated, "I believe, but I don't follow the [lifestyle]. I just don't know what they would say. . . . I love church and stuff. I just don't really follow all the [teachings]. I do sin." Jennifer's "I just don't know what they would say" demonstrates her uncertainty that a person with her lifestyle—she is an unmarried young mother, and her baby's father is in jail—would be welcome at church.

Women violating church norms have reason to fear church rejection. Writing about black churches, Taylor, Chatters, and Levin (2004) argue that congregations are particularly strong environments for negative social sanctions. Members whose behavior does not meet the expected standards of the church can be subject to reactions ranging from gossip to public censure to complete ostracism.

Women unwilling to make lifestyle changes will refrain from participating in churches that require adherence to certain norms. Juliana had a profound spiritual experience while visiting a Pentecostal church with her boyfriend's mother. However, she does not feel ready to make the strict lifestyle changes she thinks that involvement in a Pentecostal church would require.

My best friend was explaining to me if you accept the Lord as your lord and savior, you will feel like that for the rest of your life. You will feel nothing but happiness. "Well," I said, "that would be such a beautiful feeling, but it is not that easy just to go from one day to the next and just stop smoking cigarettes and stop doing everything. When I am ready to do it, I will do it." . . . I would have to get the earrings off, take all the makeup off, leave my hair out and never cut it. Wear a long skirt.

Mothers such as Juliana have strong religious beliefs and see benefits of church participation, but they do not want to make changes that they perceive churches to require. Although the Pentecostal restrictions she describes seem extreme, mothers commonly mentioned their lifestyles not being in accordance with church norms, even where church expectations are less severe.

Poor women who feel as if their lifestyles or certain life events put them at odds with church values and teachings may also experience an internal sense of shame or guilt that keeps them from participating in churches. Several African American Protestants in the study had stopped attending church due to a sense of being sinners and a heavy sense of guilt over past wrongdoing. Shantelle told me, "I used to be in church. I grew up in church, but right now they would say I am a sinner. . . . I know I'm a sinner, but I ask God to forgive me every day." As she elaborated, it became clear that Shantelle does not actually fear rejection from a church community. "People never turn you away from coming to church," she said. However, she feels guilt before God and believes she needs to seek God's forgiveness in order to get back to church. It is unclear how she will know when she has been forgiven enough that she can attend church again.

Alan Wolfe (2003) claims that a sense of sin has diminished in contemporary American religion. The notion of sin, however, had not died among my respondents (a surprising number actually used that word). Aware that they have failed to meet the standards of society, feeling like they have failed to meet God's standards, some women feel too "sinful" to attend church. Women who see themselves as deep sinners say they want to go back to church and seek forgiveness, but paradoxically, their personal sense of sin, shame, and guilt keeps them from church. Other women cognizant of themselves as sinners fear that churches may not accept them. Self-perceived sinfulness can lead to a sense of stigmatization and separation from church, often without giving actual church leaders or members a chance to stigmatize.[13]

Stigma and Types of Churches

The variety, depth, and breadth of stigma likely vary among types of churches; a small study can, of course, only suggest patterns. People in smaller, closely knit churches are more likely to be part of a church community where members know each other well. Although they are more likely to receive substantial assistance from church members in times of trouble, they also may experience more gossip, people noticing how they dress, and sometimes a feeling of unwelcome because of "lifestyle." More intimate congregations provide needed support and community, but they may also be sites of stigmatization of those deemed not to fit church norms. On the other hand, people in larger liturgical churches are more likely to not know many of the other church members well. In my study, some Catholic women who otherwise do not attend services will occasionally go to Mass when feeling stressed and depressed. They find the act of attending to be healing; other parishioners would not know or even care about their lifestyles. Catholic women were more likely, however, to perceive or experience stigmatization due to single motherhood in negative interactions with clergy.

Race and ethnicity also impact stigma. I found white mothers the most likely to perceive church-based stigma (almost half did), followed by Hispanic women. By contrast, only one African American thought her church stigmatized poor mothers (for not dressing well enough), though several other African American mothers' sense of sinfulness provided an internal sense of shame that inhibited church participation. For capacity, though, the findings were reversed, with African American mothers most likely to mention logistical challenges limiting their ability to attend church, followed by Latinas and whites.

Exit

Women's perceptions of churches not wanting "women like them" in the congregation also lead them to reject churches. When Maria felt unwelcome to participate in her congregation while she was cohabitating, in theory she could have looked for a more accepting church community (within the constraints of available time for church shopping in her schedule). In practice, she reframed her marital status by referring to her live-in partner as her husband and kept away from churches altogether. She defined her nonmarital relationship on her own terms and rejected church participation. Her quiet defiance of the norms her church seeks to impose serves as a "weapon of the weak" (Scott 1985), whereby she resists church participation at this point in her life.

Rejection of church life altogether was a common phenomenon for my respondents disappointed in their churches, whether through incidents of stigma or other situations. Hirschman's (1970) model of exit, voice, and loyalty provides a framework for analyzing those who reject church participation altogether after disappointments. This model, which has been applied across a wide variety of contexts, posits "exit" as one solution for people who are dissatisfied with a situation. Thus women who are disappointed with a pastor or some other aspect of their church may "exit" their relationship with churches overall. This phenomenon, of course, exists in the broader population but may be more prevalent among low-income populations. Very poor single mothers have many needs and thus perhaps have higher expectations from pastors and congregations; they may also have more negative experiences in congregations. Issues of self-esteem and depression may play a role as well.

Stigma or disappointment leading to "exit" is not a passive response, whereby women sit quietly and sadly, feeling rejected from or let down by their churches. Some women get angry. They assess churches and find them lacking. They offer sharp critiques of churches. The mothers in these situations see themselves as the judge of whether churches are meeting their standards and exercise their agency to exit when they do not. Lisa had no qualms contradicting the priest who told her it took a man and a woman to raise a child, and she even swore at him. This priest did not meet her standards of openness and welcome, and she "exited" formal religious participation. Peggy "exited" church participation when the church would not help with her divorce legal fees after she had financially contributed to the church as a member for nine years. In these and other situations described by the mothers, women "exited" because churches did not live up to their ideas of what a church should be.

Cultural Barriers

Religious codes are the moral and behavioral norms shared by members of a religious community (Roof 1999). Many of my respondents seemed somewhat unclear about the behavioral norms associated with churches, with the exception of women such as Maria who were involved or had been involved with evangelical or Pentecostal churches with very clear (and restrictive) codes. Mothers mentioned smoking and swearing in the same breath as out-of-wedlock pregnancies and cohabitation. Ann Marie, who is cohabiting with her child's father, indicated, "I have a lot of religious beliefs. I do believe in God. . . . I believe in burials and going to church and confessions. I made all my sacraments. . . . [But] I swear, I smoke, I'm pregnant." Several other women who were not fundamentalists brought up smoking as an example of unacceptable behavior for a churchgoer.[14] Certainly Catholicism and other mainstream faiths do not prohibit smoking. Yet some low-income single mothers hold a vision in their minds of an appropriate lifestyle for churchgoers, a high standard of behavior to which their own lives do not conform. These codes they attribute to religious communities, although not even realistic, serve to exclude them.

Their understanding points to a conflation of church norms with various middle-class cultural norms. These women share similar religious beliefs with churchgoers, they have made the same sacraments, and they believe in the same rituals. In envisioning what churchgoers should look like, however, they move beyond shared religious beliefs to manners of dress, manners of speaking, and manners of style, including things such as choices about using cigarettes. These codes are not about shared religious faith but more about markers of class. Churches are viewed as places of respectability for those living in accordance to middle-class cultural norms.[15] My interviews suggest that a number of the urban poor likely view churches as part of a middle-class culture and establishment to which they do not belong. This view is enhanced by the middle-class churches in their neighborhoods whose members commute in and go home after the services are over.[16] Many of the working-class and working-poor residents studied by Edgell (2006) in upstate New York associated local churches with middle-class culture and did not attend. Those with high school degrees or less education were much more likely to view churchgoers as hypocritical and "stuck up." Negative perceptions of churches and church members existed even among those with high levels of personal religious beliefs, practices, and salience. Another recent study suggests that low-income Catholics, who are more likely to be part of economically diverse congregations with middle-class congregants, are considerably less likely to attend Mass than their wealthier counterparts—perhaps due to feeling uncomfortable in the middle-class culture.[17]

The public housing residents surveyed by R. Drew Smith (2001) provided as a main reason for nonparticipation in churches their unwillingness to make lifestyle changes they felt churches would expect or they would expect of themselves if they were to participate. But what, exactly, are these lifestyle changes? And how many of them can be attributed to religious beliefs and how many to markers of social class? If poor single mothers view churchgoers only as people who have nice clothing, are married, are employed, do not smoke or swear, and so on, then they will feel alienated. Feeling alienated, they will keep themselves apart from churches, thinking that these "stuck-up" institutions are not for people like them and have nothing to offer them. Both actual and perceived cultural barriers contribute to the urban poor distancing themselves from churches (R. D. Smith 2001, 2003).

Religious Individualism and Mothers in Poverty

Initially, I was somewhat puzzled when I spoke with those women who seemed highly personally religious yet eschewed participation in organized religion, especially women with so many tangible needs where a church community might be able to provide support. Their personal spirituality was for the most part conventionally "religious": prayer and scripture reading; one respondent (Sarah) even fasted and prayed to "keep holy the Sabbath day" although she never attended church services. Some had been very involved in church congregations at other recent points in their adult lives. These mothers and others like them are not spiritual "seekers" rejecting traditional religion, but factors inhibit their participation in organized religion. As discussed earlier, chaotic life circumstances with housing, transportation, and job-related problems and difficulties in coping with young children as a single mother—all of these make it quite challenging for even "conventionally religious" women to attend church services.

Why Stigma?

The capacity explanation for decreased church participation among very poor single mothers is straightforward; currently a few years into researching this topic, I see that even with a supportive spouse and a church right across the street, it is challenging to get our young children up and out the door on time on Sunday mornings and quiet and still once in church. Stigma is more complicated. On the one hand, some churches proscribe certain behaviors. People may feel unwelcome in these churches due to having children out of wedlock or living with a partner out of wedlock, common occurrences in low-income urban America. On the other hand, church is a supposedly welcoming environment; Jesus reached out to the poorest of the poor. Yet some poor women cite poverty or welfare as a reason for feeling unwanted at church.

Part of the problem lies in distinguishing perception from reality. Some cases of stigma seem clear, like a pastor who refuses to baptize a child because the mother is unmarried or a pastor who insists a couple be married to continue participating in church. However, pastors may also merely preach sermons exhorting congregants to avoid drugs or sex outside of marriage, conventional teachings among many religious traditions. As described above, one mother who heard such a sermon perceived it as "nullifying" everything about her; it disturbed her so much that she felt unwelcome to return to the church even after speaking with another pastor about the incident. This church and others like it are probably not trying to make poor single mothers feel stigmatized and unwanted, driving them away. Well-meaning pastors are often trying to find a balance between upholding the tenets of their religion while not alienating the large number of potential congregants who do not adhere to these tenets. This problem is certainly not limited to inner-city pastors, but pastors in poor neighborhoods minister in areas of low levels of marriage and high levels of drugs and violence, "often feel[ing] themselves confronted by immorality all around them" (Wolfe 2003, 138). These pastors walk a fine line between being welcoming and nonjudgmental while not compromising teachings they think should be upheld.

Another part of distinguishing between perception and reality lies in assessing how women's self-perceptions may influence their perceptions of stigmatization. Mothers on welfare and other extremely poor women often suffer from depression and anxiety (Danziger et al. 2001). Under these circumstances, a woman's low self-esteem may lead her to perceive rejection in church, even if none is intended.[18] Emotionally fragile women, aware of society's prejudices against single mothers on welfare and conscious that they are not living out the American ideal of self-sufficiency, may be particularly attuned to any potential indication of church rejection. However, to dismiss poor single mothers' sense of church stigmatization as only a figment of fragile, depressed women's imaginations does not do it justice. This problem does exist in some churches, as pastors interviewed for the study confirm in the next chapter. Pastors' comments and actions, other congregants' reactions, and women's own perceptions all contribute to a sense of stigma that helps drives some low-income single mothers away from organized religion.

American Religious Culture

In studying political and civic engagement, Cliff Zukin and colleagues (2006) argue that a generational-based shift has taken place in forms of citizen engagement. We may be seeing some declines in some types of civic or political activity, but younger generations are replacing traditional forms of engagement with newer forms. A number of women I studied had older women in their lives—mothers, grandmothers, and aunts, for example—who were deeply involved in church communities. In keeping many of their elders' beliefs and personal practices, while letting go of church attendance, are younger women instead opting for newer forms of religious associational behavior? Perhaps the most pervasive "newer" form of spiritual connection is the small spiritual support group. These types of groups have flourished in recent decades, and Wuthnow (1994b) estimates that 40 percent of Americans now belong to such groups. Small support groups nurture members' spirituality, provide emotional connection, and help members gain a deeper sense of community. However, poor mothers do not appear to be rejecting church attendance in favor of alternative types of communal spiritual gatherings. Among my informants, there was little evidence of small support group behavior. A few participated in such groups: one active churchgoer participated in a Bible study for parents and children at her church, and one was in a depression support group at a community health center. In addition, a few women were recovering alcoholics and drug addicts likely undergoing the twelve-step experience. However, engagement in small groups was not widespread. Although Wuthnow asserts the small group movement reaches people of all ages, races, socioeconomic backgrounds, and geographical locations, a study based on input from black pastors claims many low-income urban residents would be unfamiliar with church-based emotional support groups (Franklin 2004). Furthermore, even though some mothers may wish to participate in spiritual support groups, the logistical problems that make church attendance challenging also affect religious small group participation. Brenda, for example, wished there were a voluntary Bible study available in the long-term shelter in which she lived:

A lot of people that are in shelters and that are drug addicts or teen parents who don't have anything or just families that are too big and that are homeless . . . those type of people need God in their life. Not to have it enforced, but to just sit around in a group. They have groups every Tuesday where a lady comes in and talks about safe sex. Another lady comes in and tells you about all types of diseases. Well, what about the woman who comes in and tells you how God can help you? Where are your options? A lot of people don't know what they are missing. Like me, I don't go to church. I really don't know what I am missing. I am guaranteeing you if I am hitting rock bottom, I am going to need God in my life and a Bible study once a week; how could that hurt you? It can't hurt you any.

I feel like a lot of women that have bad drug habits or just no self-esteem or have a bad marriage or just young or anything like that . . . don't always have God in their life. With that [Bible study], they will see that there is so much out there besides just what the government can offer you. There is a church. There are other people out there that care about you and that care about you personally. Not care about you on a level to where your time is ticking so you have to hurry up. The church is so open, and they are so there. To have a Bible study in a shelter, the mothers will feel so much better after that.

Brenda eloquently describes what she feels a Bible study run by a church could offer to struggling single mothers like her, in knowing that there are people who genuinely care about them, not just government social workers focused on the ticking welfare clock. Yet she knows that she and others in the shelter who she believes would benefit from a voluntary spiritual support group do not get out to church services and would not seek out such groups in churches. The church would literally have to come to them. Because two-thirds of all small groups have some connection to churches and synagogues (Wuthnow 1994b), women who feel distant from religious organizations would likely be distanced from spiritual support groups that take place there.

Although church participation and small support group involvement may be less likely for very poor single mothers, these women are not completely religiously isolated. Women who are not engaged in any type of communal religious activity may have friends and family members with whom they have conversations about religion. Women are spiritually encouraged through words of their mothers, grandmothers, and friends, and sometimes their partners or partners' mothers as well. I found evidence of this among the mothers studied. Informal conversations serve as sites of religious discourse, where poor mothers are encouraged by relatives or friends to persevere and trust in God. Women themselves also offer spiritual support and advice to others in their informal networks. However, the question remains whether these informal sites of religious connection can replace the social capital available in supportive sites of communal religious practice.

Poor urban mothers live in a religiously individualistic America.[19] Living as part of a modern religious culture where people change religions, choose religions, and opt for "seeking" instead of "dwelling," these women provide but one example of the way Americans experience religious fluidity. Many Americans can be characterized by the religious practices found among my informants: detaching from the churches of their childhood and choosing personal religious practices over formal participation (Wuthnow 1998; Roof 1999). Church participation is lower among younger Americans in general. Clearly, these larger cultural forces impact poor mothers' choices about religion. However, although the broader American religious landscape shapes poor women's religious participation, issues of capacity, stigma, and exit do play a particular role in their decisions, as do cultural barriers and the conflation of churchgoing with middle-class culture and lifestyle. Furthermore, women contend with multiple factors at once: marginalized women who think the middle-class churches in their neighborhoods are not for people like them also face such issues as conflicting job schedules.

Many churches exist across the country where poor mothers feel welcome and deeply engage in the life of the community. The problems described by the women interviewed are not universal phenomena. Yet they are common phenomena that for the most part have not been thoroughly addressed in sociological analyses of churches and the urban poor.

SEVEN

The Church in the City: Impressions from Urban Pastors

Although the primary goal of this book is to understand everyday religion as experienced by mothers in poverty, adding the viewpoints of urban pastors provides an essential and important counterpart. Do pastors notice poor single mothers feeling unwelcome in their churches? Is the practice of mothers sending children to church while not attending themselves a common one? What challenges do pastors face in ministry with low-income women in their communities? Incorporating the insights of pastors who collectively have worked with thousands of mothers in poverty over their many years of ministry allows findings from the mothers to be contextualized and expanded. This chapter provides a primarily narrative account of the relevant thoughts and experiences of urban pastors to add to an understanding of women's experiences.

I conducted in-depth interviews with fifteen pastors who had considerable experience in ministry in low-income urban areas. Because the mothers came from Christian religious backgrounds (or no religious backgrounds), I interviewed pastors across a variety of Christian traditions: Catholics, Pentecostals, Baptists, Methodists, and nondenominational churches. Ten were Protestant ministers, and four were Catholic priests; one was not actually a pastor but a Catholic nun with thirty years' experience working in urban parishes and providing church-based social services to poor women and their families. Four of the fifteen were women. Half of the pastors were African Americans or Latinos serving predominantly minority but diverse congregations; the white pastors also served diverse congregations. Six had twenty-five or more years of experience in urban ministry, five had between ten and twenty-five years of experience, and four had less than ten years of experience. Nine of the fifteen pastors had served in several cities during the course of their career in ministry. To maintain confidentiality, I use pseudonyms for the pastors throughout. The director of a faith-based community organizing group initially provided me with the names of pastors to contact, and I received suggestions for additional contacts from these pastors during their interviews. The pastors interviewed actively seek to include the poor into their congregations and, as such, are not representative of all urban pastors. McRoberts's (2003) research suggests that they are not the norm.

Church Participation and Mothers in Poverty

The pastors confirm a key finding from the women: although mothers in severe poverty may be personally quite religious, they often choose not to participate in formal religion. Said Father Alonzo Gonzalez, a Latino Catholic priest who had served in a parish near a large public housing complex, "They may read the Bible, they may pray every day, they believe there is a God, they believe in eternal life . . . but they don't really attend." Pastors highlighted logistical reasons, stigma, and cultural barriers, as well as other reasons, when analyzing why poor mothers who are personally religious may choose not to attend church.

Almost all of the white pastors saw logistical problems as impediments to church participation, noting the same problems related by the women: job schedules, transportation, and difficulties with children. Rev. William Anderson, a white Methodist minister who has long served poor inner-city churches in various northeastern cities, definitely thought logistics made it difficult for poor mothers to attend: " 'I've got three kids; you want me to get all three kids together, I got to walk. . . . And by the way I worked a double [shift] the night before at a nursing home, and I'm exhausted. So this is the only time I have to do laundry or go shopping.' " An African American minister of an AME Zion church, Rev. Marcus Paul, reiterated, "I feel like it's the same situation. . . . 'I have to work Sundays.' " In particular, urban pastors recognize that the fluctuating work schedules in low-wage service-sector jobs can make church attendance difficult. In addition to actual work schedules preventing attendance, as emphasized by the mothers in the study, pastors acknowledge that even those who do not have to work a Sunday morning shift every week may nonetheless feel too worn out or overwhelmed to attend. For single mothers trying to economically provide for and care for young children, Sunday mornings may be the only free time they have during the week. Pastors find these work-related obstacles to be the most plausible logistical reason for nonattendance, and they serve as a more difficult challenge for the ministers to overcome in reaching out to these women as potential church members.

Some pastors, however, particularly African American and Latino, are more likely to see other logistical reasons merely as excuses some poor mothers give for not being able to attend church. For example, fear of children disrupting the service is seen by some as an excuse. Rev. James Roberts, an African American Methodist pastor, dismissed the logistical obstacle of transportation as an excuse: "We hear those things all the time. I don't believe that's necessarily the reason, because we supply transportation like many of the churches do." These pastors believe that logistical impediments to participation, with the exception of women's work and schedules, are generally things that can be dealt with and do not need to prevent attendance.

All but four of the pastors concurred that poor women can feel stigmatized and unwelcome in church because of outward signs of their poverty. Reverend Anderson, whose congregation is composed of older working-class whites and poorer immigrants and minorities, said some people express "feeling like you have to have a certain amount of money in your pocket, or to put in the offering plate, or you have to dress in a particular way." Rev. Roberto Manuel, a Latino Pentecostal minister with twenty-nine years of ministry experience in poor neighborhoods in a number of cities, stated, "That's what I hear: 'I can't go, I don't dress right, I don't talk right.' . . . They've got all these walls already in front, and so they think that maybe the church won't accept them." Father Nathan Woods, a Catholic priest, agreed: "Excuses that I heard oftentimes when I would ask people were that I don't have anything to wear and I don't have anything to throw in the collection. And they would be very much aware of who's watching when they would reach out to put something into the basket."

Thus pastors confirm that even in congregations in poor neighborhoods, outward signs of poverty can incur stigma. Reverend Roberts has more than thirty-five years of experience as a pastor in poor urban neighborhoods and currently ministers to a working-class and lower-income minority congregation made up predominantly of African Americans. He spoke of the historical importance of dressing well in the black church: "It's about dressing up, it's about giving God your best . . . and yes, there is that stigma. I do have some poor people who will come and never take their coats off." Although this church has a meal every Sunday for the congregation after the service, some people do not want to stay and take off their coats to reveal their clothes. He tries to encourage people not to care about their attire:

One lady said to me, "Reverend, you know what, I have one dress that's what I would call a Sunday dress," she said, "so I don't want people looking at me and saying that's the same dress she wore last Sunday." I try to say, "But you're not coming for them, you know, you're really not coming for them. You're coming for God, you're coming to worship God, you're coming to be thankful for what he's done and is doing and will do for you, and you've got to push that aside."

In these situations, pastors tell impoverished women not to worry about whether people are looking at their clothing or what they put in the collection plate. Although incidents of stigma due to poverty are not necessarily overt, disapproval can be conveyed by subtle means, such as how someone is or is not welcomed. Rev. Susan Gillette, a white United Church of Christ minister, explained, "Folks who aren't able to present themselves the way that some churches think they should are not made to feel welcome. Not that anybody is barred from the door, but . . . at times it becomes obvious that there are certain moral judgments made about people in certain life situations by some churches."

However, pastors also emphasize that women can fear rejection due to their poverty even when congregation members would be welcoming. Assumptions women hold about not feeling welcome at church due to poverty can be false assumptions. Pastors see poor women's fragile self-esteem and awareness of negative stereotypes as contributing to feeling unwanted due to their poverty. Women's self-consciousness about their clothing or lack of collection-plate contribution can prove more of an impediment than the actual reaction of congregation members. Furthermore, not all pastors view actual or feared stigma as a problem. One who did not served a large Catholic parish drawing parishioners across the socioeconomic spectrum, with a long history of including poor neighborhood residents in its very active congregation and extracurricular programs. Two others led small community-based Hispanic Pentecostal churches in poor neighborhoods, and another led a large Assemblies of God congregation with many social services and support groups. If these pastors are correct, it suggests that churches may build up reputations as welcoming congregations for the very poor that dispel fears and assumptions. It is also possible that those who acknowledge this issue, some of whom also lead churches very involved in their low-income communities, may be more aware that the problem can exist.

The previous chapter discussed how some women feel unwanted at church due to being unwed mothers or living out of wedlock with a partner or because of some other aspect of their lifestyle. Pastors agree that it can be a problem in some churches. Father Woods stated, "Well, unfortunately, it does not surprise me as much as I wish it did. I've heard that kind of thing from a number of people." Reverend Paul, who had previously served a racially mixed congregation, told of a white woman with a drug problem who had experienced rejection at the church: "You know, people looked at her as a druggie. 'What is she doing here?'" He prefers the imagery of church as a hospital, where people come to be healed. "Not to be turned away from the one place that they sought refuge, that's not how it should be." Reverend Roberts noted, "Some churches are difficult. There are girls who've grown up in the church and who made mistakes and who are shunned and are treated badly." The pastors interviewed perceived themselves as personally welcoming of people whose lifestyles differ from church norms, but stated that pastors exist, particularly in fundamentalist churches, who do not embrace people whose lifestyles do not meet church standards of behavior.

In general, pastors who see lifestyle-based stigmatization as a potential problem in their congregation see it in terms of isolated occurrences. Some speak of the need to better educate congregants about the true meaning of community. However, the fact that all of the pastors had either seen such occurrences in their own congregations or knew of it in other churches affirms that the experience of being unwelcome in churches reported by some of the mothers is indeed real. Those whose lifestyles do not conform to church norms can experience lack of welcome or even outright rejection from a church community. While pastors definitely acknowledge that women's low self-esteem also may cause them to perceive stigma where none exists, church-based stigma can and does exist in some congregations.

Like the mothers interviewed, pastors are least likely to see stigmatization of poor mothers due to their lifestyle as a problem in the black church. Rev. Francis Keene, an African American Baptist minister with more than thirty years in ministry in poor urban neighborhoods, stated, "That's not in this church, not in the black churches." Reverend Roberts elaborated, "In a minority church where we had a history of young divorces, single mothers, unwed mothers, we've had a history of all that . . .

drug addiction, alcoholism. I mean there are issues we struggle with all the time, and issues that we deal with without castigating other members." However, African American pastors are also more likely to say that women's own internal sense of guilt and unworthiness can keep them away from church. Just as a sense of self-appraised stigma or being "an unworthy sinner" was pronounced among some African American respondents, African American pastors confirm this phenomenon. Reverend Roberts believes the logistical excuses that some poor mothers give for not attending church mask the true reason: they feel guilty and unworthy to attend church and falsely fear gossip or rejection due to their guilt.

I think that these are people who are wrestling with guilt and shame and who are more concerned about their plight than others would be. . . . I think that is because they are for the large part religious women, and there's a certain amount of shame that comes to an unwed mother. There is a certain amount of shame that comes to a mother who is divorced young. "My marriage failed; I broke God's law, and I had this child out of wedlock." I think because of their own religious background they automatically feel that when they walk in people are looking at them, people are talking about them, and they just don't want to go through that. So it takes a very, very brave woman to come in and be a part of the fellowship. And the same part of it is that the fellowship is open and welcoming, but it's time to get that point across to them. Because there's that inner concern, that inner guilt, that inner shame, "I know I've made mistakes, and I know people are looking at me." They're looking at themselves.

Reverend Manuel has found the same among Latinos in his almost thirty years ministering in various low-income urban locations in the United States. "At least with ethnic people, I hear them say it a lot; they'll say, 'I'm too bad, I've done too many bad things to go to church.' . . . So that's what I think we're dealing with, with the culture today, especially with ethnic people. I think the issue isn't they don't want to go to church; I think in some way they don't feel they're worthy enough." Thus urban pastors validate barriers voiced by some of the mothers in the study: guilt and "self-appraised sinfulness" (Pinhey and Perez 2000, 1) can serve to keep people away from churches. Although low-income women may be personally highly religious and even wish to participate in church, the feeling that they are too "bad" or that they have done too many wrong things in their life can keep them from participating. Among the mothers, the few African American women who were long-term welfare recipients most strongly emphasized a sense of sin and unworthiness keeping them from churches. (Like most long-term welfare recipients, these women also struggled with other serious issues, such as prolonged homelessness, domestic violence, drug addiction, and incarceration.) Only African American and Latino pastors brought up the issue of people feeling too unworthy to attend church, with Reverend Manuel attributing this phenomenon particularly to "ethnic people." This finding suggests that the issue of people feeling too sinful or unworthy to attend may be more prevalent in minority communities.[1]

Creating a Welcoming Environment

Acknowledging that obstacles stand between impoverished single mothers and churches, clergy emphasize the importance of creating an accepting environment. They believe considerable harm can be done by pastors who are judgmental or who do not truly wish to be in this kind of ministry. They emphasize that Jesus was welcoming and forgiving. Reverend Roberts explained: "We're Christians, which means we follow Christ. Christ is always welcoming. Christ is always invitational. Christ is always forgiving. You can be all of that, and you can still hold up the tenets of your religion." Yet urban pastors minister in areas with low levels of marriage and high levels of out-of-wedlock pregnancy, violence, and drug activity. As such, they need to adopt strategies that promote a welcoming atmosphere while also adhering to the moral tenets of their faith. One strategy is to choose sermon topics with care. Said Father Woods, "I didn't preach about marriage; there were people in the middle class that wanted me to do that, but I mean, what's the point? Two little words from me are not going to change that situation and will probably end up making people feel more guilty, perhaps not able to keep coming to church, and nothing changes in the situation either." Because things said from the pulpit can feel condemning to those listening, some urban pastors instead use personal interaction to encourage congregants whose lifestyles differ from church standards. Reverend Manuel gave an example of recently dealing with a couple living together out of wedlock: "I met with them for quite a while, and I shared with them what I felt the Bible says about them living together, and they said, 'Well, we understand that,' but they never changed. . . . They thanked me with tears, 'You didn't condemn us, you just worked with us, and you didn't necessarily agree with what we were doing, but you didn't condemn us.'" Reverend Manuel's strategy allowed this couple, who eventually married, to feel welcome and accepted in the church without him feeling he had compromised the moral tenets of his religion. The issue of marriage seems particularly suited to these personal pastoral interventions. Pastors say they want to encourage marriage and help those members who are married make their marriages work but without alienating or making unwelcome those who are not married.

An active "hate the sin, love the sinner" approach is a common one for urban clergy dealing with lifestyle issues. This is especially true for pastors of more fundamentalist faiths, such as evangelicals and Pentecostals, as well as African American and Latino ministers, who do not seem to hesitate to challenge congregants about their lifestyles. In contrast, Catholic priests and white mainline Protestant ministers working in poor neighborhoods seem more likely to accept lifestyle issues as part of the territory in ministry with the urban poor, and they either do not worry much about it or choose to not actively confront congregants. But evangelical, Pentecostal, Latino, and African American pastors are more likely to confront their members. They do not mince words, as Reverend Paul made clear as he related how he counsels unmarried people living together: "I say, 'Well, let's take away the falsehood behind that. You're not married, you're playing house and especially when children are involved. . . . Make it official. Get married. . . . The problem is if you're not married, you're committing fornication, and the Bible says that it is better to marry than to burn. . . . You need to lead by example, because what you're teaching your children is it's ok to be together and not be married. Is this what you want to teach them? . . . It's my job to keep you out of [God's] judgment.' "[2] But these pastors somehow seem to deliver such counsel in a spirit of acceptance and say that people who do not heed their advice are welcome to continue participating in church life. Reverend Manuel calls it "creating an atmosphere of grace." Although the pastors do not condone the behavior or hesitate to let people know what they think or what they believe the Bible teaches, they say people need to make up their own minds.

None of the clergy I interviewed turn people away from church for violations of church standards. Rev. Margarita Romero, a Latina Pentecostal minister of a small active community church serving many poor congregants, believes it "cheapens God" to either condone sin or insist on change: "I don't agree with the sin, and so my thing is to help you get out of whatever your situation is, if that's what you choose to do. . . . I introduce God to people, you're welcome to receive God into your heart, you're welcome to change whatever it is you feel that you need to change in your life, but I'm not here to do the changing for you. That's between you and God, and I don't push it. I don't push it because I believe that cheapens God." Pastors also point out that while the sins of the urban poor may be on more apparent display, in God's eyes this population has no more sinners than more affluent people, who can "hide" their sins better. Father Woods believes it is because poor people have fewer buffers available:

[It's] not necessarily because these things are more prevalent but because the whole experience is much more raw, and you're apt to see people because there are no cushions. I mean, they've got to come ask you for help, or a series of really horrible things happens in their lives, and they need the support, someone to talk to, so they have few options with distancing themselves. Where in the middle-class parish you're much more with sacramental things, prayer things, and you never even have the opportunity to find out what's going on in the personal lives of a lot of these people. Not too many people come to confession. . . . I knew a whole lot more about what was going on in the lives of the poor than I did the rich, and it's just they don't have the buffers available.

Father Woods underscores an important point. Clergy serve as an important resource for the poor in terms of counseling and mental health issues.[3] Middle-class people have access to psychotherapists and other resources and thus have less need for pastors to know details of their personal crises. Middle-class people can more effectively conceal their shortcomings and problems from their pastors. The pastors interviewed reiterate that everyone sins, and thus it is not their place to judge the urban poor, whose lives may not conform to middle-class norms of acceptable church lifestyles.

Outreach

In addition to creating a welcoming environment, the pastors emphasize the importance of outreach in helping mothers in poverty to integrate into congregational life. The churches that seemed most successful in attracting such women engaged in deliberate and time-intensive outreach efforts. Father Woods spoke of a nun in his former parish who for five years walked the streets, knocking on doors to help connect neighborhood residents to the parish: "It was pretty remarkable what she was doing because it wasn't an especially safe place, and she was single-handedly responsible for bringing a couple hundred people into contact with the parish that wouldn't have been otherwise." Both Reverend Roberts and Deacon Ernesto Ortiz, a Latino Pentecostal leading a small congregation, knock on doors, visiting the "unchurched." The amount of time such outreach takes should not be underestimated. Sometimes clergy also have help from other church volunteers (Reverend Roberts's church sends out a team of people to knock on doors on Sunday morning to invite neighborhood residents to church or to pray with them at home during the time of the service), but pastors who engage in such efforts often do a considerable amount of this outreach themselves. Deacon Ortiz manages to spend significant amounts of time going door-to-door and recruiting for his church, despite having a full-time job as a truck driver outside of the ministry. Churches may sponsor festivals or other community "fun" events to introduce neighborhood residents to the church. Reverend Manuel's relatively large, multicultural, mixed-income congregation has experienced a growing number of poor minority congregants in recent years due in part to the extensive outreach of this type that they do in a nearby public housing project. Reverend Romero, whose small and primarily Latino Pentecostal church is located in an impoverished violent neighborhood, described the ways her church seeks to connect with neighborhood residents: "We believe that church and community are as one. That we need to function together. . . . Sometimes we go door-to-door and hand out these cards, and we just say, 'Know your neighbor from the church; if there's ever anything we could do, please call and ask.'" Reverend Romero's church holds block parties for neighborhood residents and organizes yearly beach trips for them.

Door knocking, festivals, trips—these types of efforts to reach neighborhood residents or residents of nearby housing projects are labor and time intensive. More than half of the pastors interviewed do not employ such extensive and deliberate outreach to invite people to church. African American and Latino clergy were more likely to be involved in such outreach; only one white pastor currently did so. Some state they lack the volunteer or pastoral manpower to make such efforts possible. Logistically it is difficult. Sister Mary Jamison, a white Catholic nun, used to knock on doors and conduct intensive church outreach at the beginning of her ministry in the 1970s. Now, she says, no one is home during the day, the neighborhood is too dangerous to go out alone at night, and people in the neighborhood do not open their doors to strangers anyway. Pastors find it discouraging that even with outreach, it is still difficult to attract overwhelmed single mothers to congregational life. Furthermore, clergy note that as pastors, they have many other competing demands on their time and resources. The priests and ministers in this study who do engage in intensive outreach seem to do so in an attempt to genuinely connect with their poor neighbors and address their needs as whole people. They do wish to reach neighborhood residents spiritually, but they appear to view them in their full humanity, desiring to connect with them in community and help to meet some of their needs.

Social Services

As detailed in chapter 2, many churches provide social services, especially those located in poor neighborhoods. Almost all churches studied here provide some type of social services, and those few that do not provide services partner with other churches that do. Church-based social services include food pantries, clothing closets, health services, computer classes, English as a Second Language (ESL) courses, and tutoring and after-school programs, among other things. Although most of the services are provided at or near the churches and are relatively small in scale, one church had developed a large citywide social service ministry that they had incorporated as a nonprofit organization. In addition, pastors provide assistance to the many neighborhood people who call or show up looking for money, help with rent or utility bills, and counsel for personal problems. Neighborhood residents not connected with the church frequently come to them for financial assistance or counseling. Pastors cannot fulfill all of the requests made of them, especially for money. They have good knowledge of places within the city where they can refer people for social services that the church cannot fulfill. Because people often assume that churches will help them, pastors note they sometimes deal with angry people when help is denied.

Churches are more likely to provide money or more extensive help to people who are members of the church. Reverend Manuel explained why he is more likely to provide money to people who are church members as opposed to people who are not. "[People say,] 'I'm really hurting, and I can't pay my bills, and can you help us?' Our first question is, 'Well, do you go to church or not? Are you part of the church? You know, is there a church you're a part of?' We're more apt to help people that are part of our family than we are to help people who we don't know. The reason for that is because I've done that in the past and found they used the money for drugs, or they either got our money and then they got more money from four other churches." Church members are part of the "family," and pastors feel there is more accountability for the money provided. Although the clothes closets and food pantries are open to all, people are more likely to be able to access greater resources from churches if they are congregants.

Important as it is, social service provision does not usually connect neighborhood residents to congregational life, and pastors say most people who use their social services never attend church services. Most of the priests and ministers do not see their social services as a way to connect people to congregational life. There are a few exceptions; Reverend Anderson spoke of people who occasionally find their way to the congregation via first seeking out social services or children's programs. But these instances are the exceptions; for the most part, social service provision does not lead to recipients becoming involved in the church community. The pastors interviewed do not find this a bad thing; they wish to serve the needs in their neighborhoods without proselytizing or expecting recipients to attend church.

Children and Parenting

Urban churches serve poor neighborhoods by providing activities for the neighborhood's children. In studying mothers, I was struck by the finding of some mothers sending their children to church while not themselves attending. However, all the pastors confirmed this as a common occurrence in poor urban areas. Those whose churches provide transportation vans from nearby housing projects report that the vans bring many unaccompanied children. One pastor complained to me about mothers sending children as young as three to church on the van alone (he set an age limit of six to stop this practice). Pastors indicate that in churches, mothers seek a place for their children, a place where children will have activities and possibly meals and other material goods. Reverend Anderson, who estimates the number of unaccompanied children in his church at almost 50 percent, said, "Some mothers are looking for things to do that don't cost anything and a place they can see as safe, and a place that is close to home, and where there may be some material benefit, whether it's food, clothing, recreation." These clergy believe that mothers, even if they do not themselves attend church, value the community and religious education that can be found in churches. Reverend Anderson continued, "I think they're looking for some type of community life, some kind of way of engaging them with other people in a context of not feeling so isolated. . . . There is a group of moms who make sure their kids come on Sundays. . . . 'We're sending you here so you get some more direction . . . to learn a Christian way of life.'" The mothers believe in God and think it is good for their children to go to church, even if they themselves do not attend.

According to Reverend Roberts, although many of the mothers in his neighborhood are themselves young, they feel that they have already made mistakes and life choices that preclude them from church life. However, they want their children to have opportunities for church. "I think they [the mothers] see the value in church, but I think that they're convinced even at a young age that they've missed out on it. And it's not available to them, but 'I want my kids to have that experience. I want them to go to vacation Bible school, and I want them to go to confirmation class. I want that for them.'" Mothers think they have already missed out on church or did not take advantage of what they learned in church, but they think it is important for their children to be there.

Pastors note that churches often provide more programming for children than for their parents, providing more of a reason for children to be there. Children prepare for sacraments such as First Communion, take part in Sunday school classes, or otherwise participate in children's programs. Realistically, those ministering in poor neighborhoods know that sending children off to church alone on Sunday mornings provides mothers a break. For overwhelmed women who have very little free time, the opportunity to unload their children somewhere safe for a few hours is attractive. Pastors contend that it is difficult to attract mothers, even when the children are actively participating. Although the mothers may attend occasionally to see their children in specific events, they are still not interested in church for themselves. Reverend Roberts, who, like Reverend Anderson, estimates the number of unaccompanied children in his church at 50 percent, tries to attract mothers to church through children's activities. He tries to involve individual children once a month in doing something special (such as doing a reading) at the church service so that their mothers might be interested in coming to see them. He related:

I have a brother and sister who are being raised by a single mom, and the young boy, he's in the confirmation program now. He said, "It's so hard trying to get my mother to get up and come to church. I always thought it would be the other way around, and she'd have to push me out, but I'm trying to get her out. But confirmation's Sunday, and she said she'll make sure to be here." And she will, and she'll bring all her family, and they'll be just as proud of him. But I think what they [the mothers] are saying is, "I'm past that now. I'm dead to that; I can't get anything from there, but get my kids help."

Here we see the child trying to get the mother to go to church, reversing the expected scenario. These pastors' impressions and experiences resonate strongly with findings from those mothers I interviewed who feel their lives have taken directions that do not accord with a church lifestyle but still want church for their children.

Pastors believe churches have a big role to play in helping low-income mothers in parenting and, in fact, more of a role than churches are prepared to assume. Reverend Manuel remarked, "I think the biggest challenge is not only how to find ways to minister to the single mom, but how to help them raise their kids. . . . I think single moms really want you to help them raise their kids. . . . I think that's a big challenge—just Sunday school, Sunday morning learning Catechism isn't going to do it." Single mothers especially desire help and male mentors in raising their boys. Some mothers desire mentoring for themselves as well, not just their male children. Reverend Paul wants to set up a mentoring program where older women in the church mentor young single mothers. Rev. Nancy Going wants to start a special program for grandmothers raising young children in a nearby housing project.

In providing support to families, most of the churches in this study offer extracurricular after-school programs for children. Sister Jamison spoke of how the children in her neighborhood had nothing to do after school, lingering in the streets until their parents came home from work at dinnertime to open their locked apartments. She provides after-school tutoring and computer programs at the church so that these children have someplace to go. Other pastors described various after-school clubs, basketball leagues, tutoring, and other church activities geared for children.

Clergy fill the role of advocate and guide when mothers in their congregations need help. Reverend Roberts advocates for children in a variety of situations, including attending parent-teacher conferences with single mothers in his church.

I have on a number of occasions been called by a parent who feels uncomfortable going to the public schools to ask me would I go check on their child, would I go to a parent teacher meeting. . . . I went with one young lady who really wanted me to go with her. And she went, and she just froze at the door. "I just can't face going in there." I said, "Well, you don't have to face it alone; that's why I'm here. So we're gonna lock arms and go in together and sit down and talk." . . . We got through it, and I think she was happy that she had the support. A lot of these young mothers just have had such bad experiences with the school system that they just don't want to deal with it. So we try to help them there, and I think that's a major, major help that we give.

Low-income parents often feel uncomfortable negotiating with schools and other middle-class bureaucracies (Lareau 2003). Pastors can serve as a mediating figure offering support to the women and brokering interactions with schools or other institutions.

In sum, urban churches clearly play a role in helping low-income mothers raise their children. From religious education activities to extracurricular programs to parental support, churches reach out to support families. Most mothers who receive help from churches in child rearing do so without themselves participating in congregational life; they send children alone to church or sign them up for youth summer camps, after-school programs, or basketball leagues at neighborhood churches. More direct parenting support, such as mentoring of mothers or advocating for children in school and other settings, is more available to church members than to other neighborhood residents.

Challenges for Churches in Serving the Urban Poor

In reflecting on what they believe to be the greatest challenges faced by churches in genuinely serving and including poor single mothers as congregants and full members, the pastors interviewed reveal striking commonalities. Although the types of congregations they serve influence their perspectives, common challenges include welcoming the very poor, dealing with pastoral time constraints and lack of resources, battling a comfort-seeking, self-seeking view of religion in churches, and combating the disinclination of many of the urban poor to participate in congregations.

Welcome and Inclusion

Omar McRoberts's (2003) study of a low-income black neighborhood of Boston exposes the fallacy of blanket assumptions that churches in poor urban neighborhoods are dedicated to serving those in their communities. Of the twenty-nine congregations he studied in a densely populated neighborhood, most were composed of people who lived elsewhere and commuted to church. Many of the churches were in the neighborhood for the cheap rent, not to serve the neighborhood residents. On the contrary, the dominant religious interpretation of "the street" held by the majority of congregations was to view it as an "evil other" to be avoided. These churches viewed the surrounding neighborhood as a threat to church values and ordinary life, drawing a thick line between their congregations and the neighborhood and avoiding contact with the neighborhood residents. The neighborhood was perceived as a physically and spiritually dangerous place, while the church was a safe place set apart. "After services, even on the loveliest spring afternoons, congregants moved quickly to cars and church vans to avoid exposure to danger" (83). A few churches engaged neighborhood residents by attempting to "sacralize the street" through aggressive evangelization and door-to-door recruiting, viewing residents solely as potential converts. Even these churches, however, were hampered in their proselytization efforts by their fear of the neighborhood. McRoberts found only one congregation that did not view neighborhood residents as people to be avoided or merely evangelized. "They took the street neither as an inherently evil space nor as a space good only for recruitment. To the contrary, the street was the place where Jesus tested the commitment of the faithful to those poor and vulnerable" (91). McRoberts's groundbreaking research turns common wisdom on its head to show that churches in low-income neighborhoods do not necessarily or even commonly welcome their very marginalized neighbors. Other researchers who have looked at this situation have reached similar conclusions. In R. Drew Smith's (2003) study of public housing project residents, one resident leader noted that a church was right across the street but that it paid little heed to project dwellers. Another study of a public housing project with a low rate of church attendance among residents found that the outreach efforts of nearby churches would more likely reach the working poor, as opposed to the desperately poor (Price 2000).

Most of the pastors I interviewed who served congregations composed of working-class and working-poor members, as well as pastors serving more affluent congregations, expressed concern that churches did not do enough to truly welcome the very poor as members. While they contend that the lack of welcome is generally not malicious, they worry about how people are made to feel unwelcome. They noted instances of cultural and other differences that present problems. For example, when Reverend Manuel's mixed-income and racially and ethnically diverse congregation began to attract more low-income families through active outreach to a nearby housing project, some of the older members became upset by an influx of poor children they considered undisciplined and badly behaved. Reverend Manuel ended up creating a separate children's service; overall he believes that the older parishioners have accepted the outreach and the increased number of low-income families well (although perhaps they now just have less interaction).

Working-class and working-poor congregants may be unhappy when the marginalized urban poor show interest in their congregations. Reverend Roberts expressed frustration with the reaction of some of his members: "One of the ladies in the church, who spent her life in the church, said, 'Reverend, why is it that that's all we can attract? The alcoholics and the drug addicts and the people who just got out of jail? Why can't we go get doctors, and lawyers, and teachers?' So there's a mentality there that that's not what we want." He indicated that some church members look at the very poor and wonder how they will benefit the church: "[People ask,] 'What can they do for us? I mean they can't give us collection. The people are uneducated, so what can they do for us?' It's not what can they do, it's what can we do for them? They [the church members] don't ever think about that. So it's a constant struggle in trying to get people to open their heart, much less the doors. I mean, I can open the doors, I can keep the doors open, but people have to open their hearts."

The very poor are perceived by members of his predominantly African American congregation, which is itself relatively poor, as unwanted in church because they have nothing to offer the church. Church members want "respectable" people to join the church, people with education, people who can contribute to the collection. This lack of welcome can sometimes be expressed in active and overt ways. Reverend Roberts related a distressing event in which an older congregant had chased away from the church some "stereotypically ghetto-dressed youth" from a nearby youth program, whom Reverend Roberts had invited to participate in a church-run computer program. "He had a cane, and he shook it out of the door and said, 'Don't ever come back.' . . . 'But we're here for a computer class.' 'No, it's not for your type!' And they got really upset." Although the pastor went to the youth program to apologize, he was never able again to get youth program members to come back to any church activities. This scene vividly illustrates the outright rejection of the urban poor by some congregants of churches in their midst. A church member shaking a cane at a boy invited to a church computer class by the pastor, telling him that the class is not for "his type" and to never come back—just imagining that scene should raise serious and uncomfortable questions concerning church inclusion of the urban poor.

Ideals of American individualism factor into church attitudes toward the marginalized poor, especially by people just a notch or two up the social ladder from them. Because individual effort is viewed as the determinant of success, the poor are considered to have failed due to lack of effort. This framework extends in religious terms to viewing the failures of the very poor as sin (Hochschild 1995; Bane and Mead 2003). Reverend Roberts sees this clearly in his congregation: "There's the issue [among church members] that we've struggled long and hard, and we've managed to make it, and you haven't, and that's your shame. I think there's a whole idea that there's a sort of element that we want to keep away

from our children. 'We don't want that here.'" Note the emphasis on individual effort leading to success—church members have worked hard to
make it, and those who have not managed to make it should feel *shame*.
These "failures," who should feel ashamed of themselves, are certainly
not those who will be welcomed into church; the congregation does not
want its children coming into contact with their offspring. R. Drew Smith
(2003) found the same sentiment among pastors he interviewed, almost
verbatim. Church members believed they had worked hard to "escape the
ghetto." To build bridges between the churches and nearby housing projects would bring the members' children into more contact with housing
project children. Members feared that this might lead to their children
being influenced by the very things they had worked hard to escape.
Sandra Smith (2007), in addition to noting high levels of distrust and
individualism among low-income African Americans, discusses the desire
to be distanced from the stigma of being black and poor. "Respectable"
people who have struggled hard to make it wish to be distanced from the
stereotypical "ghetto poor," an attitude that carries over into churches.

Fear of crime and cultural barriers also pose problems of welcome
and inclusion. Reverend Paul, in the process of building a new church,
said his congregation of mostly middle- and upper-middle-class African
Americans wants to build on the outskirts of the city, away from crime in
the lower-income neighborhoods. Reverend Going has run into difficulty
trying to get the middle-class mothers in her church to reach out to a
nearby housing program for low-income single mothers to include them
in church activities. One time the church mothers' group did invite housing program mothers to a gathering: "I know one time the [low-income]
women were invited with their children here, and I happened to come
in, and I thought, 'This is the last time they're going to come.' It wasn't
unfriendliness, but there was an awkwardness. . . . I don't think people
were mean; I really believe that folks just don't know how to interact."
She mused, "Sometimes it's hard for me. I'm not going to say, 'Come,
you'll feel at home,' when I can't guarantee they will."

Those clergy who feel that more needs to be done to welcome the
very poor contend that some church leaders and members lack a true
understanding of the Christian gospel. Reverend Keene, whose working-
class and middle-class black Baptist church is located in a poor neighborhood, believes that churches do not "stand with open arms" for people
"whose life is on the rocks." Curious, I pressed him about why this would
be the case. "Well, it is because there is a lack of understanding of the
Gospel. . . . You have your [poor] women that are out there in a community where there are churches, but the ministers are not willing to

take on that challenge." Reverend Roberts spoke of the judgmental and superficial attitudes of some church members in the congregation: "I think that they think in terms of church membership as being something that's prestigious and that it should attract people who want a position in the church and have money to give and so forth." An emphasis on such issues as prestige and potential for collection income precludes churches from reaching out with open arms to the poorest of the poor.

These pastors try to play an educational role in helping those church members who are unwilling to welcome their low-income neighbors. About half of Reverend Anderson's congregation is composed of elderly white working-class people who are longtime members and hold most of the power in the church (about half of whom have moved out of the neighborhood and commute back to church), with the other half of the congregation composed of poorer immigrants and African Americans who live in the immediate neighborhood. He related, "When I first got there they were shunning the neighbors, so I said, 'Why is this? You need to turn this attitude around and throw your doors open and start behaving differently.'" He, like the other two white mainline Protestant ministers interviewed, sees a large part of the problem as the fact that the longer-term church members do not know how to interact with the less advantaged newcomers and need to be educated in hospitality and welcome. "I think one of the impediments is the dynamics between the elders not being trained properly in hospitality in ministries and not looking at it from a biblical or theological perspective." In these situations, pastors believe that the intent is not malicious but that congregants feel awkward interacting with those whose backgrounds differ from theirs.

Reverend Anderson helps poorer, newer congregants in navigating the church. He explains to the newcomers that they should not worry if church elders do not reach out to them or invite them to be on a church committee, and he tries himself to fill the gaps in hospitality. He assists low-income single or immigrant mothers who want to integrate more deeply into the fabric of the church life by helping them navigate the politics of the entrenched older church members. "A low-income mom, a single mom. . . . See all those church ladies, they'll eat you alive." He tells poor mothers, "I'll work with you and make sure you have a mentor, and you can work into the committee life and become a leader in that fashion." He noted to me that "there are certain places where [the newer poorer] moms would be repelled instantly." While Reverend Anderson emphasizes that the older members' intent is not malicious and talks about educating congregants in hospitality, his language seems to indicate otherwise. His talk of church ladies who would eat low-income mothers alive and mention of places in the church community where poor mothers would be instantly rejected—although not as vivid in imagery as cane shaking at the door—still conveys an active unwelcoming among some church members.

Time and resources play a strong role in the ability to reach out to poor mothers, even when pastors or congregations want to be welcoming. Reverend Romero, whose small and active church congregation is comprised mostly of residents of the surrounding impoverished neighborhood, spoke of the very real money constraints facing small churches and the time pressures on their pastors, many of whom also hold full-time jobs outside of ministry. Reverend Roberts, committed as he is to providing outreach in his neighborhood and trying to make his congregation more welcoming, believes many churches just lack the time. "We just don't have time, and, unfortunately, it's not in the top five for most of the pastors' agenda." It is most likely that many churches face dual constraints of time/resources and the more subtle issue of who is welcome.

Self-Serving Religion

Clergy members from both the small, poorer churches and larger, more affluent urban churches criticize what they see as a growing trend toward a self-serving religion. Several pastors saw this development as one of the biggest obstacles to overcome in order for churches to better include the marginalized poor as members and congregants. Reverend Romero commented that many churches and church people see reaching out to include the very poor as some type of option or special ministry that only a few are called to do: "Self-serving Christianity, that you go to church so you can feel better, you know. I need God, and I need to go to church to stay in touch with the Lord, and I just need to be fulfilled. It's all about I, I, I. It's very selfish. It's a self-serving Christianity. . . . The Bible that I read has nothing to do with that. . . . You can't just kneel before God and come and sing and forget the whole world outside. It's unbiblical. That's not what Jesus did."

On the other end of the economic spectrum, Reverend Going voiced much the same criticism: "I think our culture of religion has become self-satisfying instead of reaching out to the poor, you know. Yeah, so people will come to church expecting, you know, to find comfort, to find quiet, to find something for their children, so it's a consumer kind of thing. . . . We are consumers. People will come in, and they are looking for a church as they're looking for a school or a college. 'What do you have to offer?' And so that whole consumer religion, church is a different kind of place."

A consumer model of religion leads to church shopping for the right environment to meet one's spiritual and social needs. More than 40 percent of adults age twenty-one to forty-five who attend services at least once a month, particularly those who are married with children, have shopped for churches or synagogues. Forty-seven percent of those with college degrees have shopped for a place of worship, as have 34 percent of those without college degrees. People shop for a church as they would a product, house, or university, until they find the one that best meets their needs (Wuthnow 2007). Although in theory there is nothing inherently wrong with seeking a religious community that will best provide what people need for themselves and their children, in practice it can become self-seeking and exclusionary of those others who might intrude on one's comfort.

The blame for the distance between churches and the disenfranchised urban poor cannot be laid solely at the feet of the churches, as larger societal issues exist that make the poor less eager or even antagonistic to the idea of participation in churches (Smith 2001). In his interview, Father Gerald Hayes, a Catholic priest with forty years of experience, brought up the multilayered factors he thinks contribute to keeping impoverished single mothers from participating frequently in congregations: a multigenerational cycle of poverty and broken families, addictions, mental health issues, low self-esteem, and teenage motherhood. He astutely pointed out that these women are "not joiners in anything"—PTAs, community organizations, and so forth—so why should one expect that they would participate regularly in organized religion? The lives of women in such situations do not readily lend themselves to joining communal organizations in general, much less churches. This social capital issue is one factor contributing to decreased church participation. Cultural barriers exist between the very poor and churches when church participation is equated with middle-class norms or traditional family forms and churchgoers perceived as hypocritical. Low-income mothers may feel disinclined toward church life, especially if they think they will need to change their lifestyles in order to be accepted as church members (Smith 2001).

The Church in the City

Ministry in poor urban neighborhoods is without a doubt a challenging endeavor. As Reverend Roberts put it, "Most of the time you feel like a social worker. Some of the times you feel like a psychiatric social worker. You're a fund-raiser; you're a custodian. And if you belong to a larger denomination you have responsibilities that you've got to put in place. It's a hard thing to be true to all of that without some kind of cognitive dissonance." I came away from this research with great respect for the difficult work these pastors do.

What kinds of conclusions, then, can we draw from their observations? First, these conversations with clergy who have collectively worked with literally thousands of mothers in poverty over the many years of their ministries serve to substantiate and contextualize key findings from the women interviewed. Some pastors are more likely to see as mere excuses certain logistical challenges that mothers put forth as reasons for non-attendance, but they acknowledge that the overwhelming and difficult lives of these women make regular church attendance difficult. Problems of stigma, welcome, and inclusiveness of very poor single mothers exist in some congregations, and even where no actual problem exists, poor mothers' low self-esteem or internal sense of guilt and shame can cause them to fear such reactions and avoid church. Both longtime, very experienced pastors and mothers in poverty report these findings, lending credence to their veracity.

Some pastors distinguish between recent immigrants and the more established urban poor. They describe recent immigrants as hard working and religious, often embedded in strong family units. Problems in drawing immigrants to church services stem more from logistical constraints due to long work hours in multiple jobs. Within churches, issues arise about language and how to integrate several cultures within congregations. However, immigrants seeking community often desire to be part of church life. "I think for the immigrant women here who come over and work hard and come with family, church and their faith is very much what keeps them here in a place that's not even their home, their country," said Reverend Going, underscoring that problems involved in including recent immigrants in her congregation pales in comparison to involving other nearby impoverished urban residents in church life.[4] Even with the best resources, outreach, and welcoming attitudes, it is still difficult to include women who feel greatly distanced from and uninterested in church life.

The pastors interviewed want a broader audience of clergy to become more aware of the issues involved in doing ministry with low-income urban mothers. One noted, "I'm glad to speak to somebody focusing on that particular group. Because it's an undersold, under-identified group, and there are a lot of folk out there. . . . Seminaries and divinity schools need this kind of material. I mean they come out filled with the word of God and filled with theology, but there's no way to apply any of that." The findings from these pastors indicate the widespread nature of these issues, although they have received relatively little sociological attention.

Sample (1993) claims that "hard-living people" (whom he defines as the homeless, addicts, and so forth) face three options with regard to church. From the affluent middle-class congregation, they can mostly expect only charity. "Virtually none of its members would tolerate their presence. The arctic reception would freeze the most dauntless hard-living heart" (84). He believes conventional, "respectable" churches (perhaps with working-class or working-poor or mixed-income congregations) touch the lives of some but not the majority. Sectlike churches, he claims, have been the most successful in reaching these individuals (such as Deacon Ortiz's small Pentecostal congregation). However, my research indicates that small sectlike churches' stringent moral standards and sometimes strict codes on modes of dress and appearance mean many poor single mothers would not feel welcome. Some pastors interviewed believed that these types of churches, often small and composed of extended family members, are most likely to reject people for lifestyle issues. The experiences of the mothers interviewed dovetail with this observation: Maria, unwelcome to continue attending her church when she began cohabitating; Juliana, deeply moved by a Pentecostal service but unwilling to stop smoking and wearing jewelry, makeup, and pants, as needed to belong. These churches are also often small and unstable, with cycles of starting up, perhaps moving locations, closing down, and starting up new ones, within a short span of time. Furthermore, it was primarily sectlike Pentecostal churches that McRoberts (2003) found to avoid the poor. Isaac Laudarji and Lowell Livezey caution, "When poor people are conspicuously absent from predominantly middle-class churches near their homes, this may not mean that the poor have opted for a Pentecostal or storefront church but rather that they are absent from church altogether" (2000, 88–89).

Findings from these interviews with clergy have analytical limitations. By design, the sample was composed of those who are committed to ministry in poor neighborhoods and the social justice mission of churches. As such, these priests and ministers have considerable experience with low-income neighborhood residents and have thought in depth about the church's obligations to the poor. They were referred to be interviewed because of their commitment to working with the poor in a holistic manner. It is thus a sample more aware of and compassionate toward the problems experienced by poor families than a random sample of pastors in a city. The pastors interviewed are in this work for the long haul. These conversations do not capture the experiences of burned-out pastors fleeing this type of ministry or pastors who are in these locations for the cheap rent but do not care about the concerns of poor neighborhood residents. Nor does this sample include highly fundamentalist ministers who prevent women whose lifestyles they find objectionable from attending their churches.

However, the impressions of these experienced urban ministers lend further credence to the findings from the women interviewed. They confirm major findings from the mothers, extending generalizability. Most important, these pastors help us understand the complexities and challenges involved in their ministry and help us further see why the "everyday religion" of personally religious poor mothers may occur disconnected from regular participation in church life.

EIGHT

Conclusion: Everyday Religion and Mothers in Poverty

To study lived or everyday religion means to enter into the spaces where people live out their faith. Raising children in challenging circumstances, navigating welfare and low-wage work, and combating housing instability—for very poor urban mothers these are the spaces where they live and experience their religion. Looking at religion as "everyday" expands what it means to practice religion. Traditionally sociologists have separated the religious sphere from other spheres of life, studying religion by studying religious congregations, their participants, and their activities (Ammerman 2007). For most of the mothers I studied, religion does not usually occur in a church, because they do not generally attend church or belong to a congregation. Because obstacles exist that can inhibit mothers in severe poverty from participating regularly in organized religion, a traditional focus on churches obscures the ways in which many women practice their faith. Religion instead is woven into the fabric of their daily lives when they try to find housing, contend with their jobs, raise their children well, and seek meaning and hope amid difficult circumstances. Studies of women and religion increasingly pay attention to the lived experiences of women's everyday reality, a particularly valuable perspective when considering mothers in poverty.

Religious institutions are not absent, however, even for

those who never attend services. Case studies conducted among relatively affluent and well-educated, diverse groups who do not participate in organized religion (e.g., American Jews who do not attend synagogues, Europeans distanced from formal church participation, American teens experiencing spirituality in popular media) find that the traditions and culture of society's religious institutions nonetheless still hold influence (Ammerman 2007). People carry with them culture, ideas, and values from religious institutions in which they were raised (even if nominally raised), the religious culture of their families of origin, their environments, and American society more broadly. Religious institutions influence many poor mothers' beliefs and practices, often deeply, even for those distanced from organized religion.

Scholars of lived religion contend that religion can be found in many places; indeed, Ammerman notes, everyday religion can happen in *unpredictable* places. For poor urban mothers this is certainly true. One does not normally think of a welfare office or a housing shelter or a low-wage service job as a site for the practice of religion, unless perhaps the shelter volunteer or welfare office worker views his or her work as practicing a religious act of charity. But for those on the other end, those needing the services of the shelters and welfare offices, these places can be just as much, if not more so, sites of practicing everyday religion. Whereas a traditional understanding of religion would see a church a more likely place for the practice of religion than a fast-food cashier's stand, for the mothers I studied this was not usually the case.

Lived religion is a powerful presence in the everyday experiences of many of the mothers interviewed for this book, coming through clearly in the telling of their stories. Women grapple with integrating beliefs and living them out in daily life, bringing them to bear in shaping the moral narratives through which they construct meaning and take action. The old adage that "there are no atheists in foxholes" might well apply to very poor women who are first and foremost mothers, struggling to raise their children the best they can, often while living in dangerous neighborhoods. These are mothers trying to provide for their children by welfare or unpredictable, stressful, and low-paying jobs and suffering major anxieties related to finding safe affordable housing and child care. To take what these women say about religion seriously, not dismissing it as escapism or denial (Pargament 1997), is to understand a major cultural and material resource they bring to bear in the face of severe hardship. To take what they say about religion seriously is to understand a worldview from which women frame interpretation and action.

Poverty, Religion, and Resilience

This book has attempted to unpack how religion, largely in the absence of church participation, operates in the lives of mothers in poverty. There has been relatively little recent sociological analysis or theorizing about the role religion plays in the lives of the poor.[1] And despite many studies of low-income mothers, there has been little mention of religion. Looking at the integration of religion into daily life allows us to extend sociological theory about why and how faith practices are engaged and lived in the lives of some of our country's most disenfranchised people.

First and foremost, the mothers interviewed engaged in religious practices because they believed in God. They expressed gratitude to God despite their struggles and continued to love and worship God even as their circumstances remained difficult. Women's faith practices were not instrumental; even with parenting, the most instrumental area of religion in daily life for them, mothers genuinely wanted their children to learn about faith and have a religious community. Women did not pray only to obtain desired things or stop praying when prayers went unanswered.[2] Thus, in considering in this book the ways in which religion is engaged both helpfully and sometimes detrimentally by poor mothers, I do not wish to place their religion into a cost-benefit framework. Reducing their lived religion to a scorecard of pluses and minuses does it a huge disservice. My hope in this book is to lay forth the richness and complexity of poor women's faith practices within their lived experiences and particular social environments.

Yet in extending sociological analysis and theory about religion and poverty, it is important to understand the ways in which religion impacts people's lives. This book's analytical framework lays out the ways in which elements of religion—personal beliefs and faith practices as well as organized religion—can serve as both a positive resource and a source of potential distress for mothers in poverty. In distinguishing personal beliefs and faith practices from participation in organized religion, this framework allows for analysis of how religion operates in the lives of those who are distanced from organized religion. This way of analyzing religion is considerably more complex than seeing religion detrimentally as "compensation" for the poor (as in Marx and other older theorists) or as a problem-solving tool (as in some of the rhetoric about faith-infused social services).

Everyday or lived religion manifests itself in two primary ways for urban mothers in poverty. First, women exercise agency by drawing on their religious repertoire in confronting their numerous challenges. Religion—personal faith, cultural religious knowledge, and organized religion—helps many mothers be more resilient in their struggles. Women find faith and spiritual practices to provide them with a sense of strength, perseverance, growth, hope, and ability to act in the world. Faith gave many of my respondents a sense of self-efficacy, lived out in increased personal strength and ability to take needed actions to forge a better life and fueled by a sense of working "together with God." It provided women with hope amid suffering, an active hope that helped them combat depression and despair. Second, religion serves as a powerful cultural interpretive framework for some, guiding and constraining attitudes and actions toward welfare use, working motherhood, child rearing, and work. Marginalized and stigmatized women draw on religious interpretations to try to make sense of their suffering and their identities, a manifestation of everyday religion that was among my respondents both helpful and at times detrimental. In a positive sense, women drew on faith to reframe their suffering in a transformed light that gave them strength. Religion, for some mothers, contributed to a positive reenvisioning of how they viewed themselves in light of how society sees them.[3]

Consistent with prior research, religion was more often drawn on in helpful rather than harmful ways for the mothers interviewed. However, poor women sometimes experienced negative spiritual struggles, such as feeling abandoned by God, likely exacerbating already negative situations (Pargament and Cummings 2010). The internalization of gender role ideologies of conservative churches can produce inner conflict and guilt for poor single mothers who have to work or cause financial hardship by encouraging women not to work. Although supportive congregations play a positive role in women's lives, churches can also be the backdrop for negative incidents and interactions with pastors and other congregants for poor single mothers whose lifestyles may not accord with church norms; negative interactions in churches can increase stress and depression (Ellison et al. 2009).[4] Because one-third of my respondents felt stigmatized or unwelcome in churches, a potentially considerable number of poor single mothers may do so. Women sometimes drew on religious beliefs or ideas to interpret their situations in unhelpful ways. These interpretations compounded their shame and guilt when the women did not meet societal expectations, for instance, with regard to welfare use or motherhood. In conflating societal expectations with the will of God, women fail not only in the eyes of society but also in the eyes of God, giving them additional shame to carry (Griffith 1997).

Religion fostered resilience in the women interviewed in primarily personal ways, helping them in their quest to parent their children well, survive their jobs without getting into confrontations with unpleasant customers and supervisors, and maintain strength and growth amid hardship and setbacks.[5] As single mothers living lives consumed with raising young children, coupled with surviving the desperate struggles associated with severe urban poverty, my respondents focused on day-to-day existence. Unlike studies of low-income people who engage in faith-fueled political activism (Wood 2002; Warren 2001; Rogers 1990; Frederick 2003), the women I studied—extremely poor, almost half of them living in long-term shelters—did not engage in political activism at all. This does not mean, though, that religion serves an "opiate of the masses" function for them, despite the fact that the context shaping their lives—lack of affordable housing, poor-quality urban schools, and so on—warrants social critique and broader action. Some readers, I suspect, will still see the women in this study not primarily as engaging religion in ways that provide strength and perseverance toward goals but instead as blinding them to their miserable realities and enabling the status quo to persist. Although mothers found faith to help them in ways that provided meaning and empowerment, their faith did not provide a framework from which to draw a larger social critique or engage in social action in the ways that community organizers or feminist theorists might hope.[6]

Yet what is an isolated, low-income single mother who needs to support her young children, perhaps living in a shelter, to do? My respondents were overwhelmed dealing with the many hardships and demands of their daily lives. With the lack of other viable alternatives to the types of jobs and housing available to them, the fact that they drew on religious faith in contending with and trying to transcend their circumstances does not indicate religion serves only a role of denial and passivity. The mothers studied were for the most part disconnected from such organizations as churches, unions, or other civic groups. Efforts to effect social change begin in relationships, in community. Studies of disenfranchised people engaging in social action to better their situations show people working through their churches and community organizations. Most of the women I interviewed lacked such ties. It is through relationships and community that people learn to interpret individual interests as common interests and develop the shared resources to address these interests (Ganz 2010). Feminist theologians, social activists, and others who would critique the ways in which the mothers studied drew on their understanding of religious faith to interpret their circumstances and take action must first stop to ask several questions. How are communities being built where these women can participate meaningfully, given the difficult circumstances of their lives? Who is walking in solidarity with and building community with them? How can their narratives of individualism be surprising, given that this narrative runs though almost all parts of our society? Where would they be expected to have perhaps learned other ways of interpreting and reacting to their circumstances, given that countering narratives are not a part of their cultural repertoire (or the cultural repertoire of many Americans)?[7] Frederick's work on the black church is instructive here; she writes that considering religion as a dichotomy between accommodation and resistance does not capture the complexity of the lives of African American religious practitioners (2003, 6). She argues, "Unless agentive value is placed on the labor involved in personal transformation, what is often characterized as 'accommodation' does not take into consideration the work of individuals in forming productive personal lives within oppressive social structures" (213).

With regard to denial, one must also ask why the poor are singled out for accusations of "compensation" or denial of reality when they draw on religion for strength in hard times when wealthier people frequently turn to religion as a source of strength and meaning in hardship. Most of the existing studies on religion, coping, resilience, and meaning have in fact been done on nonpoor people. The affluent frequently draw on religion in dealing with illnesses, losses, addictions, and other hardships, in seeking both a framework for understanding their troubles and spiritual resources to help them get through them.[8] Hope, comfort, understanding—the affluent seek all of these from religion. Yet when the poor do the same thing, their religion can be dismissed as the "opiate of the masses." The mothers interviewed were not blind to their situations. Rather, they drew on faith to help them live with dignity and humanity within their social worlds (Frederick 2003).

This study is a micro analysis of religion in daily lives as lived within severe poverty. A focus on this by no means obscures the need for religion's prophetic voice to be heard. It is troubling to hear some of the theological explanations poor women put forth for their suffering, explanations associated in more affluent religious believers with difficult life events that often cannot be prevented, such as illness, accidents, and bereavement. The suffering of poor mothers could be at least ameliorated by better societal commitment to the poor by means of more affordable safe housing and child care, better schools for their children, and increased opportunities for education, training, and jobs. For low-income single mothers of young children to think they must pull themselves up "alone with God" places an untenable burden on them and their conception of the divine. It also leaves them open to feeling guilty and blaming themselves when they fail against daunting odds. Churches, civil society, and government need to contribute considerably in order to keep the hope engendered by women's religious beliefs from being a false hope. Focusing on everyday religion for mothers in poverty does not negate the need for people of faith to work to bring about changes to social structures shaping the lived experience of such women. Nor does it negate the need for faith-based and community organizations to reach out to women in solidarity and to help get their voices heard on issues affecting them. Putnam and Campbell's (2010) data show that while most Americans believe that equality of opportunity for all does not exist in today's United States, deeply religious white Americans are less likely than their nonreligious counterparts to support government policy to reduce income inequality and combat poverty.[9] Religious Americans are more likely to prefer private charity over changes in government policy and, in fact, do give and volunteer in social service more. Although some religious organizations promote greater government and societal involvement in reducing inequality and poverty, Putnam and Campbell state that unlike the social gospel reformers of the early twentieth century, the current dominant religious response to poverty and inequality has not been one of advocating for greater structural social justice. Evangelical Christianity, highly prominent in American culture and politics in recent decades, most often holds an ethos of individualism that attributes social problems to personal behavior as opposed to stemming from any structural issues.[10]

Individualism, Social Capital, and Moral Communities

A palpable sense of loneliness comes through in the narratives of many of the mothers studied. The women's words reveal a sense of isolation. They say they want to turn to God for guidance because they do not want to share their problems with friends or relatives or do not trust the advice they would receive from them. The women's discourse is highly individualistic. They speak of having to "do it myself" or "make it happen." Many feel they are responsible for dealing with their problems alone "with God's help." The majority of the women interviewed can be described as lacking in social capital. They may, in fact, have less social capital than some other poor single mothers; almost half of them were in long-term shelters, and the majority of them were on welfare, supports that are generally last resorts for those who have nowhere else to turn.

Yet in cities across the United States, there are many women in situations similar to the mothers studied: experiencing major hardships, being personally religious yet distanced from churches, residing in shelters, living on welfare, and lacking other strong sources of social support.

Although forms of personal religiosity such as private prayer, scripture reading, and religious cultural knowledge provide poor women with positive resources for living, those engaging solely in these private practices often remain fundamentally disconnected from a network of social, spiritual, and emotional support. The examples posed by the few mothers in this study involved with supportive churches make clear that women embedded in positive religious communities have greater social capital available than those drawing solely on personal faith.

Increased social capital can be a positive side benefit of participation in a supportive religious organization, but this is not, of course, the primary reason that religious organizations exist. Churches exist first of all for people to come together and worship and experience the divine. In congregations, poor mothers of faith can join together with others in prayer, song, praise, and silence, sharing in communal experiences of religious worship and receiving sacraments (Wuthnow 2004, 66). In liturgical religious traditions, a communal celebration of sacraments is at the very heart of faith. Women who participate in congregations have an opportunity to learn and appreciate more of the riches of their particular religious tradition. They may hear sermons or prayers that might encourage them, and they can deepen their knowledge of beliefs and faith practices. They could gain greater understanding of the symbolic and cultural elements of their faith. These elements (for women in this study, of the Christian faith)—a sense of divine presence and biblical stories of hope and perseverance, suffering and resurrection, and divine love and mercy—can have much to offer struggling and disenfranchised women.

In addition, supportive churches can have much to offer mothers in poverty in terms of social capital. In churches, women can experience practical support from pastors and other congregants, as well as a sense of contributing and belonging. Robert Putnam, in Bowling Alone (2000), claims that religious organizations are the largest producer of social capital in the United States. Pastors and networks of church friends provide support spiritually, emotionally, and materially (Taylor, Chatters, and Levin 2004). Controlling for factors that would influence levels of social capital including personal gregariousness, Robert Wuthnow (2004) concludes that people who are in religious congregations have access to greater levels of social capital and social support than those who are not. Church involvement is associated with less depression, less suicide, greater sense of well-being, greater life satisfaction, and more neighborliness and altruism (Johnson 2002; Putnam and Campbell 2010).[11]

Low-income mothers who are involved in welcoming congregations could come to know other members, including other church members who are not living in extreme poverty, in a variety of capacities. For example, survey data indicate that being involved in evangelical congregations is connected to greater bridging between people of different social classes. Upper-middle-class Americans who are involved in evangelical congregations and who have many friends in their congregations are more likely to report friendships with manual workers or people who have been on welfare than their secular counterparts (Putnam and Campbell 2010).[12] For low-income mothers, increased "vertical" social networks (Newman 1999) with people engaged in jobs and other aspects of mainstream society might help connect them to opportunities. Churches also play an important role in providing disadvantaged individuals with civic skills. Civic skills are the "communications and organizational abilities" that allow people to contribute effectively to political life, such as being able to communicate well and contribute to decisions. Churches are more democratic arenas for exercising civic skills than other arenas, such as the workplace or other organizations, and provide more opportunities than other organizations for the poor to learn and practice civic skills (Verba, Schlozman, and Brady 1995).[13]

Some churches provide poor women with the opportunity to engage in community-organizing efforts to improve their schools and neighborhoods. Churches have long played a prophetic role in American life. Among low-income Americans, congregationally rooted faith-based organizing is second in size only to the labor movement in organizing for justice. More than 3,500 congregations, 133 federations, and other organizations involve at least two million Americans in these types of efforts (Wood 2002). For example, congregations involved with the Industrial Areas Foundation, the Pacific Institute for Community Organization, or one of the other major faith-based organizing federations engage in social change efforts and political action. Nor are these efforts something done "for the poor" by nonpoor outsiders; working through congregations and interfaith social justice alliances, faith-based community organizing involves low-income neighborhood residents in addressing issues affecting their lives.

Supportive congregations serve as moral communities. Coming together around a shared set of "beliefs, understandings, traditions, and norms" (Wuthnow 2004, 65), healthy church communities emphasize values of caring, love, forgiveness, and trust. The shared narratives and beliefs create unique moral communities that draw people together and provide a powerful lens through which people interpret life and take actions.[14] Pastors and members of congregations often use the language of family and belonging when talking about their church communities. Shared values in churches can lead to relationships of reciprocity. Margarita Mooney (2009) argues that people who are materially disadvantaged do not wish to simply be charity recipients but desire to be in reciprocal relationships, in communion with others. When they have become a part of a moral community with others, they can offer help—even if only in the form of prayer— as well as receive it. And when they receive material aid, it is as a part of larger relationships that acknowledge their human dignity as fellow children of God.

Participation in a supportive religious community may diminish the sense of isolation and shame so clearly evident among some of the mothers interviewed. Membership in and contribution to a supportive community of shared values can allow people to understand themselves in relationship to others. Religious communities cultivate a sense of belonging that can prove transformational. "As persons experience the formative values of belonging and contributing, a dynamic process of interaction is taking place that itself alters the self-understanding of participants" (Coffin 2000, 127). The transformative interaction that can take place in a religious congregation can alter and shape self-understanding. In the case of personally religious women who are isolated from religious institutions, a sense of belonging and contribution to a larger and transcendent whole may help alleviate negative self-understanding and self-blame. Mothers who feel accepted by supportive church communities, who belong and contribute to a community of people with shared values and beliefs, may experience transformation from women who are in need to women who belong.

Thus, the paradox of distance from organized religion by highly personally religious poor mothers raises problematic implications. Churches often have a strong presence in low-income neighborhoods, and women in these neighborhoods are often personally religious. Apart from a deepened knowledge of faith and religious tradition that congregational participation provides, participation in a positive religious community works to increase social support and material aid, decrease isolation and depression, perhaps present opportunities for civic skills and community action, and provide a sense of belonging through relationships of reciprocity. Although not all of the poor lack social capital, poor individuals on average have fewer strong social networks and are more likely to live in neighborhoods with diminished resources (Smith 2007; Wilson 1987; Small 2004). It is difficult to think of many other available alternate communities that could fill these roles and meet women's needs with dignity.[15] The specter, then, of poor single mothers who are personally religious but disengaged from congregations "becomes a matter of broader social concern and not just a concern to religious leaders or others who happen to care about religious beliefs" (Wuthnow 2004, 96). Even if one views the women studied as providing just one of many examples of American religious individualism (e.g., Roof 1999; Bellah et al. 1985; Madsen 2009), this religious individualism has different implications. Middle-class people have access to many more resources. Furthermore, even with other communities middle-class people may be part of—through their work, neighborhoods, and children's schools and activities—many see churches as valuable communities that provide unique contributions, especially to the raising of their children. Low-income single mothers have comparatively few resources and fewer alternate supportive institutions in their lives.

Highlighting potential benefits to congregational participation for poor mothers who are personally religious comes with several caveats. First, the likelihood that women will experience increased social capital in welcoming congregations does not mean that churches are a panacea for the problems such women face. Second, I am not suggesting that churches should proselytize in an effort to religiously convert low-income mothers, seeing them only as objectified souls in need of salvation.[16] And, finally, to emphasize the role supportive congregations can play does not dismiss the important reality that everyday religion happens primarily outside of church walls. Even for those involved in churches, engaging their faith as part of parenting or on the job takes place primarily *in* daily life, not Sunday morning.

Churches and Class

Commenting on Martin Luther King Jr.'s well-known statement that 11:00 on Sunday morning is the most racially segregated hour of the week in U.S. Christendom, Gloria Albrecht (2005) writes that the same could be said about economic segregation. "What is much less often noticed or spoken about is that this is also an hour in which income and wealth function to separate U.S. Christians [to] file into different spaces even as they assume they share a common understanding of God" (294). Albrecht asks why American Christians are so comfortable with the idea of economic inequality and the assumption that social class and level of wealth, when shared, create comfortable commonalities and, when they differ, create uncomfortable divides. Sociologists beginning with Marx and Weber have long noted the socioeconomic stratification of religion. This has been articulated in a number of influential earlier studies from H. Richard Neibuhr's (1929) *The Social Sources of Denominationalism* to N. J. Demerath's (1965) *Social Class in American Protestantism*. Although some more recent studies note upward mobility for certain groups such as Catholics and Mormons, greater fluidity in the religious system, and slow trends toward more class convergence, sociologists still concur that the U.S. religious system is stratified by education, income, and occupation. Theology, preference for certain types of liturgical and worship practices, race, and ethnicity have been theorized as explanations.[17] Smith and Faris's (2005) analysis of General Social Survey data from 1983 to 2000 revealed stability in the socioeconomic disparity between religious groups when compared to similar data from 1972 to 1982 analyzed by Roof and McKinney (1987). Jews, Unitarians, Episcopalians, and mainline Presbyterians continue to have the highest socioeconomic status, and Jehovah's Witnesses, black Baptists, Southern Baptists, and Pentecostals occupy the low end.

A considerable number of the low-income single mothers I interviewed seemed to associate church participation with various middle-class lifestyle norms—including women from those denominations traditionally composed of members of lower socioeconomic status. These mothers who attached markers of middle-class mores to church participation believed in the same God as the churchgoers who they saw as separate from them. They engaged in similar faith practices, such as prayer or reading sacred texts. They had similar hopes to pass faith on to their children and wished for their children to have religious communities. Yet the sense of separation from a "church lifestyle" pervaded.

A key question, then, for churches to ask is: How do they see the disenfranchised poor—as charity recipients or fellow congregants? Evidence suggests that many churches in poor neighborhoods are more likely to see the urban poor as charity recipients than congregants or even see them as people to be avoided (Laudarji and Livezey 2000; Price 2000; McRoberts 2003). Even not-so-comfortable congregations comprised of the working poor may distinguish between respectable church members and the marginalized poor who cannot dress well or contribute to the collection. Most religious organizations and churches that provide aid in impoverished neighborhoods do so without regard to people's religious beliefs and do not put forth church participation as a condition for receiving aid, which I believe is a good thing. But it is problematic when church openness to the poor stops at charity. Churches provide good and needed services when engaging in charitable outreach, and their social service activity is necessary and important. However, being an occasional or even frequent charity recipient marks a completely different relationship with a church than being a member of the congregation. Charitable programs help meet basic needs for food or clothing, but they do not bring people into community (Laudarji and Livezey 2000; Smith 2001).

Sociologist Christopher Winship (2002), in his preface to the English edition of *The Poor Are the Church: A Conversation with Fr. Joseph Wresinski*, points to a radical way of understanding poverty. The founder of the Fourth World Movement, Wresinski argues that if religious believers fail to be united to the poor, they fail in relationship to God; church that is not in communion with the poor is not truly church.[18] Winship claims that seeing the poor as victims of either moral deficiency or structural injustice leads to seeing them as "other." Seeing them as morally deficient leads to charity and a sense of moral superiority; seeing them as victims of social injustice leads to seeing other people, not ourselves, as responsible for them. Expounding on Wresinski's argument further, Winship writes that only by understanding that the poor "are our moral equals and by embracing them as full members of society—neighbors, friends—can we possibly begin to deal with the problem of extreme poverty" (xii) This argument "calls us to understand poverty in a profoundly different way, not just as destitution and oppression but as social isolation. This isolation is created by us all to the degree that we live apart from the poor and fail to understand that their fate is ours" (xiii). This argument suggests that the fact that churches are more likely to view the poor as charity recipients rather than as equal members matters not primarily because church participation could help meet poor people's needs through increased social support, although that is certainly an important and positive side benefit. Rather, it matters because the poor are our brothers and sisters in the human family and, for religious believers, our brothers and sisters in faith, equal in the eyes of God.

Income inequality has dramatically increased in recent decades, as has income-based residential segregation. The social divide between socioeconomic classes has grown, with less intermarriage between people of different educational levels and fewer people of widely different educational levels working together (Putnam and Campbell 2010). The civic and fraternal organizations that once brought people of different social classes together have greatly declined (Skocpol 2003). All of these trends mean that many better-off Americans have very little contact with the poor. Relatively few social institutions have the potential to function as communities where the poor and nonpoor can interact and come to share in each others' lives on equal ground. Theologian Vincent Miller (2009) describes the few options available to meet the low-income immigrants living in his city—for example, they clean his office, he could go to their restaurants to be served as a customer, and so forth. His Catholic parish, he states, is the one place where he and they meet on equal footing and has consequently been the only place where friendships have developed. Of course, residential economic segregation means that many churches in affluent suburbs will have homogenous congregations. Variations in theology, worship style preference, race, and ethnicity also influence the socioeconomic composition of denominations and congregations. But in some types of religious contexts, congregations (such as Miller's Catholic parish or the evangelical congregations studied by Putnam and Campbell) provide perhaps one of the best possibilities for people from diverse economic backgrounds to come together on equal ground as members of a shared community.[19]

Implications

The findings of this research have practical implications across several arenas. In the following pages, I consider some of the implications of this book's findings for churches, policy makers, and social service and community workers.

Implications for Churches

Take the case of Rebecca, a white mother introduced earlier in the book who practically calls out for the sense of belonging and social capital she wishes she could find in a church congregation. Rebecca says she feels "guilt, disgust, remorse" over not working. She prays and reads the Bible nightly with her young daughters in order to teach them faith. She also brings her daughters to Mass at a local Catholic parish about half the year (only when the weather is good because they do not have transportation and have to walk). Feeling ashamed because of not supporting her family, Rebecca interacts with no one when she attends church, including the pastor. Her social isolation and her longing for community that a congregation could provide are apparent in her words.

I grew up without a family. My parents divorced when I was little, and we didn't have any family. So I have no family whatsoever. If you don't have any family and if you've been a transient, [you've] lived here, you've lived there, and you've lived in a shelter, then it's very hard to sustain normal relationships if you don't have normal outlets.

I see some people that they're very close with their church. They know everybody in their church, and if they need someone to babysit their kids sometime, they trust a church member. It's not necessarily their family, but their community. I've never had that. . . . A friend of mine, you know, she goes to church. She has a job. A lot of things have gone wrong, and she's had a lot of different church members that she trusts to watch her children.

Rebecca is personally quite religious. As a single mother who has no family and who has been a transient living in shelters, she longs for deep relationships and a sense of community. Rebecca's sense of isolation, guilt, and self-blame is palpable. Although she is actually more involved with organized religion than most of the other women I studied, Rebecca essentially practices isolated religion.

Surely there must be ways to better connect churches with the many Rebeccas in cities across the United States. Other church members could offer her a ride when the weather is bad. The church could invite her and her children to participate in some children's activities, because she is so eager to give her children religious faith and training. A concerned pastor could possibly connect her to a job-training program and encourage her to persist. Most important, church members could somehow make her feel welcome as a full and equal member. The sense of belonging to, contributing to, and participating in a supportive religious community could perhaps reduce her sense of isolation and self-blame.

Rebecca remains at least connected to church. There are many other low-income urban mothers not at all associated with churches, despite very high levels of personal religious beliefs and practices. Some of their stories have been told in this book. Vicky feels stigmatized and unwelcome in church as a single mother. Peggy left organized religion when her close-knit church became "controlling" and was unsupportive during her divorce. LaToya feels guilty over going to jail for selling drugs and stays away from church. Maria is not welcome at her church because she is living with her boyfriend. Aletta stopped church participation after facing a housing disruption and moving to a shelter. These are all women with extremely high levels of personal religiosity, women who pray several times a day, women who read the Bible frequently, and women whose religious faith infuses their daily life activities. They are all also women with tremendous needs that could in part be met by participation in a welcoming congregation.

Churches should certainly not take the full blame for whatever gap exists between churches and very poor urban residents. Low-income urban families do participate regularly in organized religion, and the cultural barriers that limit participation exist both ways (Smith 2001). With that caveat, I believe more churches could develop better approaches to help mothers in poverty to participate more in congregational life. Working within the limitations of staffing and funding, some pastors try hard to integrate the poorest in their communities into their congregations, and some succeed. But drawing on my interviews with mothers and pastors, I would argue that much room exists for churches to strategize and better welcome poor women. Although I am aware that some churches already employ many of the following suggestions, I present some recommendations here.

Basic church outreach that informs low-income neighborhood residents when church services and activities take place and invites them to participate would be a useful first step. Most churches do not seem to be doing a good job publicizing their activities to those who reside in their neighborhoods; a 2003 survey of more than twelve hundred public housing residents found that two-thirds had not been contacted in the previous year by any church to invite them to participate (R. D. Smith 2003). In particular, women moving to long-term shelters or public housing projects in new neighborhoods would probably be more likely to attend a church if they were invited to do so. Some mothers moving into long-term shelters or public housing projects leave behind vibrant church communities where they have been deeply involved. Feeling dislocated, most do not seek out churches in their new locations when the old church is too far to continue attending. Such women would likely be receptive to invitations from churches in their new neighborhoods. As suggested by my respondent Brenda, women who are personally religious but disconnected from churches would also likely be receptive to spiritual support groups or Bible studies in shelters and other locations where women live or gather. Providing transportation to churches can also help poor mothers participate more in congregational life. Either church vans or individual church members offering rides could help enable women to attend. Provision of child care during services would make it easier for single mothers of young children to participate. The fact that so many mothers are interested in involving their children in churches suggests that programs for children help connect churches with poor urban families, although pastors caution that it is still difficult to attract the mothers. Community family-fun events, such as the festivals and outings described by some of the pastors interviewed, also provide opportunities to connect churches more deeply with low-income families of their neighborhoods or nearby public housing projects.

To be sure, churches need to be careful about their motivations for engaging in outreach. Efforts conducted merely in order to proselytize, garner converts, and try to "save souls" in the inner city are unlikely to be effective. Outreach needs to be holistic, with churches willing to engage neighborhood residents on their own terms (McRoberts 2003). Churches should reach out by seeing their poor neighbors as whole people with complex needs, not as prospective converts in need of soul saving. When women do attend services, pastors and congregants should be aware that stresses in poor women's lives can make it challenging enough to get to church and participate. Their attendance is thus likely to be additionally discouraged by perceptions of criticism and other negative interactions at church. Churches need to be mindful and attentive to pastoral and congregational strategies to reduce negative interactions at churches for vulnerable women.

Different types of urban churches face different challenges with regard to reaching out to their neighbors living in severe poverty. Small churches comprised almost exclusively of low-income members, such as Reverend Romero's Pentecostal church, may not necessarily face problems of welcome and inclusion (although some still do), but they do face resource constraints and are served by pastors for whom ministry may be a second vocation outside of a regular full-time job. Although the very poor may feel at home worshipping in such communities, the lack of resources and cross-class interaction can keep such religious communities from being as effective as they could be.[20] The majority of congregations located in the poorest neighborhoods, however, are not predominantly comprised of members who are poor (Foley, McCarthy, and Chaves 2001). Nonpoor congregations in poor neighborhoods have resources, yet they may face challenges around issues of welcome and inclusion. One strong model of a congregation would be one that both is welcoming *and* has substantial programs and resources and includes both low-income members *and* those with access to greater resources who might draw the poor into greater networks of "vertical" or "bridging" social capital. An example of such a congregation noted by some of the other pastors interviewed (as well as the church's own pastor) was a large nearby Catholic parish with extensive services and programs; it attracted a good mix of poor neighborhood residents and wealthier commuter congregants. Several larger Protestant congregations in the study also seemed to be finding a good balance of inclusiveness and access to resources. And even with quite limited resources, a small church such as Reverend Romero's is engaged in alliances with other religious and civic organizations.

Predominantly nonpoor urban congregations attempting to become more inclusive and economically diverse would need to attend sensitively to issues of cultural awareness and wrestle with (perceived or valid) issues of churches as repositories of middle-class norms and culture. As several pastors noted in their interviews, involving the poor in their more middle-class congregations led to some awkward situations where people did not know how to interact with each other. Because economic residential segregation has become more pronounced in recent decades, people of widely differing socioeconomic classes are less likely to interact on a personal level (Putnam and Campbell 2010). Pastors spoke of the need to educate their congregants and, specifically, to educate them in hospitality.

Separation from their poorer neighbors is detrimental to more affluent congregations. A vision of churches providing social services to "others" who do not feel welcome or able to worship among them is surely a limited vision. Exclusive churches offering spiritual solace and mutual support among members engender a narrow vision of community. A comfort-seeking model of religion focused on one's own needs does not lead to engagement with others who may be different. Rather than functioning as bodies of like-minded and similarly situated individuals, churches open to welcoming their poor neighbors expand their concept of community and gain more understanding and solidarity with the poor (Smith 2001). As Theda Skocpol (2000) notes, "In a democratic society, fragmentary efforts to 'do for' the poor by the privileged can never be a full substitute for all of the children of God associating—'doing together'—as they struggle to move toward the promised land of a just and loving community, and a more complete democracy" (47).

Beyond better outreach and inclusion in community, more churches could also deliberately decide to better support members who are low-income mothers, either on or transitioning off welfare, across various facets of their lives. For example, a perception that some churches do not approve of working mothers can contribute to a sense of social distance from churches by low-income women who are expected by society to work. If women are to be aided by churches in their transition from welfare to work or persistence in the workforce, they must believe that religion supports them as working mothers. The perception (rightly or wrongly held) that churches do not want mothers of young children to work hinders churches' ability to play a supportive role. Churches and other religious organizations need to help women navigate the competing ideological and practical demands of commitment to both parenting and providing; women must see how religion supports them in their roles both as mothers *and* as workers. Church-based practical supports, such as help with child care and job searches, are important. Some churches do offer such programs, including welfare-to-work mentoring and assistance with job searches.

Occasional citywide meetings among religious leaders could help clergy strategize about better reaching the poor. Poor community-oriented churches that do an excellent job in holistically reaching out to and including neighborhood residents could benefit from connections with wealthier churches. Wealthier and working-class churches, in turn, could be challenged about notions of exclusive community. Involving more clergy in interfaith community-organizing alliances could more deeply engage clergy on issues of public policy affecting low-income city residents (R. D. Smith 2003).[21]

Several problems arise in consideration of how more churches can better reach poor single mothers and their children. One is capacity. Churches, which are spread thin already, may lack resources to provide outreach activities or transportation. Helping more low-income, overwhelmed single mothers become involved in church communities is difficult and takes substantial time and energy; pastors and congregations contend with many other competing responsibilities. Another problem is motivation on the part of the churches, as churches do not necessarily perceive a lack of community with the poor as a problem. McRoberts (2003) questions the extent to which inner-city churches want to deal with the urban poor and their problems. My study highlighted clergy members who all desire to serve and include the urban poor, yet even some of this highly committed group experienced problems with church members preferring a more exclusive brand of religion. Such pastors may face an uphill battle with their congregants. Among the key challenges to building bridges between congregations in poor neighborhoods and neighborhood residents is the reluctance by some church leaders to acknowledge their "personal and organizational disconnection" from the poor (R. D. Smith 2003, 30).

In addition to the very real challenges posed by lack of time, resources, and willingness of some church members and leaders to reach out to the very poor, churches also must contend with challenges posed by modern American culture. A rising individualism leads to people seeking comfort and self-satisfaction in their churches when they seek out churches. A consumer orientation leads to people shopping for churches that will meet their own needs, not challenge them to look beyond church doors. Churches must contend with how a general breakdown in community and decline in social capital and trust has deeply affected poor urban neighborhoods.

My findings of a distance between churches and impoverished urban residents further develop those of the other few studies on this topic conducted in other cities in the Northeast and Midwest (R. D. Smith 2001, 2003; McRoberts 2003; Laudarji and Livezey 2000; Price 2000) There are certainly many notable exceptions of churches actively working to bridge the distance.[22] Several of the mothers in this study were deeply involved in congregations that supported them and embraced them fully as members; several of the pastors vigorously reached out to include low-income single mothers in their congregations. It appears, however, that much remains to be done. If congregations are to fulfill the religious imperative to seek solidarity with the poor, more must find ways to better include the many religiously motivated low-income mothers living among them.

Implications for Public Policy

Whatever the causal mechanisms behind and possible solutions to the distance between churches and poor urban residents, the situation raises questions for public policy. Much of the policy debate has centered on the willingness and capacity of churches to provide social services and the constitutionality of partnering with government. These debates sidestep a central question of how churches should engage the urban poor. Furthermore, some women feel uncomfortable receiving social services from churches to which they do not belong, leading them to avoid church-based social services if they do not participate in church. Thus, in addition to contributing new scholarship in the sociology of religion and urban poverty, this study raises thought-provoking questions about the role of churches in dealing with the problems of the poor. Post-welfare-reform government policy views churches and faith-based organizations as having a key role in aiding the poor. In this view, churches and religious organizations can integrate people in poverty into a community and provide them with necessary social services and support.

Although policy makers view churches as ideally situated to aid low-income individuals, church-based efforts are less likely to be fruitful if the very poor have limited levels of participation in the actual church communities. Physical presence in a neighborhood does not mean that churches incorporate neighborhood residents into their congregation, partly because many churches do not hold a geographical conception of community (Smith 2001). Churches would be more effective in providing social services in a neighborhood—to church members and nonmembers alike—if the churches are known as warm and welcoming congregations to neighborhood residents. Policy initiatives promoting church-based solutions to the problems of the poor must first acknowledge a gap between churches and the disenfranchised urban poor.[23]

Mothers seem well aware of a gap between churches and residents of low-income neighborhoods, leading many to be suspicious of policy initiatives increasing churches' role in social service provision. While praising the good that churches already do, they also exhibit strong reservations about the capacity of churches to greatly increase their social service provision. More than 90 percent of the women I studied believe the government should have primary responsibility for helping those in need, as opposed to churches. Eleanor, a white nonpracticing Catholic, said, "The church does enough. It shouldn't even have to do any more than it does. The government should do more." Even women who think churches have "more heart" than other service providers express concern about the capacity of churches to provide more than very short-term assistance. Vicky said that churches are more tied into the community. "However, I think that they [churches] do what they can do, but they have a lot of limitations as far as funds and raising money. . . . Every church I know helps people with food banks, clothing drives, or things like that. I think they do a lot, and I think the government should be doing more."

About a quarter of respondents thought government funding of church-based social services is a good idea, because they feel churches are more compassionate and better able to help people. Lindsay believed that government funding of church social services is an excellent idea. "The churches, the pastor, could help you more. Their ideas of helping single moms are just terrific. They can help you. It's just perfect." Liz said, "They [the government] has all of this money, and they seem to not know what to do with it. I think they should give it to churches to help out people who really need it. . . . They [churches] are nicer about things, I think. They're more compassionate. . . . They're there for needy people."

But for others, concerns about inclusion and accountability override the potential for churches to provide more compassionate, humane, and effective assistance. Indeed, the majority viewed government funding of church-based social services with some suspicion. Even those who are frequent church attendees worry about the possibility of discrimination in the provision of services and church accountability. Isabella (who attends weekly) feared that those who do not attend church will be left out. "A lot of people don't go to the church, so nobody knows about the programs in the church." Rhonda (who attends monthly) echoed, "There's people who don't have a church home . . . so what happens to those people? The services wouldn't be spread among the people equally. . . . The church wouldn't send out a community-organizing group to send flyers so everyone knows that services are available to all the families in the area. . . . Both the services or money would go to the church members or to the church owners." Vicky related, "If people don't believe in God, they're not comfortable going to a church and asking for help." Women not involved in churches fear they will be left out, but those who are involved in churches also note that others will be left out.

Women bring up concerns about church accountability for funds. Said Rhonda: "My pastor and his wife drive very luxury cars. . . . Can you imagine what they would be driving if the government gave them all this money? They can fudge paperwork like you cannot believe. . . . All their family members would probably be driving around in Rolls Royces." Other mothers voice fears about churches using government social service money to fix up church buildings or to pay church salaries. Mothers in poverty thus worry that government funding of church-based social services might exclude people who do not feel comfortable with churches, and they worry about churches' financial accountability for government money. They express concern about the churches' capacity to provide more services. While they state that churches are often more compassionate, humane, and helpful than government agencies and gratefully note the good that many churches already do, poor women do not see increased government-funded church-based social services as a panacea for social problems.

In any case, most research on churches and the urban poor has focused on the issue of service provision, particularly in light of policy initiatives on faith-based social services. The question of participation in churches by the very poor is a fundamental one that is lost among the prevalent discussions of faith-based social services. Although important, issues of church capacity and willingness to provide social services, whether churches provide assistance that is more personal, holistic, or effective than government services, and issues of constitutionality of church-government partnerships, obscure this basic consideration. Rather than assuming church is a haven for the poor, policy makers need to acknowledge and be more explicit about the implications of a gap between churches and a considerable number of the urban poor.

Implications for Social Service and Community Workers

This study also raises implications for community-based workers, such as social workers, mental health counselors, teachers, and others. Religion matters. The field of social work is increasingly paying more attention to religion; the findings of this book reiterate that religion is indeed something to be paid attention to. Understanding women's motivations, interpretations, and cultural maps enables a more sensitive and informed interaction. Understanding the resources women draw on for sources of strength can help community workers better support their clients.

In talking in depth with women about religion and other sensitive areas of their lives, I had the privilege of hearing things that a busy social worker with a large caseload might not hear. Only the most religious of poor mothers might state outright that they are working "in partnership with God" or that they see the government social worker as God's instrument, yet my findings indicate that a surprising number of women may hold such beliefs. Religion may be affecting a client's job search if she holds conservative religious beliefs that it is God's will for her to be home caring for her small children; she may never share this information with a welfare caseworker. People working in human services should be sensitized to the ways in which religious beliefs and culture may be impacting their clients' motivations and actions.

Social services workers should be aware of potential religious resources their clients possess so that they can draw from and build on their cultural competencies and strengths. For example, one study of welfare-to-work programs found that women who were "highly religiously involved" (defined as at least weekly service attendance) were more likely to move successfully from welfare to full-time employment at ten dollars or more an hour by twelve months later (Monsma and Soper 2006, 154–55).[24] Although this proves nothing causal (because women with the capacity to participate in congregational life may also be those with the skills that enable them to move from welfare to sustained participation in the labor force), it provides food for thought. Without violating separation of church and state, welfare office workers may be able to indicate to clients they know to be personally religious which local churches, synagogues, or mosques offer supportive environments and services.

Those involved in providing mental health services to low-income urban mothers should remember to be mindful of the role religion can play in helping women deal with their anxiety and depression. Mental health providers who hold lingering negative biases about religion, possibly seeing religion as denial of reality or worse, should realize that religion can serve as a positive mental health resource that promotes a sense of self-efficacy. Other community-based professionals need to be aware of the role religion might play in women's lives, even women who never attend church or do not seem overtly "religious."

Everyday Religion and Mothers in Poverty

Future research on the topic of poverty and lived religion should consider differences between urban and rural poverty, as well as regional differences in the country, especially between the urban North and the South. Religious traditions outside the Christian faith need to be considered. A large sample could help further tease out differences among racial and ethnic groups and religions and denominations. Men must be considered, both in terms of how religion enters into women's dealings with the men in their lives and the role of religion in the lives of low-income men.

Listening to the vivid and intense religious language and imagery used by the mothers interviewed underscores the need for more theological attention to be paid to how mothers in poverty understand and construct theology. Their prayer narratives, their God imagery, their conceptions of Jesus, and the religious symbolism they adopt all point to the fact that the words and religious worlds of these poor and marginalized American women serve as a source for a theology "from below." How do mothers in poverty "do theology"?

Despite the need for further research, my findings provide a significant window of insight into an understudied and important area. Although I do not claim that the voices of the mothers in this book reflect the reality of all poor mothers, they are voices that need to be heard. This study makes clear that whether or not they are involved in churches, many mothers in poverty command a rich religious repertoire manifested in their daily lives. Religion is lived, often deeply and profoundly, in areas where one might not think to look: in the welfare office, behind the fast-food counter, in the family shelter. To expand an understanding of religion to a focus on the faith practices and beliefs found in everyday living is the only way to understand religion as experienced by those who hold deep faith but are distanced from organized religion. These mothers are among the poorest of the poor in contemporary American society, struggling to survive and raise their children in difficult and dangerous environments. By attending seriously to their experiences, scholars can more profoundly understand lived religion and its implications. I hope this account will also be helpful to religious leaders, community workers, activists, scholars, members of congregations, policy makers, and others in walking with mothers in poverty and working together toward a fuller human community and a more just society.

Appendix A: Background Information for Study Participants Interviewed

Adrienne. Age twenty-one. Single. White. One child age three. Raised Catholic and attended Catholic school through eighth grade. Now attends only on holidays but sends her son to Mass weekly with her mother. Studying for her GED and participating in a job training program.

Aletta. Age twenty-two. Mixed-race black/Hispanic. Married. Three children ages five, three, and one. Seventh-Day Adventist (but stopped twice-weekly attendance on moving to a shelter). On welfare, living in a family shelter.

Ann Marie. Age twenty-four. White. Single. One child age three and pregnant with another. Catholic who rarely attends Mass. On welfare, living with her children's father.

Annie. Age nineteen. White. Single. One child age eight months. Nonattending Catholic. In a program to obtain her GED.

Brenda. Age twenty-one. White. Single. One child age three. Raised nominally Catholic, does not attend Mass. On welfare, in a job training program, and living in a family shelter.

Carrie. Age thirty-five. White. Separated, getting divorced. Two children ages six months and eleven. Nonattending Catholic. Receiving Supplemental Security Income and living in a family shelter.

Claire. Age twenty-eight. White. Single. One child age eighteen months. Raised Catholic, now attends a Baptist church once or twice a month. On welfare, living in a family shelter.

Eleanor. Age nineteen. White. Single. One child age one. Nonattending Catholic. On welfare, living with her mother.

Elisa. Age twenty-three. Hispanic. Single. Three children ages three, two, and four months. Nonattending Pentecostal. On welfare, living in a family shelter, and participating in a job training program.

Gabriella. Age seventeen. Hispanic. Single. One child age one. Raised Pentecostal, stopped attending her Pentecostal church at age eleven. On welfare, studying for her GED, and living with her mother.

Gwen. Age twenty-two. White. Single. One child age five. Raised Catholic but does not practice; says all organized religion is hypocritical. Participating in a job training program.

Isabella. Age twenty-seven. Hispanic. Single. Two children ages two and five. Catholic. Attends Mass weekly as part of a promise she says she made to God when her daughter recovered from an asthma-related coma. On welfare, living in a family shelter.

Jamila. Age twenty-eight. Black. Single. Two children ages five and seven months. Raised Catholic (graduated from Catholic school); now attends Mass occasionally with her mother. Sends her daughter to Mass every week with her mother. On welfare, living in a family shelter.

Jane. Age forty. White. Married. Four children ages fifteen, twelve, eleven, and three. Devout born-again evangelical Christian who stopped attending church services when her family became homeless. Receiving Supplemental Security Income and living in a family shelter.

Jennifer. Age twenty. White. Single. One child age seventeen months. Raised Catholic, now attends only on holidays. On welfare, in a job training program.

Juliana. Age twenty. Hispanic. Single. Two children ages one and two. Did not grow up in church and now attends a Pentecostal church about once a year as a guest of her boyfriend's mother. On welfare, living in a family shelter.

LaToya. Age thirty-five. Black. Single. Seven children ages six weeks to thirteen years old. (Currently only the baby is living with her; the others are being cared for by relatives). Baptist, not currently attending services. Formerly imprisoned for selling drugs. Not working, living in a family shelter.

Lenora. Age twenty-two. Hispanic. Single. One child almost two years old. Occasionally attends an evangelical church. On welfare, living in a family shelter.

Lindsay. Age twenty-three. Black. Single. Three children ages three, five, and seven. Attends a black Protestant church every week with her children. On welfare, living in a family shelter.

Lisa. Age thirty. White. Single. Two children, ages one and six. Nonattending Catholic. On welfare, participating in a job training program.

Liz. Age twenty-one. White. Single. One child age six months. Raised Catholic; attends only on holidays now. On welfare.

Magda. Age twenty-two. Mixed-race black/white. Single. One child age sixteen months. Episcopal but nonattending. On welfare, living in a family shelter.

Maggie. Age thirty-two. White. Single. Two children ages ten and three. Catholic; attends Mass several times a week. Attends weekly Bible study at church. Not working, receiving Supplemental Security Income.

Maria. Age twenty-four. Hispanic. Single. Three children ages three, two, and six months. Highly religious Pentecostal who stopped her previously frequent church involvement after she began cohabitating with the father of her children. Living in a family shelter.

Maribel. Age thirty-five. Hispanic. Single. Three children ages two, nine, and seventeen. Raised nominally Catholic; does not attend. Went on welfare after a fifteen-year career with the government ended when she lost her job after the computer system was upgraded. Living in a family shelter.

Marilyn. Age thirty-two. White. Single. One child age three. Raised Catholic; not practicing. Working as a union painter.

Martina. Age forty-three. Hispanic. Single. One child age eleven removed by child protective services. Working at a self-service laundry.

Peggy. Age forty-three. White. Divorced. Two children ages five and fifteen. Devout evangelical who stopped her previously frequent church attendance when she got divorced. On welfare.

Rebecca. Age thirty-four. White. Separated from her abusive husband. Two children ages nine and three. Catholic; attends Mass (with her children) about half the year, when the weather is nice (they have to walk). On Supplemental Security Income and not working. In a day treatment program for severe clinical depression.

Rhonda. Age twenty-nine. African American. Single. One child age five. Attends Baptist services about once a month. Employed as a human services worker.

Rosalyn. Age twenty-eight. Mixed-race black/Hispanic. Single. One child age four. Nonattending Catholic. On welfare, working part-time as a hotel housekeeper, and living in a family shelter.

Sally. Age twenty-nine. Mixed-race black/white. Single. One child age six. Catholic. Not attending Mass. Social service worker.

Sarah. Age thirty-one. Black. Single. One child age three. Nonattending Pentecostal, although she sends her daughter regularly with her sister. On welfare, in a job training program.

Shantelle. Age thirty-eight. African American. Single. Seven children (three children ages five, seven, and nine, and four older children). Domestic violence survivor and homeless for ten years. Protestant (raised Pentecostal); rarely attends. On welfare, living in a family shelter.

Sheila. Age twenty-one. African American. Single. One child age two. Neither raised with nor currently practices organized religion. On welfare, in a job training program, and taking community college classes.

Tamika. Age twenty-six. African American. Single. Two children ages nine and one. Neither raised with nor involved in organized religion. On Supplemental Security Income, receiving child support, and participating in a job-training program.

Vicky. Age thirty-four. Native American. Divorced. One child age four. Nonattending Catholic. Recovering alcoholic and drug addict. Attending college full-time.

Appendix B: Methodology

I recruited mothers from long-term family shelters (five transitional living facilities that also provided other services, such as housing search assistance, job training and search assistance, GED, and child care), non-live-in welfare-to-work job training and job search assistance programs (two programs), and other social service agencies (three agencies). Women had to have at least one child under six and be currently on or have recently transitioned off welfare. Given the difficulty in gaining access to social service programs, it was not possible to set up a perfect balance of race/ethnicity and religious background in the study, but I did obtain a sample of diverse racial, ethnic, and religious backgrounds.

It took a substantial amount of effort to find appropriate social service programs and gain access. In beginning this research, I assumed that because I planned to compensate people twenty-five dollars for their participation, I would easily find low-income mothers wanting to be interviewed. The difficulty lay mostly in gaining access to social service facilities, because once I was "in," eligible women wanted to do the study. Getting in, however, was not easy. I finally gained access to a group of three affiliated government transitional housing facilities through an aunt who knew the social workers there. With the help of an able research assistant, I was able to then gain access to a number of other social service programs throughout the city. After gaining access to an agency, I advertised for participants by putting up posters and by asking agency staff to let others know about the study.

I emphasized that women did not need to be religious to participate in the study and that I was there as an academic researcher not representing any religious view. Although the likelihood always exists of some self-selection bias in any study, I do not think it played a significant role in this case. I emphasized that it was important for me to include those who did not have a religious background or who did not see faith as important in their lives. The mothers perceived the financial incentive of $25 for the interview to be substantial, and often I would interview every eligible person at the particular social service agency on a given day. Participants included those who said that faith and religion were not important to them. In trying to combat the phenomenon of interviewees saying what they thought the interviewer would want to hear, I was careful to emphasize that there were no "right" answers. The mothers put forth a full range of ideas and opinions, and the tenor of the interviews was such that it seemed people were speaking genuinely and honestly. Said one respondent (Rebecca) at the end of the interview, "I think everything that I have to say isn't preconceived, it's just honest, even though it's mixed." I conducted the vast majority of the interviews myself; a research assistant conducted a few in the cases where there were a considerable number of women to be interviewed in a limited amount of time at an agency.

I interviewed pastors working in a nearby city with considerable urban poverty comparable to the environment of the mothers interviewed. To find pastors for the study, I began with names of clergy members given to me by a leader of a faith-based community-organizing coalition. From there, I developed a sample based on further recommendations from pastors interviewed. I interviewed most of the pastors at their offices. Interviews of mothers and pastors were approximately one hour, many longer. I fully transcribed all the mother and pastor interviews and coded the data.

Interview Schedule: Mothers

(Note: This interview schedule covers only a portion of topics that were discussed during the interview. Although these questions reflecting my initial research interests in issues of religion vis-à-vis work and motherhood were the ones asked of respondents, women brought up numerous issues that I did not expressly ask. For instance, I never asked why women did not attend religious services or how religion affects how they contend with and interpret their circumstances, yet these evolved as major themes of the book. Many women offered information that I then pursued in further depth by appropriate follow-up questions. In general, I asked a lot of follow-up questions, both to responses to the interview questions and to the other information women offered.)

1. Background Information
   a. Are you from the area? How long have you lived here (if shelter or program)?
   b. How many children do you have—how old?
   c. What is the highest level of education you have completed?
   d. What is your marital status—married, single, divorced?
   e. How would you define your race/ethnicity (e.g., white, black, Latina, Asian, other)?
   f. How old are you?

2. Work History
    a. Are you currently working?
    b. What is your current job (or most recent)? What are your responsibilities there?
    c. What other kinds of jobs have you held in the past?
    d. Have you received public assistance (welfare or other)? When and how long?
3. Religion—Background Information
    a. Were you raised in a religion; if yes, which one?
    b. Do you currently practice a religion; if yes, which one?
    c. How frequently do you attend services?
    d. How important is religion to you (very, moderately, little)?
    e. Do you have close friends and acquaintances from your church? If yes, how many?
    f. Do you pray privately? If yes, how frequently?
    g. Do you read the Bible or other religious writings? If yes, how frequently?
    h. Could you call on your minister or others at church if you needed help with day care? Transportation? A family problem? Food? Housing? If yes, have you?
4. Religion and Work
    a. What do you think your religion (or your pastor/priest) teaches about work?
    b. Have you ever heard a sermon about work or had other religious teaching about work? Have jobs ever been announced in church?
    c. What, if anything, do you think the Bible/scriptures say about work?
    d. Do you think your religion affects how you do your work? Do you ever think about God or pray during work?
    e. What do you think your religion says/thinks about not working—times in people's lives when they aren't working? What do you think your religion (or pastor/priest) thinks about welfare?
    f. (For religious respondents who talk about God): This may be an odd question, but if you put yourself in the mind of God as you understand God, what do you think God thinks about you working or not working? Your receiving welfare? About welfare in general?
    g. What do you think are the responsibilities of the employer/boss to the employee in a job? Do you think your faith/your religion would say anything about this?
5. Political Questions
    a. When people have times in their lives when they might need assistance (for example, single mother with young children), who do you think should assist them (government? church?)?
    b. What do you think the role of government should be? The role of the church? The role of the individual person herself?
    c. What do you think your faith teaches (or your church thinks) about single mothers with financial needs—what should the church do? Do you think churches are doing enough?
    d. Some politicians want to cut back the government role in aiding people and have the churches do more—do you think that is a good idea or a bad idea? Why?

e. Some politicians want the government to give money to the churches to help people when they need it—do you think that is a good idea or bad idea—why?

f. Some politicians want to give money to churches to run programs like job training or education. These programs could have religious components like a Bible study that were not paid for by the government. Do you think that is a good idea or a bad idea—why? Would you like a job training program, for example, that had a religious component?

6. Children

a. What kinds of child-care arrangements have you used in the past? (If they say children shouldn't go to day care until a certain age, ask what age.)

b. Were you satisfied with them?

c. What kind of child care do you use/will you use when you begin working?

d. How do you think your work affects your children? Is there a positive component? A negative component?

e. Does your religious faith influence how you want to raise your children; how? (There were a lot of follow-up questions here for those who said they wanted to raise their children in a religion: why, what will it give your child, why do you want them to have this, what did being raised in a religion give you, what does faith give you, and so forth.)

f. Some people think that in an ideal situation, mothers of young children should stay home and take care of them. What do you think about this? What do you think your religion would say about this? Your pastor/priest?

g. What do you think the best way is to balance working with caring for your children (schedule wise)? Do you think your faith influences your thoughts about how to balance working with your children's needs; how?

7. Miscellaneous

(For religious respondents who talk about God): This is another odd question, but do you think there is something God wants you to do with your life—do you think God has a calling for you and your life? (If yes, ask what and follow up.)

Interview Topic Guide: Pastors

(Note: As with the mothers, other topics came up, though not to such a large extent as with the women.)

1. Denomination, years as a pastor
2. Pastor's background in working with poor urban women
3. Demographic composition of current/applicable congregation; size of congregation
4. Demographic composition of neighborhood
5. Participation in congregation by poor single mothers
6. Participation in other church activities by poor single mothers
7. What factors might impede church participation by poor single mothers?
    (Logistics? Stigma?)

8. Why stigma—real or perceived?

9. How do pastors deal with lifestyle issues—the fact that many women are unmarried mothers, living out of wedlock—not in accordance with church norms?

10. Mothers sending children but not attending themselves?

11. Does church provide social services; if yes, what and how? Are social services used by neighborhood residents who are not church members? Does social service use help connect people to become congregation members?

12. (Describe to pastors the assessment of Omar McRoberts's book—that churches in poor urban areas are not necessarily interested in incorporating the very poor as members): Is this a fair assessment?

13. Is it practical/feasible for churches to provide transportation, reach out to homeless shelters—things suggested by the mothers interviewed?

14. What is the greatest challenge to churches in incorporating very poor single mothers into the congregation?

15. Do you think other congregants would want to include the very poor (if not already discussed)?

Notes

CHAPTER ONE

1. I am grateful to Omar McRoberts for this observation.
2. For further reading on the role of church-based resources, see, for example, Morris 1986 (civil rights movement); Seybold and Hill 2001; Ellison 1995 (mental health and companionship); Taylor, Chatters, and Levin 2004; Krause et al. 2001 (pastoral assistance); Warren 2001; Wood 2002 (community organizing and social justice); and Wuthnow 2004; Bradley 1995 (friendship and support).
3. I am indebted to Misty Koger-Ojure for this insight.
4. Overall, conclusions on income and attendance are somewhat mixed. Earlier studies find that lower income is associated with less participation in organized religion (Demerath 1965; Fukuyama 1961; Stark 1972). In a 2003 review of survey research from the 1950s onward, Stark finds that the poorest and least-educated Americans are least likely to participate in churches. Robert Putnam and David Campbell (2010) find no effect of income on church attendance, based on their nationally representative Faith Matters survey. However, with regard to education, another marker of social class, they find that less-educated people are less likely to attend church. Using the General Social Survey cumulative 1972–2006 data, Schwadel, McCarthy, and Nelsen (2009) find that income has a relatively small but positive effect on church attendance for all Christians together, little effect for non-Catholic Christians, and a strong positive effect on Catholics, particularly white Catholics. Schwadel (2008) notes that in earlier studies that found income effects on church attendance, the effects are often not large and may be partially due to other factors; however, he claims income

does have a clear and positive effect on participation in other church activities (see Schwadel 2002).

5.   Data about rates of attendance for African Americans is from Putnam and
Campbell 2010. The profile of African Americans who never attend church
is from Taylor 1988. African Americans who never attend church are more
likely to have lower levels of education and income, be younger and never
married, and reside in the Northeast.

6.   I am grateful to Brad Wilcox (pers. comm. 2010) for this information
drawn from the Fragile Families survey.

7.   See, for example, Davidson 1977; Fukuyama 1961; and Stark 1972. Research findings on this topic, though, are not consistent.

8.   Putnam and Campbell (2010) argue for a modest decline in attendance and
highlight the decline among young adults. Presser and Chaves (2007) examine religious service attendance levels and trends from 1990 to 2006 using three types of survey data on attendance, including the General Social
Survey and time-use diaries. They argue that attendance has been stable
in that time period. Also see Putnam's (2000) *Bowling Alone*; he pulls together evidence from five surveys to conclude that church attendance rose
in the decades after World War II and declined from the late 1950s to the
1990s.

9.   Putnam (2000, 71–72) estimates that involvement in church activities outside of attending formal worship services has fallen by one-third since the
1960s and by one-half or more since the 1950s.

10. For reviews of the benefits of social capital, see Putnam 2000. Small (2009,
230) describes the wide literature on the relationship between social ties
and access to resources in poor urban areas. For review articles, see Small
and Newman 2001 and Newman and Massengill 2006.

11. Ironically, Small (2004) finds that people in poor neighborhoods with
strong resources have fewer outside ties because they do have resources in
their neighborhoods.

12. The information in this paragraph is drawn from several sources, including the official White House website on the faith-based initiative during
Bush's presidency; the Center for Public Justice's (1997) website describing
Charitable Choice; and David J. Wright's (2009) "Taking Stock: The Bush
Faith-Based Initiative and What Lies Ahead." Wright's ninety-one-page
report provides a comprehensive look at the Bush faith-based initiative:
the background leading up to the initiative; legislative and legal issues and
regulatory changes; programmatic initiatives; and a discussion of its scope
and effectiveness. It is recommended for further background reading on
the Bush faith-based initiative, as well as for a brief discussion of the out-
look of faith-based initiatives in the Obama administration. With regard
to nondiscrimination laws and religious exemptions in hiring, the Obama
administration is studying this unresolved matter, both at the Justice
Department and in the faith-based office. In a February 18, 2010, speech at

the Brookings Institution, Joshua Du Bois said: "We also continue to work with our colleagues in government to take a clear-eyed approach to other difficult issues, including religious hiring. We know that there is a tremendous desire for finality on this topic, but we also know that due to its importance, decisions must be made carefully and with all due diligence. That's a process we are in, and one we take very seriously." See http://www .whitehouse.gov/blog/2010/02/18/a-vision-faith-based-and-neighborhood-partnerships.

13. This information comes from the Office of Faith-Based and Neighborhood Partnership's website, http://www.whitehouse.gov/administration/eop/ofbnp.

14. The survey also reports that areas where religious organizations are not seen as being able to provide the best services include child care, drug treatment, health care, and job training.

15. I am grateful to Omar McRoberts for this observation.

16. Madsen (2009, 1297) uses this metaphor, although not talking about poverty. Omar McRoberts first suggested this metaphor to me.

17. This congregation, whose members are low-income individuals who mostly speak Creole, provides the largest number of participants in the political events organized by a citywide faith-based community organizing group to address social problems.

18. I am grateful to Misty Koger-Ojure for this insight.

19. I did conduct a pilot interview with the one Jewish woman who showed up to be interviewed at a government-subsidized housing facility. She turned out to be an upper-middle-class woman with a master's degree whose mental health issues had brought her into hardship. Because her background was quite different from the rest of the respondents and she did not have children, I did not include her. I also found no Muslims or people of other faiths. I thus concentrated on women from Christian or no religious traditions.

20. I focused on mothers of young children because of my initial interest in the potential tension among religious views, working motherhood, and welfare reform requirements, assuming that mothers of children who were not yet of school age faced the greatest difficulties in managing child care and balancing work and family.

21. See Karp 1996 (page 13) for similar dynamics when conducting in-depth interviews on potentially sensitive topics.

22. Although approximately one-third of the respondents were in social service programs that were in some way religiously affiliated, none of the programs were overtly religious, "faith infused," or church based. I found no difference in respondents' religiosity.

23. Two of the mothers receiving Supplemental Security Income (disability benefits for those with little or no income or resources) offered to disclose the nature of their disability, which was mental health (depression, attention deficit disorder).

24. Estimates vary widely, but many studies calculate that between 20 and 30 percent of women on welfare have experienced domestic violence. See Raphael 2002.
25. I thank Jocelyn Crowley for highlighting this fact for me.
26. Because of the relatively large number of low-income whites and Hispanics of Catholic heritage in the area where I conducted the interviews, more than half of the sample had some Catholic background (although it was often quite nominal). About a quarter of the sample had been raised in an evangelical, Pentecostal, Seventh-Day Adventist, or Baptist tradition; two women were raised in mainline Protestant traditions, and three women were raised with no religious tradition.
27. I am thankful to Omar McRoberts for this observation.
28. The recession has increased the number of homeless families in some cities, putting even more women into situations similar to the women studied in this book. For example, between 2008 and 2010, the number of homeless families increased by 50 percent in New York City (*New York Times*, March 21, 2010).
29. See, for example, Zinnbauer, Pargament, and Scott 1999; Hill et al. 2000; Zinnbauer et al. 1997; and Schlehofer, Omoto, and Adelman 2008.

CHAPTER TWO

1. Jane was receiving Supplemental Security Income at the time of the interview.
2. See Werner and Smith 1992. Their important longitudinal study of children in poverty looked at individual factors, environmental factors, and social network factors in resilience. Also see Jackson et al. 2007 for a good literature review on resilience.
3. For discussion of sustainability see Zautra 2009. See also Bonanno (2004).
4. See Pargament and Cummings 2010.
5. These factors, of course, exist within and are shaped by one's social environment. There is a vast literature on "religious coping," and "positive religious coping" is a factor that promotes resilience (Kenneth Pargament, pers. comm., February 10, 2010). Pargament's (1997) framework of religious coping distinguishes between "positive religious coping" and "negative religious coping," or spiritual struggle. "Positive religious coping" includes a sense of meaning in life, a sense of spirituality, and spiritual connectedness with others, embodied in collaborative religious coping, religious forgiveness and helping, and benevolent religious reprisals. On the other hand, "negative religious coping" or "spiritual struggle" represents a negative religious worldview, feeling punished by God, demonic religious reappraisals, personal and interpersonal religious discontent, and a sense of disconnection from God (Folkman and Moskowitz 2004, Pargament 1997). The framework of religious coping differs from the framework of religion as compensation, and

there is no clear-cut connection between the religious coping framework and theories of compensation. Various "religious coping" strategies can be either proactive or defensive and compensatory. For example, seeking and finding comfort in faith is a "positive religious coping" strategy, but it could also be used in a defensive, passive, compensatory way. "Negative religious coping," involving spiritual struggle, possibly feeling abandoned by or angry at God, also differs from compensation. The religious coping framework aims to articulate a more nuanced and balanced view of religion that acknowledges the depth and breadth of religious motivations and actions (Pargament, pers. comm., February 10, 2010.) I choose to avoid the language of "coping" because the vernacular meanings of the word "coping" (thesaurus definitions: "survive," "get by," "muddle through," and so forth) are too easily conflated with compensation and do not accurately reflect what I found among my respondents. Pargament and Cummings's (2010) chapter in the *Handbook of Adult Resilience* discusses how religious coping connects to resilience. Pargament has also noted that "harmful spiritual struggles" is another term for negative religious coping (pers. comm., February 10, 2010).

6.   Faith in God, sacred reading, and attendance at church services proved sustaining forces in light of adversity in a study of resilience among African American women exiting street prostitution (Prince 2008). A study of fifty employed but low-income African American women found that for two-thirds of them, religion and spirituality were important factors contributing to resilience and well-being (Todd and Worrell 2000). Religion is theorized to be a cultural factor impacting resilience to adverse health outcomes for low-income Latinos (Gallo et al. 2009) and adverse mental health outcomes for African Americans (Keyes 2009). Half of the respondents in a study of resilience in post-Katrina New Orleans stated that faith in God was critical in helping them deal with the hurricane and its aftermath (Glandon, Miller, and Almedom 2009).

7.   This is Pargament's (1997) "negative religious coping."

8.   As indicated in note 5 above, Pargament (pers. comm. February 10, 2010) contends that the religious coping framework aims to present a more nuanced view of religious motivations and actions.

9.   See Gallup and Lindsay 1999, Baker 2008, and Ellison and Taylor 1996.

10. A study of 753 single mothers on the Michigan welfare rolls found welfare mothers to have much higher rates of mental health problems such as clinical depression, personal physical health problems, health problems among their children, and domestic violence than did similar women in national samples (Danziger et al. 2000). Major mental health problems such as clinical depression or severe anxiety can affect a woman's ability to secure and keep a job and hinder her negotiation of the journey from welfare to work.

11. Eighty percent (n = 36) of my sample prayed about mental and emotional health, which includes 79 percent (n = 30) of those who never or rarely

attend church services and 86 percent (n = 6) of those who attend once a month or more.

12. See Johnson 2002 for a review. Also see Koenig and Larson 2001. Studies on the relationship between religiosity and emotional health are somewhat inconsistent, as the relationship may be curvilinear. See Tabak and Mickelson 2009 for a recent discussion.

13. See Mooney 2009, Black 1999, and Frederick 2003.

14. See Hayes 2003 for a discussion of the discretionary role of welfare social workers under the Temporary Assistance for Needy Family program.

15. Unless otherwise noted, all biblical citations refer to the New American Bible.

16. Frederick (2003) finds that gratitude helped her respondents see themselves as people who had something to give to others.

17. See Pargament 1997.

18. As it turns out, Sally's faith rebounded as her situation improved.

19. This may be the case, or they may be answering in ways that seem acceptable.

20. Margarita Mooney (2009) found a similar phenomenon among Haitian immigrants; for an illuminating quote from one of her respondents, see page 133. In this view, religion aims to make earth better, more like heaven.

21. Also see Wuthnow 2007.

22. Carrie paraphrases here a poem, "Footprints in the Sand," known to many American Christians, particularly evangelical women. It is often printed on little wallet-sized prayer cards or on posters.

23. Also see Pargament and Park 1995 and Pargament and Cummings 2010.

24. In the General Social Survey (Davis and Smith 1972–2002), poor and borderline-poor white women are more likely than their nonpoor counterparts to wonder whether God has abandoned them (24 percent versus 11 percent) and to feel God is punishing them (36 percent versus 19 percent), n = 520, p < 0.005. The data also suggest that poor and borderline-poor black women may also be more likely than their nonpoor counterparts to wonder whether God has abandoned them (13 percent versus 10 percent) and feel God is punishing them (32 percent versus 26 percent), n = 109. Although the differences are not statistically significant, the sample size is small, and the percentages are suggestive.

25. In a two-year longitudinal survey study of 596 hospitalized patients age fifty-five and over, items that indicated religious struggle (e.g., "Wondered whether God had abandoned me," "Questioned God's love for me") predicted mortality after controlling for demographic, physical health, and mental health variables (Pargament 2001, cited in Folkman and Moskowitz 2004).

26. See McGuire 2002 for an overview.

27. Among the religious media mentioned by my respondents were Seventh-Day Adventist take-home pamphlets talking about money, family, and love; a prayer book at a Catholic church given out to mothers; daily (pos-

sibly twelve-step) meditations; the Serenity Prayer; the movie *The Ten Commandments*; and televangelists (indirectly, via others).

28. I am indebted to Misty Koger-Ojure for this analysis.

29. The *Merriam-Webster Online* Dictionary defines faith as "belief and trust in and loyalty to God" and "firm belief in something for which there is no proof." The definition of optimism is "an inclination to put the most favorable construction upon actions and events or to anticipate the best possible outcome." The definition of hope is "to desire with expectation of obtainment" or "to expect with confidence." http://www.merriam-webster.com.

Psychologist C. R. Snyder and colleagues (2002) have defined hope as "a cognitive set involving an individual's beliefs in his or her capability to produce workable routes to goals (waypower or pathways) and beliefs in his or her own ability to initiate and sustain movement toward those goals (willpower or agency)" (666).

In the Christian tradition, faith and hope are two of the three theological virtues providing the foundation of Christian moral activity ("faith, hope, and love"). From the *Catechism of the Catholic Church* (1993): "Faith is the theological virtue by which we believe in God and believe all that he has said and revealed to us, and that Holy Church proposes for our belief, because he is truth itself. By faith 'man freely commits his entire self to God.' For this reason the believer seeks to know and do God's will. 'The righteous shall live by faith.' Living faith 'work[s] through charity'" (para. 1814).

"Hope is the theological virtue by which we desire the kingdom of heaven and eternal life as our happiness, placing our trust in Christ's promises and relying not on our own strength, but on the help of the grace of the Holy Spirit. 'Let us hold fast the confession of our hope without wavering, for he who promised is faithful.' . . . The virtue of hope responds to the aspiration to happiness which God has placed in the heart of every man; it takes up the hopes that inspire men's activities and purifies them so as to order them to the Kingdom of heaven; it keeps man from discouragement; it sustains him during times of abandonment; it opens up his heart in expectation of eternal beatitude. Buoyed up by hope, he is preserved from selfishness and led to the happiness that flows from charity" (para. 1817–18).

For Christians, hope is grounded in the resurrection of Jesus. After Jesus's suffering and death came resurrection; after Good Friday comes Easter Sunday. Jesus's resurrection after suffering shows believers that they do not hope in vain. Mooney's (2009) study provides an excellent discussion for how this theology operates in the lives of Catholic Haitian immigrants.

From the Old Testament on hope: "They that hope in the LORD will renew their strength, they will soar as with eagles' wings; they will run and not grow weary, walk and not grow faint" (Isa. 40:31).

30. Johnson's (2002) study provides a review of studies of religion and hope; twenty-five of the thirty studies reviewed found a positive relationship between measures of religiosity and hope.

31. Scheier and Carver's definition of optimism, discussed in Rand's (2009) article.

32. Most (though not all) of the relatively regular attendees received such assistance from their churches. In addition, a few women who no longer attended church turned infrequently to their old congregations.

33. Maggie was receiving Supplemental Security Income at the time of the interview; I did not inquire why but presume it is likely because of her severe clinical depression, which substantially impacts her daily life.

34. Taylor, Chatters, and Levin (2004) explain why the poor are more likely to seek out clergy members than mental health professionals, with African Americans often consulting pastors as their only mental health resource. The poor lack access to mental health professionals or distrust them. There is stigma associated in seeking assistance from mental health professionals. In contrast, clergy are known and respected. Clergy do not charge for their services and do not require insurance forms or other types of deterring paperwork hassles. Clergy are available. Parishioners generally seek the assistance of a pastor in the context of an ongoing personal relationship.

35. See, for example, Krause et al. (2001); Taylor, Chatters, and Levin (2004); and Taylor and Chatters (1988) for their studies of how church members receive support from other members. African Americans who attend church more frequently and are formal members of the church are more likely to receive assistance from church members. Catholics are less likely to report receiving assistance from fellow congregants than Baptists.

36. The social integration associated with churches aids mental health; church-based social support has independent effects on mental health outcomes above and beyond secular social support (Ellison 1995).

37. Also see Nooney and Woodrum 2002, especially page 360; Krause et al. 2000; and Taylor, Chatters, and Levin 2004. Taylor, Chatters, and Levin (2004) analyzed two large national data sets, which showed negative church interactions to be relatively rare for black Americans.

38. Catholics are less likely to receive social support from fellow church members than Baptists. Catholic parishes tend to be larger than many Protestant churches, as well as lack many "fellowship" type activities that would enable congregants to get to know one another better. (See n. 35, above.)

39. In looking at 1,044 congregations in the Philadelphia area, Cnaan and Boddie (2001) noted that nine out of ten helped their community in some way, estimating that it would cost a quarter of a billion dollars were government to provide all the social services that the churches do in Philadelphia. Also see Unruh and Sider 2005.

40. Six mothers, like Brenda, use church-based social services such as food pantries or clothing banks; all but one use them only sporadically. About one-third of respondents receive social services from nonprofit organizations that are religiously affiliated to some degree (but do not include religion as

part of service provision), and almost all receive some type of government assistance.

41. This is the study of twelve churches within one mile of a Chicago housing project mentioned in the first chapter of the book (Price 2000). Although the churches provided social services, only one included project residents as members.

CHAPTER THREE

1. In Colossians 3:23 (King James Version), the passage reads, "And whatsoever ye do, do it heartily, as to the Lord, and not unto men."

2. The information in the paragraph was drawn from Zedlewski and Golden 2010. Almost half of the states sanction families 100 percent of their benefits for some period of time at the first breach of work participation requirements. For an ethnographic description of programs designed to divert potential recipients from the welfare rolls, see Hayes 2003.

3. See Hudson and Coukos 2005 for an interesting analysis of the Protestant ethic with regard to the 1996 welfare reform movement and the nineteenth-century campaign to abolish outdoor poor relief. They argue that under certain conditions, such as a tight labor market and political mobilization by reform advocates, the Protestant ethos can produce severe retrenchments in aid to the poor.

4. Mead wrote this before the economic downturn of 2008 and was referring to adults choosing not to work and receiving public assistance, not those who have been laid off and are looking for work.

5. In giving talks on this material, I have been asked if perhaps mothers were just saying they believed that religion called for people to work hard, presenting a face they wanted a researcher to see. Responding to similar possible skepticism about her research with welfare mothers, Sharon Hayes (2003) points to Goffman's (1959) claim that all people construct their life narratives to some degree so as to convince hearers that they are worthy people: "The fact that welfare mothers may not always practice the ideals they proclaim, I would suggest, makes them neither more nor less morally virtuous than anyone else" (141). Because the Protestant work ethic is ingrained in American culture, it is unsurprising that women reflecting on religion and work, even those on welfare, would draw connections between morality, religion, and hard work. And, as we shall see below, mothers do not always connect "work" with paid employment, because they also believe God calls them to work hard in their "primary" jobs as mothers.

6. Hayes (2003) notes this as well. This observation is particularly true in a recession. The American Recovery and Reinvestment Act of 2009 created a $5 billion TANF emergency fund, where states can apply for funding to provide basic assistance, short-term and nonrecurrent emergency aid, and

subsidized employment; states must match 20 percent of the funds. States with growing caseloads under this law must increase the number of people in welfare-to-work activity by a comparable percent. TANF caseloads have increased in a number of states since the recession, but have stayed flat or even declined in some states with high unemployment rates. Welfare reform time limits remain in effect. Food stamp (SNAP) use has increased at a much greater rate than TANF. Some analysts speculate that the requirements of welfare reform (for example, the need to engage in extensive job searches in areas of very high unemployment) may be discouraging people from applying. Many low-wage workers cannot qualify for unemployment insurance (Zedlewski and Golden 2010; also see Parrott 2009). I conducted the interviews before the current economic downturn, but the welfare system's time limits, sanctions, diversion tactics, and work-related requirements remain.

7. There is an initial two-year time limit in the state where this research was conducted, with a lifetime limit of five years.

8. See Marie Griffith 1997 for a similar notion for evangelical women violating societal expectations for women.

9. Mothers familiar with several religious traditions sometimes contrast how they believe different traditions view welfare. Juliana thinks the Catholic Church would disapprove of welfare, whereas the Pentecostal church would encourage her to get the assistance. "It seems to me that they [Catholics] think they are too good to have something, to have help. They already have help from God. . . . I think they [the Pentecostals] say get all the help you can get and just keep the faith." Claire, who personally believes that God views welfare use negatively, thinks the Catholic Church in which she was raised would be more judgmental about welfare use, whereas the Baptist church she attends twice a month would be more understanding. Women perceive some religious traditions as more compassionate and accepting of welfare than others.

10. Although the majority of participants were receiving public assistance at the time of the study, few were long-term welfare recipients, and many were involved in job training programs.

11. See Skocpol 1995. These pensions did not apply to women considered unworthy, such as African American women or unwed mothers.

12. See "'Welfare Queen' Becomes Issue in Reagan Campaign," New York Times, February 15, 1976.

13. This figure comes from Williams 2000 (199). She notes that whereas more than a third of poor women were full-time homemakers in 1994, less than 25 percent of working-class women were.

14. The labor force participation rate includes people who are employed or looking for work; the percentage of mothers of children under age eighteen actually employed in 2008 was 67.6 percent. See U.S. Bureau of Labor Statistics 2009b.

15. Also see Edin and Kefalas 2005.
16. Mormon mothers, especially those with strong religious values, have also been found to be less likely to be employed (Chadwick and Garrett 1995) or to work part-time as opposed to full-time (Heaton 1994). Putnam and Campbell (2010) argue, using General Social Survey data and controlling for age composition, that women's religious tradition and religiosity have had relatively little impact on women moving into the labor force in increased numbers. The most religious and most secular women entered the labor force at approximately the same trajectory between 1973 and 2008, and the gap between the groups is relatively small (4 percentage points in 2008). Although the most religious American women are still more likely to endorse traditional gender roles as compared to their secular counterparts, they too have experienced a dramatic change in gender ideologies since the 1970s.
17. See, for example, Blair-Loy 2003 and Stone 2007, which profile upper-middle-class women grappling with work-family decisions.
18. The study Stone cites is Sylvia Ann Hewlett and Carolyn Buck Luce (2005), Off-ramps and on-ramps: Keeping talented women on the road to success, *Harvard Business Review* 83 (3): 43–54.
19. Peek, Lowe, and Williams (1991) found women's personal religious beliefs are more important than denominational doctrine in affecting their gender role ideology (cited in Glass and Nash 2006.)
20. Sharon Hayes (2003) notes that although wealthier women who choose to stay home may struggle with issues of career identity, they find support for their child-rearing role. Also see Stone 2007 and Blair-Loy 2003 for ethnographies of well-educated upper-middle-class women who have made this decision and find validation. In a religious sense, wealthier mothers of young children who opt out of the labor force for a while to provide caregiving may at times miss aspects of their former lives, but they also find encouragement and support for their new role in their churches and social circles.
21. Hayes (2003) finds that most low-income single mothers of young children see work in the paid labor force as "a central ticket to social membership" (235) and want to reconcile employment and caring for children.
22. Examples include Princeton University's Center for the Study of Religion, Faith and Work Initiative and Yale Divinity School's Yale Center for Faith and Culture, Ethics and Spirituality in the Workplace Program.
23. Miller (2007, 109–10) cites two of these books and others.
24. See Macdonald and Merrill 2009 for a good discussion of the intersectionality of race, ethnicity, class, and gender in such jobs.
25. See Ehrenreich 2001 for examples of how management demeans low-skilled workers. See Wharton 2009 as well.
26. Yet the differences between religious people and nonreligious people in these areas of workplace ethics are small (Wuthnow 1994a). One could also

question whether there are actual behavioral differences or mere reporting differences.

27. Given some of the ethnographic studies on maid work (e.g., Ehrenreich 2001), the attitude of housecleaning as a gift and act of love is touching and somewhat sad; one would hope home owners might take note.

28. In particular, material success was considered a sign of God's favor with regard to predestination (Wuthnow 1994a).

29. Hayes (2003) has a good discussion in chapter 7 of how the types of jobs available for low-skilled women make motherhood as a social role all the more valued.

30. The fourth category, enrichment, describes prayer and stress relief as part of a broader package of self-realization, meditation, personal growth, and so forth from various religious and New Age perspectives. It did not capture the desperate prayers for survival of poor women in the low-wage work-place.

31. See Volf 1991 for an excellent discussion on theology, work, and justice.

CHAPTER FOUR

1. I am grateful to Ed Thompson for some of these thoughts. Also, exceptions include Wiley, Warren, and Montanelli 2002, McAdoo 1995, and Cain 2007.

2. Ammerman points readers to an essay by Anne Brown and David Hall in Hall 1997.

3. Some of the main studies discussed in this review are Bartkowski and Wilcox 2000; Wilcox 1998; Brody et al. 1994; and Pearce and Axinn 1998.

4. This study measured maternal responsiveness by interviewers observing emotional and verbal responsiveness, provision of adequate play materials, and parental involvement. The study found personal religiosity but not church attendance to be associated with greater parental responsiveness. Also see Wiley, Warren, and Montanelli 2002: among poor rural African Americans, religious mothers (measured by church attendance and per-sonal beliefs) reported using fewer coercive parenting techniques.

5. The authors put forth church-based social support, pro-family church norms, and the imbuing of parenting with sacred significance as possible reasons explaining increased child well-being; they note that the reverse explanation that parents of better-behaved children are more likely to take them to church is also possible.

6. The authors find that parental religious participation, not belief, buffers disadvantage. But parental belief is narrowly measured in terms of such items as literal belief in the Bible and does not speak to religious practices in the home. Another pertinent study is Furstenberg and Hughes (1995), who found that increased levels of family social capital predicted markers of economic success in early adulthood in a longitudinal study of disadvan-taged youth.

7. Also see Edin and Kefalas 2005 (165); the young women they spoke with saw their children as gifts from God.
8. Some of those who did not say this were already highly personally religious.
9. Twelve women also had children over age six.
10. See Ellison 1997, Ellison and Levin 1998, and Cain 2007. Ellison posits a framework of religious role taking whereby people identify with figures in religious texts and parent in accordance with what a divine being would expect.
11. See Wiley, Warren, and Montanelli 2002 for a review.
12. McAdoo's (1995) study of 318 single and employed middle-class and working-class African American mothers in Baltimore, women who were personally religious but basically unchurched, found the most noted benefits of prayer indicated by the women were emotional and moral support to the women and their families; only 6 percent of the sample highlighted family unity.
13. Half of the women who want their children in churches give protection as a reason.
14. This pertinent study of religious involvement among unmarried adolescent mothers sheds some theoretical light on this question. They present two competing hypotheses: (1) religious affiliation could provide positive social support to unmarried adolescent mothers, and (2) the prohibition of nonmarital fertility implicit in religious teachings could actually increase the young mothers' distress. Using a longitudinal study of pregnant adolescents in Canada, they found support for the second hypothesis. Unmarried adolescent mothers who attended more conservative churches or churches with clearly enunciated positions on traditional religious sexual norms experienced significantly higher levels of distress. "It appears that traditional religious organizations cannot claim a supportive role in the adaptation of unmarried teenage mothers in the period shortly after their babies were born" (80).
15. Dehejia et al.'s (2009) study, the only one specifically on disadvantaged children, finds that parental religious participation, not belief, buffers disadvantage. But parental belief is narrowly measured in terms of such items as literal belief in the Bible and does not speak to religious practices in the home. Bartkowski, Xu, and Levin (2008) find benefits to child well-being associated with parents attending church and discussing religion with children, but this study does not analyze religion in the home in depth.
16. For example, Mahoney et al. 2001.

CHAPTER FIVE

1. A thorough examination of the concept and history of theodicy is beyond the scope of this book. In this chapter I seek to understand theodicy from the point of view of mothers in poverty, and as a sociologist, not a theologian.

2. Scott (2008) provides a clear discussion of theodicy and social theorists. Also see Musick 2000. Musick finds that among black respondents, no relationship exists between a theodicy that emphasizes sin and evil and life satisfactions. For whites, a theodicy emphasizing sin and evil is associated with worse life satisfaction; for whites, church attendance and stressful circumstances moderate this relationship.

3. Pargament (1997) categorizes various religious attributions for suffering into the following: (1) religious reframing of the event: suffering as part of God's will or plan, suffering as a spiritual opportunity; (2) religious reframing of the person: human sinfulness, human's limited ability to understand; and (3) religious reframing of the sacred: a punishing God, the devil's doing, a limited God.

4. The only one of my respondents who even brought up prosperity gospel thinking joked about wanting God to help her win the lottery.

5. As a twentieth-century example, Pinn analyzes Martin Luther King Jr.'s theology of redemptive suffering as one whereby black suffering due to human evil, dealt with nonviolently, could be fruitfully used by God. In addition to providing inner transformation for the oppressed, God would use a nonviolent yet powerful response to unearned suffering to bring about racial reconciliation in American society (77).

6. Pargament (1997) discusses the view of suffering leading to character development. In terms of being able to comfort others in similar situations, this is referenced in the New Testament: "The God of all encouragement, who encourages us in our every affliction, so that we may be able to encourage those who are in any affliction with the encouragement with which we ourselves are encouraged by God" (2 Cor. 1:3–4). Also see Marie Griffith (1997); suffering enables one to help others, and helping others may bring further healing. Thus, "suffering may be discerned as a gift rather than as a punishment from God" (91).

7. See Baker 2008 regarding the poor being more likely to pray for forgiveness of sins. The other findings, discussed in more detail in chapter 2, note 24, draw on my analysis of the General Social Survey.

8. This includes Elisa. She goes on to address how prayer helps her feel God is with her again.

9. See Pargament 1997.

10. This differs from some of the findings of Seccombe (1999), whose welfare mother respondents invoked structural explanations for their own welfare use and personal attributions for welfare use of others. For more about "God's plan," see Frederick (2003).

11. And by extension, one could include poor marginalized white women such as the white women in my study.

12. See Helen Black 1999. She also argues that her elderly African American respondents found their traditional Christian framework for interpreting suffering to be helpful to them.

13. Juliana highlights her lack of church upbringing, which she believes led to negative adolescent behaviors and her current situation (see chapter 4). Lack of church participation is viewed by her and others as indirectly leading to undesirable outcomes. Ironically, for some women, the arrow also goes the other way, as their difficult life situations hinder them from participating in churches.

14. Pargament (1997) categorizes two ways in which religion can be used to make meaning of negative events: (1) positive religious reframing, that is, thinking there is a higher purpose in the suffering, and (2) negative religious reframing, such as feeling punished by God. The ways in which people engage in reframing their situations can have consequences; positive religious reframing is associated with greater life satisfaction and better emotional health outcomes, and negative reframing is associated with depression and poorer quality of life (Pargament et al. 1998). It seems plausible that the causal arrow also may go in the opposite direction.

CHAPTER SIX

1. Smith (2001) reports that the concentrated urban poverty of inner-city housing complexes leads to such social isolation that many residents are not exposed to churches and people in churches. He describes "a lack of church-related interaction by persons whose social isolation confines them to networks of family, friends, and acquaintances who may have had little or no involvement with church matters. Where multiple households conforming to this pattern are concentrated in the same area, the chances increase that patterns of church non-affiliation may quickly multiply" (311).

2. Nineteen of my respondents brought up logistical barriers impeding church participation.

3. Weisbourd also notes that in very low-income schools in Chicago, 80 percent of children change schools each year.

4. "Abominations of the body" are various physical deformities. "Blemishes of individual character" are weak will, domineering or unnatural passions, treacherous and rigid beliefs, or dishonesty. Blemishes of character are inferred from, for example, mental disorder, imprisonment, addiction, alcoholism, homosexuality, unemployment, suicidal attempts, or radical political behavior. "Tribal stigma of race, nation, and religion" are beliefs that are transmitted through lineages and equally contaminate all members of a family.

5. Other strategies for reconciling differentness from societal norms include rejecting the norms and thus not being bothered by failing to live up to them (which Goffman believed to be uncommon) and trying to correct the blemish (for example, through plastic surgery or an illiterate person learning to read).

6. Previous research finds welfare use to be associated with social stigma (Jarrett 1996; Rogers-Dillon 1995; Seccombe, James, and Walters 1998).

Jarrett's (1996) focus groups with mothers on welfare find both economic and family-related dimensions of these mothers' experience of social stigma. On the economic front, mothers on welfare experience stigma from deviating from norms of employment. In addition to economic sources of stigma, they experience stigma because of their family situations. Both their welfare status and single-parent status are used as evidence that they do not live up to economic or family norms. Seccombe, James, and Walters (1998) find that women on welfare are overwhelmingly aware of negative stereotypes and stigma associated with welfare receipt. Almost all of their respondents had personally experienced stigma and criticism directed at them due to being single mothers on welfare. In a study of stigma and social services, Spicker (1984) finds that poverty itself is stigmatizing but that welfare receipt is even more stigmatizing. Racial attitudes are intertwined with welfare stigma. American hatred of the welfare system is interconnected with the racial perceptions of welfare recipients, and welfare mothers are incorrectly viewed to be primarily African American (Gilens 1999).

7. One study on social services discussed in Unruh and Sider (2005, 5) found that churches balk at serving particularly disenfranchised groups such as people with AIDS and people who receive welfare. (The study they discuss is Susan Grettenberger [2001], Churches as a community resource and source of funding for human services [Working Paper Series, Aspen Institute Nonprofit Sector Research Fund].)

8. Also see Sample (1993) for a longer discussion of the importance of clothing as a barrier for the poor in church attendance. Weissbourd (2000) addresses this as well.

9. Timothy Nelson's excellent 2005 ethnography, *Every Time I Feel the Spirit*, details how he felt intimidated by the financial expectations of the low-income African American church he studied as a graduate student. In addition to expecting tithing and participating in other church fund-raisers, congregants filed to the front of the church to put their collection in the basket, and the amount of each contributor was published and handed out the following Sunday.

10. People of low socioeconomic status, particularly black Americans, are increasingly less likely to marry (Goldstein and Kenney 2001). Women of low socioeconomic status are at greatest risk for single motherhood (Catanzarite and Ortiz 2002). Catanzarite and Ortiz (2002) extend Wilson's hypothesis across racial and ethnic groups. Cultural factors, which are linked to socioeconomic issues, have also contributed to the decline of marriage in low-income minority communities (Catanzarite and Ortiz 2002; Wilcox and Wolfinger 2007; Mare and Winship 1991).

11. Sorenson, Grindstaff, and Turner (1995) found that church attendance among unwed adolescent mothers who attended churches with conservative or clearly enunciated views on marriage actually elevated their distress instead of buffering it.

12. Thornton, Axinn, and Hill (1992) note that because cohabitation publicly acknowledges a sexual relationship, it highlights the individual's nonconformity to certain church norms: "With fewer positive interactions, and many negative messages from religious sources, cohabiting individuals would have less motivation to attend services" (632). The effects of cohabitation on attendance were strongest among Catholics and fundamentalist Protestants. Theologian Brent Coffin's (2005) study of an evangelical church in an affluent suburb of Boston found that cohabiting couples with children were not allowed to become members of the church unless they married.

13. The term "self-perceived sinfulness" comes from Pinhey and Perez 2000.

14. Interestingly, a number of respondents mentioned cigarette smoking. Smoking was given as an example either of negative behavior not congruent with a church lifestyle or (by nonsmokers) of positive behavior demonstrating a "morally worthy" lifestyle. In the latter case, not smoking was mentioned at the same time as other behaviors, such as not drinking or doing drugs.

15. I am grateful to Misty Koger-Ojure for this insight.

16. See also Lausanne Committee for World Evangelization 1980. Lausanne is an international movement of evangelicals founded by the Reverend Billy Graham. Also see Sample 1993.

17. Poor white Catholics are especially less likely to attend. Schwadel, McCarthy, and Nelsen (2009) believe this may be due to discomfort with middle-class culture. They also posit that poor white Catholics may fear they would lack the financial resources to contribute, deterring attendance.

18. When I told an acquaintance training to be a minister how a respondent felt unwanted in church because she was on welfare, she expressed shock and dismay, saying she would never want someone to feel unwelcome due to being on welfare.

19. Bellah et al. (1985) trace the roots of religious individualism back to the beginnings of the United States; individuals could find the form of religion that best suited their interests as early as the 1700s. Bellah et al. contend that in recent decades, religious individualism, which was once associated with elites such as Jefferson, Thoreau, Walt Whitman, and others has become part of the American middle-class norm.

CHAPTER SEVEN

1. With small numbers the data are, of course, only suggestive. In some religious traditions one is not supposed to receive sacraments while in a state of sin. Although this practice is often disregarded, for example among middle-class Catholics, perhaps it weighs more heavily among certain ethnic groups.

2. From Edgell and Docka (2007): "Cohabiting relationships were greatly frowned upon by the community and the pastor and several respondents proudly told me about the couples within the congregation that had been

persuaded to marry by constant efforts on behalf of the leadership and laity alike" (36).

3. Taylor, Chatters, and Levin 2004 discuss this in some detail in terms of the black church.

4. Her congregation has come to include a growing number of recent African immigrants.

CHAPTER EIGHT

1. Margarita Mooney (2009) and Marla Frederick (2003) are excellent exceptions.

2. See Margarita Mooney 2009 (46–47) for similar findings among the Haitian immigrants she interviewed.

3. Also see Mooney 2009; Frederick 2003; and Pargament 1997.

4. Ellison et al. use longitudinal data to establish deleterious effects to mental health of negative interactions in congregations.

5. Although the rural African American churchgoing women Marla Frederick (2003) studied sometimes ventured into political action fueled by religious convictions, religion more often fueled transformation in personal matters.

6. The only exception among the interviewees was Jane, whose social critique is recounted in chapter 2. Also, I am indebted to Misty Koger-Ojure for this insight. I write this, by the way, with sympathy toward community organizing, having taught organizing to undergraduates since 1997.

7. Misty Koger-Ojure contributed this analysis. Also see Hochschild 1995.

8. See Pargament and Park 1995 and Pargament and Cummings 2010 for reviews of studies. I am grateful to Ann Braude for pointing out that the poor should have as much right to derive comfort from religion as anyone else.

9. This is not true of deeply religious African Americans and Latinos, who support government policy to reduce poverty and inequality (Putnam and Campbell 2010).

10. In an ironic twist, the phrase "what would Jesus do," associated with personal behavior decisions by modern evangelicals, actually originated in the late nineteenth century in connection with social injustice (Putnam and Campbell 2010). Also, to say that modern evangelicals are not too concerned with issues of social structure and injustice does not include exceptions such as Jim Wallis's Sojourners organization or Ron Sider's work, for example.

11. There is a large body of literature assessing the relationship of religion to these outcomes. Johnson (2002) includes a review of 103 studies on religion and depression, 70 studies on religion and suicide, and 99 studies on religion and measures of well-being (happiness, life satisfaction, and so forth). The majority, though not all, of the studies indicate religious involvement is associated with less depression; the vast majority found religion associated with measures of life satisfaction. Johnson notes that the studies

reviewed tend to be cross-sectional, but a significant number are prospective cohort studies.

12. These friendships are not concentrated among volunteers, so it is not social service provision that leads to these relationships. Rather, it is people who are very involved in church and who have many friends in church who report these cross-class friendships.

13. Schwadel (2002) contends that higher-income individuals still receive the majority of civic skills training and practice in churches. Membership in charity, social justice, and public policy organizations in churches are least likely to be income stratified, suggesting they offer opportunities for lower-income members to learn civic skills. In general, however, organizations in churches are strongly stratified by income. Schwadel also notes that it is possible that even with this degree of stratification, churches may still be better than other institutions in offering the poor the opportunity for learning and practicing civic skills.

14. See Margarita Mooney 2009 (44–46) for a discussion of churches as unique moral communities as opposed to other types of organizations.

15. Mario Small (2009) shows that child-care centers can function to provide greater social networks and access to more resources to mothers using them. Margarita Mooney (2009) contends, however, that churches are unique moral communities.

16. See Omar McRoberts's (2003) *Streets of Glory* for further description of churches that see their low-income neighbors only as potential converts.

17. Roof and Kenney (1987), while concurring that American faith communities continue to be divided along class lines, argue that "the ascriptive bases of the religious communities have declined, creating a more fluid and voluntary religious system" (145). Park and Reimer (2002) also concur that major class differences remain, although they note a slow convergence toward more similar class statuses of various groups. Wuthnow (1988) analyzes the role of education in restructuring American religion. See Smith and Faris 2005 for a good overview and discussion of literature on socioeconomic inequality in the American religious system. Also see Nelson 2009 on worship practices and class segregation in American religion.

18. According to their website, the Fourth World Movement is "a network of people in poverty and those from other backgrounds who work in partnership towards overcoming the exclusion and injustice of persistent poverty" (http://www.4thworldmovement.org/fwusa.php). It began in France in the 1950s, came to the United States in 1964, and now operates in about twenty-five countries on five continents. Their priorities are to learn from the poor, understand how they become trapped in persistent poverty, and develop and plan projects with them. Their advisory committee includes Nobel Peace Prize laureate Elie Wiesel, author Jonathan Kozol, and Harvard sociologists William Julius Wilson and Christopher Winship, among others.

19. Recall Putnam and Campbell's (2010) finding that evangelical congregations are places where cross-class social interaction occurs.

20. Churches composed of predominantly poor members are smaller and less likely to have linkages with outside sources of assistance or larger denominational bodies (Foley, McCarthy, and Chaves 2001).

21. Getting more clergy members and neighborhood residents working together in an organized way to address issues of violence, school quality, and affordable housing would strengthen relationships between churches and neighborhoods. R. Drew Smith (2003) notes this as well. Several pastors interviewed for my book stated that clergy within cities often do not work in collaboration; they feel their ministries would be more effective if more pastors met together to address common concerns.

22. See, for example, McRoberts 2003 for a discussion of the Azusa Christian Community and their involvement with neighborhood residents.

23. In the 1999 National Congregations Study, 3 percent of congregations received government money for their social service provision, though one-fifth of congregations collaborated with government agencies in providing service. Thirty-six percent of congregations indicated that they would be interested in applying for government funds to support social service projects (Chaves 2001). In a 2007 national stratified random sample of American congregations, less than one-tenth of all congregations reported seeking government grants for social services in the past four years. Overall, 7.1 percent of the congregations reported having applied for a government grant, with a mean of 10.1 applications (with a standard deviation of 30.4 applications). The congregations received a mean of 3 government grants during this period (with a standard deviation of 13.7 grants) and a mean of nearly $400,000 per grant (and a standard deviation of almost $1 million). Less than 25 percent were familiar with Charitable Choice provisions. However, almost half the congregations said they were likely to increase government grant activity in the future (Green 2007).

24. Because of the small sample size, the authors did not try to determine whether different types of welfare-to-work programs (i.e., government, faith-based, secular nonprofit, and so forth) were more effective at moving more or less religiously active people from the Temporary Assistance for Needy Families program to sustained employment at ten or more dollars an hour a year later.

References

Albrecht, Gloria. 2005. Class on Sunday. *Crosscurrents*, Fall.

Ammerman, Nancy. 1997. Golden rule Christianity: Lived religion in the American mainstream. In *Lived Religion in America: Toward a History of Practice*, edited by David D. Hall, 196–216. Princeton, NJ: Princeton University Press.

———. 2007. *Everyday Religion: Observing Modern Religious Lives*. Oxford: Oxford University Press.

Baker, Joseph O. 2008. An investigation of the sociological patterns of prayer frequency and content. *Sociology of Religion* 69 (2): 169–85.

Bane, Mary Jo. 2000. Faith communities and the post–welfare reform safety net. In *Who Will Provide: The Changing Role in American Social Welfare*, edited by Mary Jo Bane, Brent Coffin, and Ronald Thiemann, 286–99. Boulder, CO: Westview Press.

Bane, Mary Jo, and Lawrence M. Mead. 2003. *Lifting Up the Poor: A Dialogue on Religion, Poverty and Welfare Reform*. Washington, DC: Brookings Institution Press.

Barna Group. 2001. Annual study reveals that America is spiritually stagnant. http://www.barna.org/barna-update/article/5-barna-update/37-annual-study-reveals-america-is-spiritually-stagnant?q=read+bible.

———. 2009. Study: Americans customize their religion. http://www.barna.org.

Bartkowski, John. 2001. *Remaking the Godly Marriage: Gender Negotiation in Evangelical Families*. New Brunswick, NJ: Rutgers University Press.

Bartkowski, John, and Helen Regis. 2003. *Charitable Choices: Religion, Race, and Poverty in the Post-Welfare Era*. New York: New York University Press.

Bartkowski, John, and W. Bradford Wilcox. 2000. Conservative Protestant child discipline: The case of parental yelling. *Social Forces* 79 (1): 265–90.

Bartkowski, John, Xiohae Xu, and Martin Levin. 2008. Religion and child development: Evidence from the Early Childhood Longitudinal Study. *Social Science Research* 37 (1): 18–36.

Bellah, Robert, Richard Madsen, William M. Sullivan, Ann Swidler, and Steven M. Tipton. 1985. *Habits of the Heart: Individualism and Commitment in American Life*. Berkeley: University of California Press.

Belle, Deborah. 1982. Social ties and social support. In *Lives in Stress: Women and Depression*, edited by Deborah Belle, 133–44. Beverly Hills, CA: Sage Publishers.

Berger, Peter L. 1967. *The Sacred Canopy: Elements of a Sociological Theory of Religion*. New York: Anchor Books/Random House.

Black, Helen K. 1999. Poverty and prayer: Spiritual narratives of elderly African-American women. *Review of Religious Research* 40 (4): 359–74.

Blair-Loy, Mary. 2003. *Competing Devotions: Career and Family among Women Executives*. Cambridge, MA: Harvard University Press.

Bonanno, G. A. 2004. Loss, trauma, and human resilience: Have we underestimated the human capacity to thrive after extremely aversive events? *American Psychologist* 59: 20–28.

Bradley, Don E. 1995. Religious involvement and social resources: Evidence from the data set Americans' Changing Lives. *Journal for the Scientific Study of Religion* 34 (2): 259–67.

Brody, Gene, Zolinda Stoneman, Douglas Flor, and Chris McCrary. 1994. Religion's role in organizing family relationships: Family process in rural two-parent African-American families. *Journal of Marriage and the Family* 56: 878–88.

Cain, Daphne. 2007. The effects of religiousness on parenting stress and practices in the African American family. *Families in Society* 88 (2): 263–72.

Catanzarite, Lisa, and Vilma Ortiz. 2002. Too few good men? Available men and single motherhood among Latinas, African Americans, and Whites. *Hispanic Journal of Behavioral Sciences* 24 (3): 278–95.

Catechism of the Catholic Church. 1993. http://www.vatican.va/archive/ENG0015/index.htm.

Center for Public Justice. 1997. A guide to Charitable Choice. http://www.cpjustice.org/charitablechoice.guide/.

Chadwick, Bruce A., and H. Dean Garrett. 1995. Women's religiosity and employment: The LDS experience. *Review of Religious Research* 36 (3): 277–93.

Chaves, Mark. 1999. Religious congregations and welfare reform: Who will take advantage of "Charitable Choice"? *American Sociological Review* 64: 836–46.

———. 2001. Religious congregations and welfare reform. *Society* 38 (2): 21–27.

Chaves, Mark, and William Tsitsos. 2001. Congregations and social services: What they do, how they do it, and with whom. *Nonprofit and Voluntary Sector Quarterly* 30 (4): 660–83.

Cnaan, Ram, and Stephanie Boddie. 2001. *Black Church Outreach: Comparing How Black and Other Congregations Serve Their Needy Neighbors*. Philadelphia: Center for the Research on Religion and Urban Civil Society at the University of Pennsylvania.

Coffin, Brent B. 2000. Where religion and public values meet: Who will contest? In *Who Will Provide: The Changing Role of Religion in American Social Welfare*, edited by Mary Jo Bane, Brent Coffin, and Ronald Theimann, 121–43. Boulder, CO: Westview Press.

———. 2005. Moral deliberation in congregations. In *Taking Faith Seriously*, edited by Mary Jo Bane, Brent Coffin, and Richard Higgins, 113–45. Cambridge, MA: Harvard University Press.

Cohen, Jere. 2002. *Protestantism and Capitalism*. New York: Aldine de Gruyter.

Cone, James H. 1997. *God of the Oppressed*. Maryknoll, NY: Orbis Books.

Danziger, Sandra, Mary Corcoran, Sheldon Danziger, Colleen Heflin, Ariel Kalil, Judith Levine, Daniel Rosen, Kristin Seefeldt, Kristine Siefert, and Richard Tolman. 2000. Barriers to the employment of welfare recipients. Poverty Research and Training Center, University of Michigan, Ann Arbor. http:www.fordschool/umich.edu/research/poverty/pdf/wesappam.pdf.

Davidson, James D. 1977. Socioeconomic status and ten dimensions of religious commitment. *Sociology and Social Research* 61: 462–85.

Davidson, James, and D. P. Caddell. 1990. Religion and the meaning of work. *Journal for the Scientific Study of Religion* 33 (2): 135–47.

Davis, James Allan, and Tom W. Smith. 1972–2002. *General Social Surveys*. Storrs, CT: Roper Center for Public Opinion Research, University of Connecticut.

Davis, Kingsley. 1949. *Human Society*. New York: Macmillan.

Dehejia, Rajeev, Thomas De Leire, Erzo F. P. Luttmer, and Joshua Mitchell. 2009. The role of religious and social organizations in the lives of disadvantaged youth. In *The Problems of Disadvantaged Youth: An Economics Perspective*, edited by Jonathan Gruber, 237–74. Chicago: University of Chicago Press.

Demarath, N. J., III. 1965. *Social Class in American Protestantism*. Chicago: Rand McNally.

Dobson, James. 2005. Family news from Dr. James Dobson. *Focus on the Family*. August. www.focusonthefamily.com.

Dollahite, David C., and Jennifer Y. Thatcher. 2007. How family religious involvement benefits adults, youth, and children and strengthens families. In *Family Law: Balancing Interests and Pursuing Priorities*, edited by Lynn D. Wardle and Camille S. Williams, 427–36. Buffalo, NY: William S. Hein.

Edin, Kathryn, and Maria Kefalas. 2005. *Promises I Can Keep: Why Poor Women Put Motherhood before Marriage*. Berkeley: University of California Press.

Edin, Kathryn, and Laura Lein. 1997. *Making Ends Meet: How Single Mothers Survive Welfare and Low-Wage Work*. New York: Russell Sage Foundation.

Edgell, Penny. 2006. *Religion and Family in a Changing Society*. Princeton, NJ: Princeton University Press.

Edgell, Penny, and Danielle Docka. 2007. Beyond the nuclear family? Familism and gender ideology in diverse religious communities. *Sociological Forum* 22 (1): 26–51.

Ehrenreich, Barbara. 2001. *Nickel and Dimed: On (Not) Getting By in America*. New York: Henry Holt.

————. 2009. *Bright-Sided: How the Relentless Promotion of Positive Thinking Has Undermined America*. New York: Henry Holt.

Ellison, Christopher G. 1994. Religion, the life stress paradigm, and the study of depression. In *Religion in Aging and Health: Theoretical Foundations and Methodological Frontiers*, edited by Jeffery S. Levin, 78–121. Thousand Oaks, CA: Sage Publications.

————. 1995. Race, religious involvement, and depressive symptomatology in a southeastern U.S. community. *Social Science and Medicine* 40: 1561–72.

————. 1997. Religious involvement and the subjective quality of family life among African Americans. In *Family Life in Black America*, edited by R. J. Taylor, J. S. Jackson, and L. M. Chatters, 117–31. Thousand Oaks, CA: Sage Publications.

Ellison, Christopher, and Linda George. 1994. Religious involvement, social ties, and social support in a southeastern community. *Journal for the Scientific Study of Religion* 33 (1): 46–61.

Ellison, Christopher, and J. S. Levin. 1998. The religion-health connection: Evidence, theory, and future directions. *Health Education and Behavior* 25 (6): 700–720.

Ellison, Christopher, and R. S. Taylor. 1996. Turning to prayer: Social and situational antecedents of religious coping among African Americans. *Review of Religious Research* 38 (2): 111–31.

Ellison, Christopher, Wei Zhang, Neal Krause, and John P. Marcum. 2009. Does negative interaction in church increase psychological distress? Longitudinal findings from the Presbyterian Panel Survey. *Sociology of Religion* 70 (4): 409–31.

Fay, Martha. 1993. *Do Children Need Religion? How Parents Today Are Thinking about the Big Questions*. New York: Pantheon Books.

Foley, Michael, John McCarthy, and Mark Chaves. 2001. Social capital, religious institutions, and poor communities. In *Social Capital and Poor Communities*, edited by Susan Saegert, J. Phillip Thompson, and Mark R. Warren, 215–45. New York: Russell Sage Foundation.

Folkman, Susan, and Judith Telie Moskowitz. 2004. Coping: Pitfalls and promises. *Annual Review of Psychology* 55: 745–74.

Francis, Ara. 2008. Bearing imperfect children: Raising kids with problems in an era of medicalization and anxious parenting. Ph.D. diss., University of California, Davis.

Franklin, Robert M. 2004. Healthy marriages in low-income African-American communities, part 1: Exploring partnerships between faith communities and the marriage movement: A thematic summary. Annie E. Casey Foundation, Baltimore.

Frederick, Marla F. 2003. *Between Sundays: Black Women and Everyday Struggles of Faith*. Berkeley: University of California Press.

Freud, Sigmund. (1927) 1961. *The Future of an Illusion*. Translated and edited by James Strachey. New York: W. W. Norton.

Fukuyama, Yoshio. 1961. The major dimensions of church membership. *Review of Religious Research* 2: 154–61.

Furstenberg, Frank, Jr. 2001. The fading dream: Prospects for marriage in the inner city. In *Problem of the Century: Racial Stratification in the United States*, edited by Elijah Anderson and Douglas Massey, 224–46. New York: Russell Sage Foundation.

Furstenberg, Frank, Jr., and Mary Elizabeth Hughes. 1995. Social capital and successful development among at-risk youth. *Journal of Marriage and the Family* 57 (3): 580–92.

Gallo, Linda C., Frank Penedo, Karla Espinosa de los Monteros, and William Arguelles. 2009. Resiliency in the face of disadvantage: Do Hispanic cultural characteristics protect health outcomes? *Journal of Personality* 77 (6): 1707–46.

Gallup. 2009. Religion. http://www.gallup.com/poll/1690/religion.aspx.

Gallup, Alec, and Wendy W. Simmons. 2000. Six in ten Americans read Bible at least occasionally. Gallup Organization. http://www.gallup.com/poll/2416/six-ten-americans-read-bible-least-occasionally.aspx.

Gallup, George, and Timothy Jones. 2000. *The Next American Spirituality: Finding God in the Twenty-First Century*. Colorado Springs, CO: Cook Communications.

Gallup, George, and D. Michael Lindsay. 1999. *Surveying the Religious Landscape: Trends in U.S. Beliefs*. Harrisburg, PA: Morehouse Publishing.

Gallup Organization and Center for Research on Religion and Civil Society, University of Pennsylvania. 2003. The spiritual state of the union. www.gallup.com.

Ganz, Marshall. 2010. Leading change: Leadership, organization, and social movements. In *Handbook of Leadership Theory and Practice*, edited by Nitin Nohria and Rakesh Khurana, 509–50. Cambridge, MA: Harvard Business School Press.

Gilens, Martin. 1999. *Why Americans Hate Welfare: Race, Media, and the Politics of Anti-Poverty Policy*. Chicago: University of Chicago Press.

Glandon, Douglas M., Jocelyn Miller, and Astier Almedom. 2009. Resilience in post-Katrina. *Social Policy* 39 (1): 51–55.

Glass, Jennifer, and Leda E. Nash. 2006. Religious conservatism and women's market behavior following marriage and childbirth. *Journal of Marriage and Family* 68: 611–29.

Glock, Charles Y. 1964. The role of deprivation in the origin and evolution of religious groups. In *Religion and Social Conflict*, edited by Robert Lee and Martin E. Marty, 24–36. New York: Oxford University Press.

Goffman, Erving. 1959. *The Presentation of Self in Everyday Life*. Garden City, NY: Doubleday.

———. 1963. *Stigma: Notes on the Management of Spoiled Identity*. Englewood Cliffs, NJ: Prentice Hall.

Goldberg, Wendy A., JoAnn Prause, Rachel Lucas-Thompson, and Amy Himsel. 2008. Maternal employment and children's achievement in context: A meta-analysis of four decades of research. *Psychological Bulletin* 134 (1): 77–108.

Goldstein, Joshua R., and Catherine T. Kenney. 2001. Marriage delayed or marriage forgone? New cohort forecasts of first marriage for U.S. women. *American Sociological Review* 66: 506–19.

Grant, D., K. O'Neil, and L. Stephens. 2004. Spirituality in the workplace: New empirical directions in the study of the sacred. *Sociology of Religion* 65: 265–84.

Green, John C. 2007. American congregations and social service programs: Results of a survey. Roundtable on Religion and Social Welfare Policy, Nelson A. Rockefeller Institute of Government, State University of New York, Albany. http://www.religionandsocialpolicy.org/docs/public_resources/AmericanCongregationsReport.pdf.

Griffith, R. Marie. 1997. *God's Daughters: Evangelical Women and the Power of Submission.* Berkeley: University of California Press.

Griffith, Wendy. 2009. Know your Bible? Many Christians don't. Christian Broadcasting Network. http://www.cbn.com/cbnnews/us/2009/June/Do-You-Know-Your-Bible-Many-Christians-Dont/.

Hall, David. 1997. Introduction. In *Lived Religion in America: Toward a History of Practice,* edited by David D. Hall, vii–xiii. Princeton, NJ: Princeton University Press.

Hamilton, Brady E., Joyce A. Martin, and Stephanie J. Ventura. 2009. Births: Preliminary data for 2007. *National Vital Statistics Reports* 57, no. 12. March 18. http://www.cdc.gov/nchs/data/nvsr/nvsr57/nvsr57_12.pdf.

Hayes, Sharon. 1996. *The Cultural Contradictions of Motherhood.* New Haven, CT: Yale University Press.

———. 2003. *Flat Broke with Children: Women in the Age of Welfare Reform.* Oxford: Oxford University Press.

Heaton, Tim B. 1994. Familial, socioeconomic, and religious behavior: A comparison of LDS and Non-LDS women. *Dialogue* 27 (2): 169–83.

Hill, Peter, Kenneth Pargament, Ralph Wood Jr., Michael McCullough, James Swyers, David Larson, and Brian Zinnbauer. 2000. Conceptualizing religion and spirituality: Points of commonality, points of departure. *Journal for the Theory of Social Behavior* 30 (1): 51–77.

Himmelfarb, Gertrude. 1995. *The De-Moralization of Society: From Victorian Virtues to Modern Values.* London: IEA Health and Welfare Unit.

Hirschman, Albert O. 1970. *Exit, Voice, and Loyalty: Responses to Decline in Firms, Organizations, and States.* Cambridge, MA: Harvard University Press.

Hochschild, Arlie Russell. 1983. *The Managed Heart: Commercialization of Human Feeling.* Berkeley: University of California Press.

Hochschild, Jennifer. 1995. *Facing Up to the American Dream: Race, Class, and the Soul of the Nation.* Princeton, NJ: Princeton University Press.

Holloway, Susan D., Bruce Fuller, Marylee F. Rambaud, and Costanza Eggers-Pierola. 1997. *Through My Own Eyes: Single Mothers and the Cultures of Poverty.* Cambridge, MA: Harvard University Press.

Hout, Michael, and Claude S. Fischer. 2002. Why more Americans have no religious preference: Politics and generations. *American Sociological Review* 67 (2): 165–90.

Hudson, Kenneth, and Andrea Coukos. 2005. The dark side of the Protestant ethic: A comparative analysis of welfare reform. *Sociological Theory* 23 (1): 1–24.

Jackson, Debra, Angele Firtko, and Michel Edenborough. 2007. Personal resilience as a strategy for surviving and thriving in the face of workplace adversity: A literature review. *Journal of Advanced Nursing* 60 (1): 1–9.

Jarrett, Robin, L. 1996. Welfare stigma among low-income African American single mothers. *Family Relations* 45 (4): 368–74.

John Paul II. 1984. On the Christian meaning of human suffering. http://www.vatican.va/holy_father/john_paul_ii/apost_letters/documents/hf_jp-ii_apl_11021984_salvifici-doloris_en.html.

Johnson, Byron. 2002. Objective hope: Assessing the effectiveness of faith-based organizations: A review of the literature. Center for Research on Religion and Urban Civil Society, University of Pennsylvania, Philadelphia.

Karp, David A. 1996. *Speaking of Sadness: Depression, Disconnection, and the Meanings of Illness*. New York: Oxford University Press.

Keyes, Corey L. M. 2009. The black-white paradox in health: Flourishing in the face of social inequality and discrimination. *Journal of Personality* 77 (6): 1677–1706.

Kim, Eunjeong. 2003. Maternal employment and parenting stress among unmarried mothers with a welfare history. Ph.D. diss., University of Texas at Austin.

Koenig, Harold G., and David B. Larson. 2001. Religion and mental health: Evidence for an association. *International Review of Psychiatry* 13: 67–78.

Krause, Neal, Linda Chatters, Tina Meltzer, and David Morgan. 2000. Negative interactions in the church: Insights from focus groups with older adults. *Review of Religious Research* 41 (4): 510–33.

Krause, Neal, Christopher G. Ellison, Benjamin A. Shaw, John P. Marcum, and Jason D. Boardman. 2001. Church-based social support and religious coping. *Journal for the Scientific Study of Religion* 40 (4): 637–56.

Lamont, Michele. 1992. *Money, Morals, and Manners*. Chicago: University of Chicago Press.

Lareau, Annette. 2003. *Unequal Childhoods: Class, Race, and Family Life*. Berkeley: University of California Press.

Laudarji, Isaac B., and Lowell W. Livezey. 2000. The churches and the poor in a "ghetto underclass" neighborhood. In *Public Religion and Urban Transformation: Faith in the City*, edited by Lowell W. Livezey, 83–106. New York: New York University Press.

Lausanne Committee for World Evangelization. 1980. Christian witness to the urban poor. Occasional Paper 22. http://www.lausanne.org/all-documents/lop-22.html.

Lee, Jerry W., Gail T. Rice, and V. Bailey Gillespie. 1997. Family worship patterns and their correlation with adolescent behavior and beliefs. *Journal for the Scientific Study of Religion* 36 (3): 372–81.

Lehrer, Evelyn. 1995. The effects of religion on the labor supply of married women. *Social Science Research* 24: 281–301.

————. 2004. Religion as a determinant of economic and demographic behavior in the United States. *Population and Development Review* 30 (4): 707–26.

Lenski, Gerhard. 1961. *The Religious Factor: A Sociological Study of Religion's Impact on Politics, Economics, and Family Life.* Garden City, NY: Doubleday.

Lincoln, C. Eric, and Lawrence H. Mamiya. 1990. *The Black Church in the African-American Experience.* Durham, NC: Duke University Press.

Loser, Rachel W., E. Jeffrey Hill, Shirley R. Klein, and David C. Dollahite. 2009. Perceived benefits of religious rituals in the Latter-Day Saint home. *Review of Religious Research* 50 (3): 345–62.

Luthar, Suniya, D. Cicchetti, and B. Becker. 2000. The construct of resilience: A critical evaluation and guidelines for future work. *Child Development* 71: 543–62.

Macdonald, Cameron Lynne, and David Merrill. 2009. Intersectionality in the emotional proletariat: A new lens on employment discrimination in service work. In *Service Work: Critical Perspectives*, edited by Marek Korczynski and Cameron Lynne Macdonald, 113–33. New York: Routledge.

Macdonald, Cameron Lynne, and Carmen Sirianni. 1996. The service society and the changing experience of work. In *Working in the Service Society*, edited by Cameron Macdonald and Carmen Sirianni, 1–26. Philadelphia: Temple University Press.

Madsen, Richard. 2009. The archipelago of faith: Religious individualism and faith community in America today. *American Journal of Sociology* 114 (5): 1263–1301.

Mahoney, Annette, Kenneth Pargament, Nalini Tarakeshwar, and Aaron B. Swank. 2001. Religion in the home in the 1980s and 1990s: A meta-analytic review and conceptual analysis of links between religion, marriage, and parenting. *Journal of Family Psychology* 15 (4): 559–96.

Mare, Robert D., and Christopher Winship. 1991. Socioeconomic change and the decline of marriage for blacks and whites. In *The Urban Underclass*, edited by Christopher Jencks and P. Peterson, 175–96. Washington, DC: Brookings Institution Press.

Marks, Loren. 2004. Sacred practices in highly religious families: Christian, Jewish, Mormon, and Muslim perspectives. *Family Process* 43 (2): 217–31.

Marx, Karl. (1843) 1978. Contribution to the critique of Hegel's *Philosophy of Right*: Introduction. In *The Marx-Engels Reader*, 2nd ed., edited by Robert C. Tucker, 16–65. New York: W. W. Norton.

Maslow, Abraham. 1943. A theory of human motivation. *Psychological Review* 50 (4): 370–96.

McAdoo, Harriette Pipes. 1995. Stress levels, family help patterns, and religiosity in middle- and working-class African American single mothers. *Journal of Black Psychologists* 21 (4): 424–49.

McGuire, Meredith. 2002. *Religion: The Social Context*, 5th ed. Long Grove, IL: Waveland Press.

————. 2008. *Lived Religion: Faith and Practice in Everyday Life.* Oxford: Oxford University Press.

McRoberts, Omar. 2003. *Streets of Glory: Church and Community in a Black Urban Neighborhood*. Chicago: University of Chicago Press.

Miller, David W. 2007. *God at Work: The History and Promise of the Faith at Work Movement*. Oxford: Oxford University Press.

Miller, Vincent J. 2009. *Consuming Religion: Christian Faith and Practice in a Consumer Culture*. New York: Continuum.

Monsma, Stephen. 2004. *Putting Faith in Partnerships: Welfare-to-Work in Four Cities*. Ann Arbor: University of Michigan Press.

Monsma, Stephen, and J. Christopher Soper. 2006. *Faith, Hope, and Jobs: Welfare-to-Work in Los Angeles*. Washington, DC: Georgetown University Press.

Mooney, Margarita. 2009. *Faith Makes Us Live: Surviving and Thriving in the Haitian Diaspora*. Berkeley: University of California Press.

Moreton, Bethany. 2009. *To Serve God and Wal-Mart: The Making of Christian Free Enterprise*. Cambridge, MA: Harvard University Press.

Morris, Aldon D. 1986. *The Origins of the Civil Rights Movement: Black Communities Organizing for Change*. New York: Free Press.

Murray, Charles. 1984. *Losing Ground: American Social Policy 1950–1980*. New York: Basic Books.

Musick, Marc A. 2000. Theodicy and life satisfaction among black and white Americans. *Sociology of Religion* 61 (3): 267–88.

Nash, Laura, and Scotty McLennan. 2001. *Church on Sunday, Work on Monday: The Challenge of Fusing Christian Values with Business Life*. San Francisco: Jossey-Bass.

Nason-Clark, Nancy. 2001. Making the sacred safe: Woman abuse and communities of faith. In *Feminist Narratives and the Sociology of Religion*, edited by Nancy Nason-Clark and Mary Jo Neitz, 7–27. Walnut Creek, CA: Rowman and Littlefield.

Neibuhr, H. Richard. 1929. *The Social Sources of Denominationalism*. New York: Henry Holt.

Nelson, Timothy. 2004. Low-income fathers. *Annual Review of Sociology* 30: 427–51.

———. 2005. *Every Time I Feel the Spirit: Religious Experience and Ritual in an African American Church*. New York: New York University Press.

———. 2009. At ease with our own kind: Worship practices and class segregation in American religion. In *Religion and Class in America: Culture, History, Politics*, edited by Sean McCloud and William Mirola, 45–68. Leiden, The Netherlands: Koninklijke Brill.

Newman, Katherine, and Rebekah Peeples Massengill. 2006. The texture of hardship: Qualitative sociology on poverty, 1995–2005. *Annual Review of Sociology* 32 (18): 1–24.

Newman, Katherine S. 1999. *No Shame in My Game: The Working Poor in the Inner City*. New York: Alfred A. Knopf and the Russell Sage Foundation.

Newport, Frank. 2006. Religion most important to blacks, women, and older Americans. http://www.gallup.com/poll/25585/Religion-Most-Important-Blacks-Women-Older-Americans.aspx.

———. 2007. Americans more likely to believe in God than the devil, heaven more than hell. http://www.gallup.com/poll/27877/americans-more-likely-believe-god-than-devil-heaven-more-than-hell.aspx.

Nooney, Jennifer, and Eric Woodrum. 2002. Religious coping and church-based social support as predictors of mental health outcomes: Testing a conceptual model. *Journal for the Scientific Study of Religion* 41 (2): 359–68.

Olasky, Marvin. 1992. *The Tragedy of American Compassion.* Washington, DC: Regnery Gateway.

Orsi, Robert. 1985. *The Madonna of 115th Street: Faith and Community in Italian Harlem, 1880–1950.* New Haven, CT: Yale University Press.

———. 1996. *Thank You, St. Jude: Women's Devotion to the Patron Saint of Hopeless Causes.* New Haven, CT: Yale University Press.

———. 1997. Everyday miracles: The study of lived religion. In *Lived Religion in America: Toward a History of Practice,* edited by David D. Hall, 3–21. Princeton, NJ: Princeton University Press.

———. 2002. *The Madonna of 115th Street: Faith and Community in Italian Harlem, 1880–1950,* 2nd ed. New Haven, CT: Yale University Press.

Pargament, Kenneth. 1997. *The Psychology of Religion and Coping: Theory, Research, and Practice.* New York: Guilford Press.

Pargament, Kenneth, and Jeremy Cummings. 2010. Anchored by faith: Religion as a resilience factor. In *Handbook of Adult Resilience,* edited by John W. Reich, Alex J. Zautra, and John Stuart Hall, 193–210. New York: Guilford Press.

Pargament, Kenneth, and Crystal L. Park. 1995. Merely a defense? The variety of religious means and ends. *Journal of Social Issues* 51 (2): 13–32.

Pargament, Kenneth, Bruce Smith, Harold Koenig, and Lisa Perez. 1998. Patterns of positive and negative religious coping with major life stressors. *Journal for the Scientific Study of Religion* 37 (4): 710–24.

Park, Jerry, and Samuel Reimer. 2002. Revisiting the social sources of American Christianity, 1972–1988. *Journal for the Scientific Study of Religion* 41 (4): 733–46.

Parrott, Sharon. 2009. Despite critics' overheated rhetoric, the economic recovery bill does not undermine welfare reform. Center on Budget and Policy Priorities, February 17. http://www.cbpp.org/cms/index.cfm?fa=view&id=2648.

Pearce, Lisa, and William G. Axinn. 1998. The impact of family religious life on the quality of mother-child relations. *American Sociological Review* 63: 810–28.

Peek, Charles W., George D. Lowe, and L. Susan Williams. 1991. Gender and God's word: Another look at religious fundamentalism and sexism. *Social Forces* 69: 1205–21.

Pew Forum on Religion and Public Life. 2008. *U.S. Religious Landscape Survey.* http://religions.pewforum.org/reports.

Pew Forum on Religion and Public Life and Pew Research Center for the People and the Press. 2009. Faith-based programs still popular: Democrats now more supportive than Republicans. November 16. http://pewresearch.org/pubs/1412/faith-based-programs-popular-church-state-concerns.

Pew Research Center. 2007. Fewer mothers prefer full-time work from 1997 to 2007. July 12. http://pewresearch.org/pubs/536/working-women.

Pineda-Madrid, Nancy. 2001. In search of a theology of suffering Latinamente. In *The Ties That Bind: African American and Hispanic American/Latino/A Theology in Dialogue*, edited by Anthony Pinn and Benjamin Valentin, 187–99. New York: Continuum.

Pinhey, Thomas, and Michael Perez. 2000. Recounting the wages of self-appraised sinfulness: A research note on divorce, cohabitation, and guilt. *Deviant Behavior: An Interdisciplinary Journal* 21: 1–13.

Pinn, Anthony B. 1995. *Why, Lord? Suffering and Evil in Black Theology*. New York: Continuum.

Poloma, Margaret, and George Gallup. 1991. *Varieties of Prayer*. Philadelphia: Trinity Press International.

Presser, Stanley, and Mark Chaves. 2007. Is religious service attendance declining? *Journal for the Scientific Study of Religion* 46 (3): 417–23.

Price, Matthew J. 2000. Place, race, and history: The social mission of downtown churches. In *Public Religion and Urban Transformation: Faith in the City*, edited by Lowell W. Livezey, 57–82. New York: New York University Press.

Prince, Lola Marie. 2008. Resilience in African American women formerly involved in street prostitution. *ABNF Journal* 19 (1): 31–36.

Prothero, Stephan. 2007. *Religious Literacy: What Every American Needs to Know—and Doesn't*. New York: HarperCollins.

Public Broadcasting System. 1987. *Eyes on the Prize: America's Civil Rights Movement, 1954–1985*. http://www.pbs.org.

Putnam, Robert. 1993. The prosperous community: Social capital and public life. *American Prospect* 4. http://www.prospect.org/cs/articles?article=the_prosperous_community.

———. 2000. *Bowling Alone*. New York: Touchstone.

Putnam, Robert, and David Campbell. 2010. *American Grace: How Religion Is Reshaping Our Civic and Political Lives*. New York: Simon and Schuster.

Rand, Kevin L. 2009. Hope and optimism: Latent structures and influences on grade expectancy and academic performance. *Journal of Personality* 77 (1): 231–60.

Raphael, Jody. 2002. Keeping battered women safe during welfare reform: New challenges. *JAMWA* 57 (1): 32–35.

Reeves, Thomas. 1996. *The Empty Church: The Suicide of Liberal Christianity*. New York: Free Press.

Riccio, J. A. 1979. Religious affiliation and socioeconomic achievement. In *The Religious Dimension: New Directions in Quantitative Research*, edited by Robert Wuthnow, 199–226. New York: Academic Press.

Rogers, Mary Beth. 1990. *Cold Anger: A Story of Faith and Power Politics*. Denton: University of North Texas Press.

Rogers-Dillon, Robin. 1995. The dynamics of welfare stigma. *Qualitative Sociology* 18 (4): 439–56.

Roof, Wade Clark. 1999. *Spiritual Marketplace: Baby Boomers and the Remaking of American Religion*. Princeton, NJ: Princeton University Press.

Roof, Wade Clark, and W. McKinney. 1987. *American Mainline Religion*. New Brunswick, NJ: Rutgers University Press.

Sakalas, Joan. 1999. Face to face: Transforming faith-based outreach. In *Welfare Policy, Feminist Critiques*, edited by Elizabeth M. Bounds, Pamela K. Brubaker, and Mary E. Hobgood, 201–12. Cleveland: Pilgrim Press.

Sample, Tex. 1993. *Hard Living People and Mainstream Christians*. Nashville: Abingdon Press.

Schieman, Scott. 2010. Socioeconomic status and beliefs about God's influence in everyday life. *Sociology of Religion* 71 (1): 25–51.

Schlehofer, Michele, Allen Omoto, and Janice Adelman. 2008. How do "religion" and "spirituality" differ? Lay definitions among older adults. *Journal for the Scientific Study of Religion* 47 (3): 411–25.

Schwadel, Philip. 2002. Testing the promise of the churches: Income inequality in the opportunity to learn civic skills in Christian congregations. *Journal for the Scientific Study of Religion* 41 (3): 565–75.

———. 2008. Poor teenagers' religion. *Sociology of Religion* 69 (2): 125–49.

Schwadel, Philip, John D. McCarthy, and Hart M. Nelsen. 2009. The continuing relevance of family income for religious participation: U.S. white Catholic church attendance in the late twentieth century. *Social Forces* 87 (4): 1997–2030.

Scott, James. 1985. *Weapons of the Weak: Everyday Forms of Peasant Resistance*. New Haven, CT: Yale University Press.

Scott, Mark S. M. 2008. Cosmic theodicy: Origin on the problem of evil. PhD diss., Harvard University.

———. 2009. Theorizing theodicy in the study of religion. Martin Marty Center for the Advanced Study of Religion, University of Chicago Divinity School. http://divinity.uchicago.edu/martycenter/publications/webforum/112009/ Theorizing%20Theodicy%20.pdf.

Seccombe, Karen. 1999. *"So You Think I Drive a Cadillac": Welfare Recipients' Perspectives on the System and Its Reform*. Boston: Allyn and Bacon.

Seccombe, Karen, Delores James, and Kimberly Battle Walters. 1998. "They think you ain't much of nothing": The social construction of the welfare mother. *Journal of Marriage and the Family* 60 (4): 849–65.

Seybold, Kevin S., and Peter C. Hill. 2001. The role of religion and spirituality in mental and physical health. *Current Directions in Psychological Science* 10 (1): 21–24.

Sherkat, Darren. 2000. "That they be keepers of the home": The effect of conservative religion on early and late transitions into housewifery. *Review of Religious Research* 41 (3): 344–58.

Skocpol, Theda. 1995. *Protecting Soldiers and Mothers: The Political Origins of Social Policy in the United States*. Cambridge, MA: Harvard University Press.

———. 2000. Religion, civil society, and social provision in the U.S. In *Who Will Provide: The Changing Role of Religion in American Social Welfare*, edited by Mary Jo Bane, Brent Coffin, and Ronald Thiemann, 21–50. Boulder, CO: Westview Press.

———. 2003. *Diminished Democracy: From Membership to Management in American Civic Life*. Norman: University of Oklahoma Press.

Skocpol, Theda, and Morris Fiorina, eds. 1999. *Civic Engagement in American Democracy*. Washington, DC: Brookings Institution Press.

Small, Mario L. 2004. *Villa Victoria: The Transformation of Social Capital in a Boston Barrio*. Chicago: University of Chicago Press.

———. 2009. *Unanticipated Gains: Origins of Network Inequality in Everyday Life*. Oxford: Oxford University Press.

Small, Mario L., and Katherine Newman. 2001. Urban poverty after *The Truly Disadvantaged*: The rediscovery of the family, the neighborhood, and culture. *Annual Review of Sociology* 27: 23–45.

Smith, Christian. 2003. Theorizing religious effects among American adolescents. *Journal for the Scientific Study of Religion* 42 (1): 17–30.

Smith, Christian, and Melissa Lundquist Denton. 2005. *Soul Searching: The Religious and Spiritual Lives of American Teenagers*. New York: Oxford University Press.

Smith, Christian, and Robert Faris. 2005. Socioeconomic inequality in the American religious system: An update and assessment. *Journal for the Scientific Study of Religion* 44 (1): 95–104.

Smith, R. Drew. 2001. Churches and the urban poor: Interaction and social distance. *Sociology of Religion* 62 (3): 301–13.

———. 2003. Beyond the boundaries: Low-income residents, faith-based organizations, and neighborhood coalition building. Faith Communities and Urban Families Project, Leadership Center at Morehouse College. Annie E. Casey Foundation, Baltimore. http://www.aecf.org/publications/data/3_btbreport.pdf.

Smith, Sandra Susan. 2003. Exploring the efficacy of African-Americans' job referral networks: A study of the obligations of exchange around job information and influence. *Ethnic and Racial Studies* 26 (6): 1029–45.

———. 2005. "Don't put my name on it": Social capital activation and job-finding assistance among the black urban poor. *American Journal of Sociology* 111 (1): 1–57.

———. 2007. *Lone Pursuit: Distrust and Defensive Individualism among the Black Poor*. New York: Russell Sage Foundation.

Snow, David A., and Leon Anderson. 1993. *Down on Their Luck: A Study of Homeless Street People*. Berkeley: University of California Press.

Snyder, C. R., and Shane J. Lopez, eds. 2002. *Handbook of Positive Psychology*. Oxford: Oxford University Press.

Sorenson, Ann Marie, Carl F. Grindstaff, and R. Jay Turner. 1995. Religious involvement among unmarried adolescent mothers: A source of emotional support? *Sociology of Religion* 56 (1): 71–81.

Spicker, Paul. 1984. *Stigma and Social Welfare*. London: Croom Helm.

Stack, Carol. 1974. *All Our Kin: Strategies for Survival in a Black Community*. New York: Harper and Row.

Stark, Rodney. 1972. The economics of piety: Religious commitment and social class. In *Issues in Social Inequality*, edited by Gerald W. Thielbar and Saul D. Feldman, 483–503. Boston: Little, Brown.

———. 2003. Upper class asceticism: Social origins of ascetic movements and medieval saints. *Review of Religious Research* 45 (1): 5–19.

Stone, Pamela. 2007. *Opting Out? Why Women Really Quit Careers and Head Home*. Berkeley: University of California Press.

Strayhorn, Joseph, Carla Weidman, and David Larson. 1990. A measure of religiousness and its relation to parent and child mental health variables. *Journal of Community Psychology* 18: 34–43.

Swidler, Ann. 1986. Culture in action: Symbols and strategies. *American Sociological Review* 51: 273–86.

———. 2001. *Talk of Love: How Culture Matters*. Chicago: University of Chicago Press.

Tabak, Melanie A., and Kristin D. Mickelson. 2009. Religious service attendance and distress: The moderating role of stressful life events and race/ethnicity. *Sociology of Religion* 70 (1): 49–64.

Taylor, Robert Joseph. 1988. Correlates of religious non-involvement among black Americans. *Review of Religious Research* 29 (4): 126–39.

Taylor, Robert Joseph, and Linda M. Chatters. 1988. Church members as a source of informal social support. *Review of Religious Research* 30: 193–203.

Taylor, Robert Joseph, Linda M. Chatters, and Jeff Levin. 2004. *Religion in the Lives of African Americans*. Thousand Oaks, CA: Sage Publications.

Thornton, Arland, William Axinn, and Daniel Hill. 1992. Reciprocal effects of religiosity, cohabitation, and marriage. *American Journal of Sociology* 98 (3): 628–51.

Todd, Janet L., and Judith Worrell. 2000. Resilience in low-income, employed, African American women. *Psychology of Women Quarterly* 24: 119–28.

Townes, Emilie. 1993. Living in the new Jerusalem: The rhetoric and movement of liberation in the house of evil. In *A Troubling in My Soul: Womanist Perspectives on Evil and Suffering*, edited by Emilie M. Townes, 78–91. Maryknoll, NY: Orbis Books.

Unruh, Heidi Rolland, and Ronald J. Sider. 2005. *Saving Souls, Serving Society: Understanding the Faith Factor in Church-Based Social Ministry*. Oxford: Oxford University Press.

U.S. Bureau of Labor Statistics. 2009a. Employment characteristics of families in 2008. http://www.bls.gov/news.release/famee.nr0.htm.

———. 2009b. Women in the workforce: A databook. http://www.bls.gov/cps/wlf-databook-2009.pdf.

Verba, Sidney, Kay Lehman Schlozman, and Henry E. Brady. 1995. *Voice and Equality: Civic Voluntarism in American Politics*. Cambridge, MA: Harvard University Press.

Volf, Miroslav, 1991. *Work in the Spirit: Toward a Theology of Work*. New York: Oxford University Press.

Wacquant, Loic, and William Julius Wilson. 1989. The cost of racial and class exclusion in the inner city. *Annals of the American Academy of Political and Social Science* 501: 8–25.

Warren, Mark. 2001. *Dry Bones Rattling: Community Building to Revitalize American Democracy*. Princeton, NJ: Princeton University Press.

Weber, Max. 1930. *The Protestant Ethic and the Spirit of Capitalism*. London: Routledge.

———. (1922) 1963. *Sociology of Religion*. Translated by Ephraim Fischoff. Boston: Beacon Press Books 1963.

———. (1915) 1991. *From Max Weber: Essays in Sociology*. Edited with an introduction by H. H. Gerth and C. Wright Mills. London: Routledge.

Weissbourd, Richard. 2000. Beyond villages: New community building strategies for disadvantaged families. In *Who Will Provide? The Changing Role of Religion in American Social Welfare*, edited by Mary Jo Bane, Brent Coffin, and Ronald Theimann, 219–37. Boulder, CO: Westview Press.

Werner, Emmy E., and Ruth Smith. 1992. *Overcoming the Odds: High Risk Children from Birth to Adulthood*. Ithaca, NY: Cornell University Press.

Wharton, Amy S. 2009. The sociology of emotional labor. *Annual Review of Sociology* 35: 147–65.

Wilcox, W. Bradford. 1998. Conservative Protestant child rearing: Authoritarian or authoritative? *American Sociological Review* 63: 796–809.

Wilcox, W. Bradford, and Nicholas Wolfinger. 2007. Then comes marriage? Religion, race, and marriage in urban America. *Social Science Research* 36: 569–89.

Wiley, Angel, Henriette Warren, and Dale Montanelli. 2002. Shelter in a time of storm: Parenting in poor rural African American communities. *Family Relations* 51 (3): 265–73.

Williams, Joan. 2000. *Unbending Gender: Why Family and Work Conflict and What to Do about It*. Oxford: Oxford University Press.

Wilson, William Julius. 1987. *The Truly Disadvantaged: The Inner City, the Underclass, and Public Policy*. Chicago: University of Chicago Press.

———. 1996. *When Work Disappears: The World of the New Urban Poor*. New York: Alfred A. Knopf.

Winship, Christopher. 2002. Preface to *The Poor Are the Church: A Conversation with Fr. Joseph Wresinski, Founder of the Fourth World Movement*, by Gilles Anouil. Mystic, CT: Twenty-Third Publications.

Witten, Marsha G. 1993. *All Is Forgiven: The Secular Message in American Protestantism*. Princeton, NJ: Princeton University Press.

Wolfe, Alan. 2003. *The Transformation of American Religion: How We Actually Live Our Faith*. New York: Free Press.

Wood, Richard, L. 1994. Faith in action: Religious resources for political success in three congregations. *Sociology of Religion* 55 (4): 389–97.

———. 2002. *Faith in Action: Religion, Race, and Democratic Organizing in America*. Chicago: University of Chicago Press.

Wright, David J. 2009. Taking stock: The Bush faith-based initiative and what lies ahead. Roundtable on Religion and Social Welfare Policy, Nelson A. Rockefeller Institute of Government, State University of New York, Albany. http://www.religionandsocialpolicy.org/final_report/full_report_060809.pdf.

Wuthnow, Robert. 1988. *The Restructuring of American Religion*. Princeton, NJ: Princeton University Press.

———. 1994a. *God and Mammon in America*. New York: Free Press.

———. 1994b. *Sharing the Journey: Support Groups and America's New Quest for Community*. New York: Free Press.

———. 1998. *After Heaven: Spirituality in America since the 1950's*. Berkeley: University of California Press.

———. 2002. Religious involvement and status-bridging social capital. *Journal for the Scientific Study of Religion* 41 (4): 669–84.

———. 2004. *Saving America? Faith-Based Services and the Future of Civil Society*. Princeton, NJ: Princeton University Press.

———. 2007. *After the Baby Boomers: How Twenty- and Thirty-Somethings Are Shaping the Future of American Religion*. Princeton, NJ: Princeton University Press.

Wuthnow, Robert, Conrad Hackett, and Becky Y. Hsu. 2004. The effectiveness and trustworthiness of faith-based and other service organizations: A study of recipients' perceptions. *Journal for the Scientific Study of Religion* 43: 1–17.

Wuthnow, Robert, and Tracy Scott. 1997. Protestants and economic behavior. In *New Directions in American Religious History*, edited by H. S. Stout and D. G. Hart, 260–95. New York: Oxford University Press.

Zautra, Alex J. 2009. Resilience: One part recovery, two parts sustainability. *Journal of Personality* 77 (6): 1935–42.

Zedlewski, Sheila, and Olivia Golden. 2010. Next steps for temporary assistance for needy families. Brief 11, Urban Institute. http://www.urban.org/uploadedpdf/412047_next_steps_brief11.pdf.

Zinnbauer, Brian, Kenneth Pargament, Brenda Cole, Mark Rye, Eric Butter, Timothy Belavich, Kathleen Hipp, Allie Scott, and Jill Kadar. 1997. Religion and spiritual: Unfuzzying the fuzzy. *Journal for the Scientific Study of Religion* 36 (4): 549–64.

Zinnbauer, Brian, Kenneth Pargament, and Allie Scott. 1999. The emerging meanings of religiousness and spirituality: Problems and prospects. *Journal of Personality* 67 (6): 889–19.

Zukin, Cliff, Scott Keeter, Molly Andolina, Krista Jenkins, and Michael X. Delli Carpini. 2006. *A New Engagement? Political Participation, Civic Life, and the Changing American Citizen*. Oxford: Oxford University Press.

Index

abuse. *See* domestic violence

activism. *See* political action; social action

ADC. *See* Aid to Dependent Children (ADC)

addiction. *See* alcoholism; drug addiction

adolescent mothers. *See* teenage mothers

Adrienne, 113, 126–27, 227

AFDC. *See* Aid to Families with Dependent Children (AFDC)

African American churches. *See* black churches

African Americans: and church attendance, 7, 236n5; high levels of distrust and individualism among, 11; marriage, low levels of, 163, 166; prayers by, 32; resilience among, 239n6; theology, 141

African American women. *See* black women

African immigrants, 252n4. *See also* immigrants

African Methodist Episcopal (AME) church, 166–67, 179. *See also* black churches

afterlife, 15–16, 26, 43, 86, 134, 138. *See also* heaven

agency: and church attendance, 171; creative, 17; and fortitude, 107; and hope, 55, 241n29; and prayer, 39; and protector, role of, 120; and religion, 204–5; and self-confidence, 111; and self-

efficacy, 47; sense of, 35, 47, 55, 111; and willpower, 77, 241n29; women as actors with, 39

AIDS/HIV, 30, 250n7

Aid to Dependent Children (ADC), 81

Aid to Families with Dependent Children (AFDC), 81

Albrecht, Gloria, 212

alcoholism, 41, 119, 140, 149, 175, 182–83, 194, 229, 249n4

Aletta, 60, 92, 101, 116, 122, 136–37, 139, 157, 216, 227

altruism, 210

AME church. *See* African Methodist Episcopal (AME) church

American dream, 52–53, 69, 77

American Recovery and Reinvestment Act of 2009 (ARRA), 243–44n6

Ammerman, Nancy, 4, 55, 66, 110, 202–3, 246n2

Anderson, Leon, 147, 154

Anderson, Rev. William, 179–80, 189–90, 196

Annie, 112–13, 122, 227

Ann Marie, 33, 46, 57, 73, 125, 159, 171, 227

anthropology, of religion, viii, 4

ARRA. *See* American Recovery and Reinvestment Act of 2009 (ARRA)

Aspen Institute Nonprofit Sector Research Fund, 250n7

Assembly of God church, 27, 52, 88

atheists, 203

MORALITY AND SOCIETY SERIES
Edited by Alan Wolfe

Moral Communities in Medical Science: Managing Risk in Early Human Experiments
Sydney Halpern

Cultural Dilemmas of Progressive Politics: Styles of Engagement among Grassroots Activists
Stephen Hart

For the Sake of the Children: The Social Organization of Responsibility in the Hospital and the Home
Carol A. Heimer and Lisa R. Staffen

Money, Morals, and Manners: The Culture of the French and the American Upper-Middle Class
Michèle Lamont

Streets of Glory: Church and Community in a Black Urban Neighborhood
Omar Maurice McRoberts

The Making of Pro-life Activists: How Social Movement Mobilization Works
Ziad Munson

God and Government in the Ghetto: The Politics of Church-State Collaboration in Black America
Michael Leo Owens

The Catholic Social Imagination: Activism and the Just Society in Mexico and the United States
Joseph M. Palacios

Citizen Speak: The Democratic Imagination in American Life
Andrew J. Perrin

Speaking of Abortion: Television and Authority in the Lives of Women
Andrea L. Press and Elizabeth R. Cole

The Ironies of Affirmative Action: Politics, Culture, and Justice in America
John David Skrentny

Public and Private in Thought and Practice: Perspectives on a Grand Dichotomy
Edited by Jeff Weintraub and Krishan Kumar

Soft Patriarchs, New Men: How Christianity Shapes Fathers and Husbands
W. Bradford Wilcox

Faith in Action: Religion, Race, and Democratic Organizing in America
Richard L. Wood